Dear Mom:
I haven't been doing anything special, just flying
a lot and doing a lot of letter writing. I have
flown over 200 combat hours now, as much time
as I got all through flight school. I don't have
much to say. I just wanted to write and tell you
I'm fine.

I felt we were like a huge, green clay pigeon suspended
in the air inviting someone to take a pot shot at us.
Charlie must have had the same idea. At two hundred
feet on final approach, the ridge line on my side of the
aircraft lit up with green tracer rounds flying in our direction. The crew chief began firing his M-60. Several
grunts in the back began firing their weapons too. Bernie threw the aircraft hard left and dove at the trees but
not before we took several hits. I scrunched down, waiting for one of the bullets to rip into my body . . .

Dear Mom, I'm Alive

RANDOLPH P. MAINS

AVON BOOKS ◆ NEW YORK

DEAR MOM, I'M ALIVE is an original publication of Avon Books. This work has never before appeared in book form.

AVON BOOKS
A division of
The Hearst Corporation
1350 Avenue of the Americas
New York, New York 10019

Copyright © 1992 by Randolph P. Mains
Published by arrangement with the author
Library of Congress Catalog Card Number: 91-92454
ISBN: 0-380-76568-3

First Avon Books Printing: June 1992

AVON TRADEMARK REG. U.S. PAT. OFF. AND IN OTHER COUNTRIES, MARCA REGISTRADA, HECHO EN U.S.A.

Printed in the U.S.A.

RA 10 9 8 7 6 5 4 3 2 1

"Death has but one terror,
that it has no tomorrow."

Eric Hoffer,
The Passionate State of Mind

CONTENTS

Author's Note

The idea for this book came to me one evening when my mother and I were drinking coffee after dinner in the living room of her tiny California apartment. She stood up from her chair, suddenly remembering something and, with the aid of a cane to help steady her, following a stroke that had left one leg partially paralyzed, she made her way to an antique desk in a corner of the room. With trembling hands she reached into one of the cluttered alcoves and pulled out a thick stack of letters wrapped neatly with rubber bands.

"I thought that one day you might like to read these. They are all the letters you sent me while you were in Vietnam," she said, placing the packet in my lap.

I looked at the postmark of the top letter. It was dated 20 October 1968. The return address was Cam Ranh Bay. It was the first letter I had sent home. I unwrapped the rubber bands and carefully thumbed through the faded envelopes. The addresses were written in my hand, the small picture of Vietnam occupying the left side of many of those purchased in the PX there, and in the right-hand corner, where the stamp would normally be, the word "FREE." The suddenly renewed acquaintance with these letters spirited my mind back to a time saturated with electric emotions, the source of my most personal memories.

Mom had told me many times over the years that she still had them. But I had never before had the interest or the inclination to reread what I'd written during those turbulent times. Twenty years had passed. I was now curious.

I did not read the letters that night. Instead, I saved

them for the long airplane flight back to the Middle East. Something unexpected happened to me when I did finally read those letters. Their contents triggered recollections and feelings that had been pushed back in the deep recesses of my mind and left dormant over the last twenty years. The memories were always there, unexamined, I knew that. My memory, like a mirror that had been etched in the distant past by a year of diamond-hard experiences, only needed to be dusted off to reveal the scars the ordeal had left. Reading those letters was like dusting off that mirror. They brought back almost entirely the adventures as if an instant replay of my year over there as a twenty-two-year-old warrant officer helicopter pilot was suddenly brought into focus.

Those letters had been something more tangible than mere words scribbled on a page. Twenty years ago each letter arrived in turn to 21601 Kaneohe Lane, Huntington Beach, California to give strength to an anxiously waiting family at home. Some of the letters described in great detail what I was doing at the time I wrote them. Many did not. As I read each one on the plane, I remembered the name we had for such letters in Vietnam. "I'm Alive" letters. Everyone over there wrote them. The most important thing about them was the date in bold letters written on the upper right-hand corner. Each letter had one. When my family received a letter they knew I was alive on that date. That was the significance of each letter. That was their true value.

When I returned to civilian life after the army, I quickly learned what the public's sentiment was toward veterans of that war. During my first week back at college a nineteen-year-old girl, who could not have been more than sixteen at the time I was serving over there, called me a "baby killer" to my face when she found out I'd flown helicopters in Vietnam. After that experience I decided not to tell anyone I had fought in the war. It was better to consider the ordeal a closed chapter in my life and begin again. It was senseless to argue. It was easier to remain silent than to have confrontations with people who did not understand.

Now veterans are beginning to talk. Many people who

did not share in the Vietnam experience and who at one time may have condemned us are now curious to learn and want to listen. I am frequently asked now, "What was it *really* like over there?" In this book I have attempted to supply the answer. It is the true story of one helicopter pilot's year in Vietnam. The events happened exactly as I have detailed them here and are chronologically correct to the best of my recollection. The people described in this work are real people. I have changed many of the names to preserve their anonymity.

I dedicate this book to the one person who's always stood by me, who has never lost faith in me. I dedicate this book to you, Mom.

CHAPTER 1

October 15, 1968

Point of No Return

The inside of the stretch DC-8 looked like a sea of green. There were 288 of us flying somewhere over the Pacific, bound for the same destination—Vietnam. Most of the men were infantrymen, "grunts." A few of us were pilots.

Bob Lawson, my roommate through flight school, was seated next to me, staring out the window into the blackness. Stu Lindsey, another classmate, was sitting on my right, thumbing through a *Time* magazine and chewing aggressively on a Life Saver. The tension building up among the men was thick enough to slice with a bayonet. We were traveling more than nine miles a minute, each minute bringing us that much closer to war.

Up until now the war had been an intangible thing, hairy stories told by instructor pilots who had been there and were lucky enough to return. The war headlines in the newspapers, or moving pictures on the six o'clock news. The war was statistics, numbers, a daily tally of the men fighting over there. Cold numbers, not warm-blooded fighting men. The war was body counts. Men killed on both sides. It was not yet real. But it was about to become our reality. Soon we would become part of it, irrevocably affected by it. In less than two hours we would become part of the statistical machine.

I looked around at my fellow passengers, most of whom were exactly like myself—young and inexperienced, leaving home soil for the first time and heading for this totally alien assignment. I imagined that their heads were also filled with questions right now. Questions like, what in the

1

holy fuck am I doing here? Would I ever see my family again? My mom, my seventeen-year-old sister, Nancy, my five-year-old sister, Andrea, my stepfather, Howard, or my real father? Would I ever take carefree drives in my sports car up Coast Highway again? Had I seen my girlfriend, Michelle, for the last time? What about my closest friend, college buddy, and surfing companion, Greg Omberg? Would I ever ride a wave with him again? But the main question gnawing at my gut was what would it be like to fly in combat?

I'd heard the stories in flight school, plenty of them, of how helicopters fell from the Southeast Asian sky like raindrops, brought down by everything from rocket-propelled grenades RPGs, to spears and arrows. Would I be brave enough to face the enemy's bullets in hot landing zones, "LZs," or would I chicken out and, finally, one day rip the wings off my chest and, refusing to fly, throw them on my commanding officer's desk? The only way a man can answer those kinds of questions is trial by fire. I would know soon enough.

The words "One in three, candidate, one in three!" kept ringing in my ears. The men sitting on either side of me, Bob Lawson, and Stu Lindsey, were buddies of mine since we took our oath to join the army at the reception station in Los Angeles a year ago. Two months before we had stood with twenty other warrant officer candidates braced at attention in the polished halls of the candidate's billets at Fort Rucker, Alabama. Wearing stiffly starched fatigues and spit-shined combat boots, our backs and heads were pressed hard against the walls, bodies rigid, eyes locked forward. Chief Warrant Officer Wilson, our hard-ass tactical officer, walked down the hall and screamed into each of our faces, "Look around you, candidates, and look around good, cuz one in three ain't comin' back. That's one in three, gentlemen!" He held up a stubby finger for effect. "That's a statistic you'd better learn to live with!"

I would not now be facing the one-in-three odds of being killed if it had not been for my love of flying, I thought. Most small boys grow up with a fascination for airplanes and flying. That's normal. Some say it's a disease caused by the "flying bug." Like most childhood diseases the body's defenses take over, kill the offending organism, and you get well. I had my fair share of childhood maladies—mumps, measles, chicken pox, flu, and colds—but I never recovered when I was attacked by the flying bug. I was not merely bitten by the little sucker, I was devoured by him.

By the time I was four years old I knew I was going to be a pilot, and that was that, Period. At four years old I owned a rusty old airplane that my dad bought me secondhand. I used to spend hours pedaling it around the back yard. That two-tone, silver and rust airplane with the bent wings and broken propeller used to fuel my childhood fantasies for hours. It would fly me around the world and always deliver me back home safely just before Mom would call me to dinner.

When I was a little older, and not building airplane models in my bedroom, I used to sneak off to the local airport. I would sit under the approach path and watch the F-86 Saber jets come in for landings.

One afternoon I found a hole in the airport fence. I crawled under it and discovered I could make a game out of dodging airport security guards on patrol. I made my way across the airport and found an area surrounded by a chain-link fence. On the other side sat several scrapped B-25 Mitchell bombers with gear up, lying on their bellies. They were the type of airplane my dad used to fly during the Second World War. Trying to contain my excitement, I quickly scaled the fence and climbed into the cockpit of one of the planes. It had that unmistakable aircraft smell of dripping oil, leaking hydraulic fluid, and old sweat. The odor somehow signified it was a *real* airplane, not the make-believe machines I used to fabricate in my friend's attic out of cardboard boxes and the steering wheel from an old car.

Once I'd made the discovery of the old planes, I would often sneak to the airport to experience the thrill of sitting in the pilot's seat. I'd flick on the overhead switches, imagining I was starting the two radial engines and hearing them roar to life. I'd imagine taxiing for takeoff, take the wheel in my hands, push the throttles to the fire wall, then pull back on the control yoke and fantasize about soaring to altitude and flying combat missions over foreign lands somewhere far, far away. I would be fighting side by side with men like John Wayne, Van Johnson, or Jimmy Stewart. But in the end, in my mind, it was always just me, and me alone, locked in some deadly air battle. The battle had to be won for God and country. The stakes were always all or nothing. I had to win it, or freedom for all would be lost. And in my childhood daydreams, as I had learned from the movies, because I was an American on the side of God and righteousness, I could never lose.

My overwhelming urge to fly was never satisfied by my vivid imagination. I tried all the usual stunts kids try to defy gravity. I tied one end of a sheet to the belt loops of my Levis and held the free ends over my head. I then jumped off the garage roof to the grass with my makeshift parachute. Before that I ruined my grandfather's umbrella by jumping off the same roof holding it over my head. It immediately inverted and collapsed as in a Road Runner cartoon.

When I was twelve I thought I had the ultimate answer for getting airborne. In the secrecy of my garage I constructed a crude airplane from an equally crude soapbox racer I'd made a week earlier. With wooden wings covered in fabric, old sheets that my mom had given me, I pulled the contraption up Plummer Hill for a test flight.

Sitting in the cockpit at the top of the hill, with a rock wedged under the rear wheel, I made my preparations. I cinched the seat belt tight around my waist. It was a Cub Scout belt cut in half and nailed to each side of where the driver (pilot) sat. I gave one last tug on the chin strap of my Los Angeles Rams football helmet thinking that it would protect me in the event of a crash from the great height I knew I would attain.

I took a firm grip on the rope steering, which I held like the reins of a horse. There was no way to guide the craft if it did get airborne, but I hadn't thought of that. I figured I would just lean in the direction I wanted to fly. The object was to get airborne. Steering in flight was a secondary consideration that I would deal with later.

Once ready, I yanked out the rock wedged under the

rear wheel. The craft began to roll down the steep hill and gained speed quickly. In no time I was rocketing down the hill on the narrow tarmac road. The wings bowed and flapped wildly as they tried to take the weight of the craft. The steering began to buffet as if the front wheels were trying to lift off the ground. I bent over in my seat and pulled the steering reins tighter to hold on for liftoff. Halfway down the hill one wing reached its structural limit and snapped off, causing the plane to ground loop and hurl me, and machine, down a steep embankment and through a barbed wire fence. It was only by the grace of God, and with a hell of a lot of luck, that the back axle caught on a fence post to stop the remains of the contraption from hurling itself off into the never-never over a two-hundred-foot cliff.

It turned out to be a good safety measure to wear the football helmet. After the dust and debris had settled I took it off and noticed that there was a long, deep groove carved along the top by a rusty barb from the fence I had just crashed through. Orville and Wilbur had nothing to fear that day.

My first real flight in an airplane took place when I was fifteen. It occurred a short time after my mom remarried to an air force colonel. The best part of the arrangement was that he owned an airplane—not just any airplane, but a World War II trainer. It was a two-seat, open-cockpit Waco UPF-7 biplane he had rebuilt. Its fabric covering was painted canary yellow. She was a real beauty. He knew how much I loved airplanes and how, some day, I wanted to be a pilot. I think that first flight was his way of testing me.

Because it was an open-cockpit airplane I had to wear a leather helmet, goggles, and a seat parachute, just in case. We took off from Torrance airport and flew over Long Beach Harbor and began a slow climb over the California coastline. Once we reached four thousand feet he yelled, ''Ready?''

''Ready!'' I hollered back into the wind from the front seat and gave him the thumbs up sign as he'd told me to do. Before I could get my hand back into the cockpit to grab onto something, the world suddenly started to spin.

The control stick gyrated wildly between my legs as he threw the craft into loops, snap rolls, split-s's, stalls, and spins. My body was squished into the seat by invisible G (gravity) forces. My eyelids felt like they were drooping down around my lower lip, my cheeks to my chin. Then I felt an incredible tickling sensation in the pit of my stomach and I thought I was going to wet my pants. The Gs suddenly changed direction and I became weightless. The only things keeping me from floating out of the cockpit and into eternity were the shoulder harness and seat belt. It was wonderful!

He dove the machine to gain airspeed, then threw the aircraft into a loop. My body compressed under the strain of the Gs. I remember seeing the horizon disappear from under me, then blue sky, several puffy clouds, then the sun, and finally the ocean appearing as we came out of the loop and dove straight for a tanker anchored in the harbor. The yellow airspeed needle rocketed through 120 knots and beyond. The biplane's wing wires hummed as the wind resistance increased. The ship in the harbor seemed like it was caught in a vortex when we started to spin. I could hear the engine change pitch when he chopped the throttle in the dive to keep the aircraft from gaining too much airspeed and ripping the wings off. The spinning stopped and the wings leveled. Looking at the ship below through the windmilling prop reminded me of a scene out of an old war movie from Saturday morning television.

I think my stepfather thought I would be begging for mercy, pleading for him to stop within the first thirty seconds. I think he thought I'd throw up, wet my pants, or both. But I didn't. I could not get enough. He flung the machine through the sky in every conceivable attitude for fifteen minutes. From that day on I knew I could hack it as a pilot.

"One in three, candidate, one in three!"

It was never any secret where I was going once I finished flight training. Every prospective army helicopter pilot knew before joining why he was being trained. It was part of the deal. A common saying among the candidates in flight school if you fucked-up at anything was,

"What can they do to you, send you to Vietnam?" I guess there was no worse punishment than to face the one-in-three odds of being killed.

After the graduation ceremony at Fort Rucker our company was assembled for one last formation outside our billets. A full colonel, with a voice as rough as a gravel road, stood on a box and spoke to us. He looked out at all us 124 brand new warrant officers with our new rank gleaming on our shoulders in the sun, a pair of shiny silver wings pinned on each chest. It was a proud day.

"Men!" he barked. "Today you've joined the most elite aviation fraternity in the world. You've all worked damn hard to get where you are today, and you should be proud, damn proud, of that accomplishment. Army aviators are the best trained pilots in the world and the cost of your training reflects that fact. Uncle Sam has spent more than sixty-thousand dollars on each and every one of you to make you what you are today. That's sixty-thousand dollars!" He made it sound as if we should all be grateful for the government's generosity in training us to become expensive cannon fodder.

Somewhere in the back of the crowd one of the new members of the most elite aviation fraternity in the world cupped his hands and yelled, "Yes, sir! And you can shove that sixty-thousand dollars up your ass a nickel at a time!" Everyone laughed. What could the colonel do to the guy? Send him to Vietnam? I chuckled again at the memory.

The questions continued to run through my mind. What about my instrument training? Will I need to use it? I'd been told the weather was shitty half the year over in Vietnam. There were a million ways to die, but bad weather and flying into clouds had killed more aviators than bullets ever had.

I had flown fifty hours of instrument training in flight school. We all had. The ticket we were issued was called a tactical instrument ticket. Like bayonet training, which taught you just enough to get you killed on the ground, the tactical instrument ticket was supposed to get you out of a jam if you accidentally flew into the clouds. I had my doubts. It was a standing joke that the tactical instrument ticket had a hole punched in the upper right-hand corner.

If you contemplated going flying you took it out of your wallet, held it toward the sky, and if you did not see blue sky you did not take off. I hated stories like that.

Bob, Stu, and I had 210 hours total flight time. Bayonet training again. We were like newborn birds kicked from the nest. Our experience level was even pointed out to us in our rank. We were WO-1s out of flight school, warrant officer ones. We were affectionately called "Wobbly Ones." That about summed it up. At our experience level we just might be able to fly the aircraft out of a hot LZ if the aircraft commander got shot and get him to a hospital without damaging the aircraft—maybe.

Of the 210 hours I had only 50 hours in the Bell Huey, the aircraft I would be flying over there. Was 50 hours enough? I thought not. The machine could be a handful. I remember my flight instructor trying to drill into me the importance of keeping the tail of the Huey straight when maneuvering it in a small LZ surrounded by high trees. The tail rotor pedals on the Huey are hydraulically assisted, and you only have to "think" about moving them to get a response to turn the nose right or left in a hover.

"Goddamn it, Mains," he would yell. "You let the tail go squirrelly like that over in Nam you'll stick the tail rotor into a tree. Some of the LZs over there are tighter than your first piece of ass, and if you let the tail dance around like that you'll kill yourself, your crew, and anybody else unlucky enough to be flying with you. Now watch how I do it. I have the controls."

"You've got it, sir."

He took control of the aircraft. The machine hovered as if frozen in time and space. "See there, nothing to it. Just 'think' about making those movements. Now you take it and I don't want to see the ship's heading vary by more than a couple of degrees either side of our present heading or I'll pink you for flight safety, understand?"

"Yes, sir."

"You got it then."

"I've got it, sir."

With my right arm resting on my leg I took the cyclic stick in my right hand. The cyclic looks like the conventional stick you would see in a modern jet fighter. Its function is to tilt the rotor disk in the direction the pilot moves the stick. If I move it left the rotor disk tilts left and the aircraft flies left. Move it forward, the rotor disk tilts forward and the aircraft moves forward and so on. In the tight area we were now hovering in I concentrated on making minute movements with the cyclic to keep the aircraft over one spot on the ground.

My left hand held the collective pitch lever which stuck up out of the floor at a thirty-degree angle. Approximately the diameter of a small baseball bat, the collective, as it's called, changes the pitch of the blades collectively. When pulled up it causes the rotor blades to take a bigger bite out of the air and the helicopter rises. Conversely, if lowered, the helicopter descends. I had a relatively good control touch on the cyclic and collective. I could hold the position over the ground with the cyclic and the three-foot hovering altitude with the collective. It was the damn pedals I had difficulty with.

I concentrated on just thinking about moving the pedals as the instructor had told me. I thought about it too much. I was sweating profusely. I pushed in right pedal. The nose swung right. It was too much. I overcorrected, making the aircraft yaw in the opposite direction. The high trees around us were only about a rotor's length away. Shit, settle down. I tried to relax. Again I tried to just "think" about moving the pedal controls. I concentrated on making the tensed muscles in my legs relax. He grabbed the controls away from me again. "This is hopeless," he said in disgust. "I've got it. Let's go home."

"You've got it, sir."

He told me I was going to get a pink slip for unsatisfactory pedal control. It was the first pink slip I had received in flight school.

Walking from the parked aircraft to the briefing room he said to me, "You know, Mains, some people are not cut out to be helicopter pilots."

Uh-oh, here it comes, I thought.

"We all have our strong points. If you don't make it through flight school maybe your strong point rests somewhere else. Maybe you'd make a good mechanic." He talked as if I were going to be washed out of flight school that afternoon. I tried to sound convincing when I told him I could do it. I just needed a little time, that was all.

We flew the next day. I was graded unsatisfactory once again and assigned to fly with another instructor for a second opinion. I knew what that meant. If the second instructor failed me, action would be taken to either wash me out of flight school or recycle me to the class two weeks behind mine for further training. What was, in my eyes, a small problem of pedal control was growing out of all sensible proportion. The worry caused by my weak pedal control was turning into more of a problem than the original problem itself.

I flew with the other instructor the following day. To my great relief I did fine. His only recommendation was a change of instructor, evaluating the real problem to be a clash of personalities and not my actual flying ability.

My flying skills in that area were weak, and it still concerned me. Nearly all my classmates had the same trouble with overcontrolling the pedals of the Huey. If I were going to be assigned to a peacetime position somewhere stateside it would not make much difference if I mastered the rock-steady hovering technique. But I was being trained to go into combat. In Vietnam the consequences of poor technique would be far worse. It could cost me my life. Shit, bayonet training again!

A stewardess walked down the aisle. She was offering dried out sandwiches, turkey wedged between white bread. She smiled and held out the aluminum tray. "Sandwich?"

"No thanks." I waved her off.

Stu reached across and took a handful. "I'll eat yours for you then."

Stu's appetite never waned. That's why his uniform was so snug. Even at Fort Polk, Louisiana, during basic training, he was the only one in the company who gained weight. He looked over at me and stuffed a quarter of a turkey sandwich into his mouth. He smiled as he chewed trying to keep his lips shut over the huge mouthful. My appetite had left me when we took off from Fort Lewis, Washington, twenty hours ago. I smiled, looking at my friend's bulging cheeks, shook my head, and thought about Michelle.

I'd kept an 8-x-10 photo of her on my desk at Fort Wolters and Fort Rucker. Her letters and her support had helped me make it through a lot of the hard times. Her picture was with me now packed in my duffel bag stuffed somewhere in the plane's belly. The picture captured Michelle as the classic California girl she was—tanned, her broad smile exposing perfect, white teeth, her long blonde hair being lifted by the gentle sea breeze. She cradled my green flight helmet under her arm while standing in front of a Bell-47 helicopter at Orange County Airport. The picture had been taken on one of my leaves.

Two nights before I left, Michelle and I rented a room at the Sheraton on Coast Highway overlooking the ocean in order to make love for the last time. Something happened, or, I should say, did not happen, which left me humiliated. I could not make love to her. My mind was racing, full of too many questions. I felt I had ruined our last precious evening together. Sensing my anxiety, she suggested we just talk instead.

Our only plans for the future were to just get through the next twelve months. October 15, 1968 to October 15, 1969—just 365 days. Her words soothed me and eased the anxiety I tried to hide, but had done such a lousy job of covering up. We did not talk of death that night. At our age dying was barely conceivable. But we both knew it was a very real possibility. Too real in my line of work.

As we sat on the bed, she made me lie on my back and place my head on her lap. She stroked my face with her long, polished fingernails. I closed my eyes and drank in her tenderness knowing it would be a long, long time before I would experience this kind of love and affection again.

Michelle had a light and breezy manner that I had come to love. She was nineteen, three years younger than I. As we talked in soft whispers, I opened my eyes and studied her face under the flickering glow of candles we'd lit for the occasion. As the evening progressed into the early hours of the morning, she seemed to take on a maturity I had never noticed before.

She told me that she'd miss me and would wait for me, that I could count on receiving her letters. We passed much of the time in silence. I would occasionally take in a deep breath to capture her lightly perfumed scent. I wanted to remember that smell. I reached up and lightly stroked her hair. I tried to etch the soft image of her face on my mind so I could recall her beauty at will. It would give me strength to help me through the long year. She would be one of the things I would be fighting for, I told myself.

I closed my eyes and could see her again.

I had always thought as I grew up that I would join the air force, as my dad did during World War II. But it was because of my stepfather that I joined the army instead. I was attending college and working as a baggage handler (we were called "ramp rats") for Air California at Orange County Airport when I received a letter from my draft board informing me that my student deferment had changed from 2-S, student status, to 1-A. It was the kind of letter students dreaded. It meant I was next in line to go.

Several days after I received the news from my draft board, Howard, my stepfather, an active duty colonel in the California Air National Guard, walked through the door holding a brochure he'd picked up from an army recruiter. He unfolded it on the living room coffee table to reveal a shot taken from behind, showing two pilots sitting in the cockpit of a Huey. It was impressive. "This is the way to go, Randy," he told me. "You want to fly? This is how you can do it. They'll draft you before you get your college degree to qualify for air force flight training, so why not try to get into this program?"

My current situation offered me three options: I could flee to Canada and dodge the draft, as I had heard some guys were beginning to do, but such an idea was unthinkable. I could take my chances, get drafted, and probably end up a foot soldier. Definitely not my style. Or I could enlist in the warrant officer flight-training program and satisfy my dream of one day becoming a pilot. The decision was easy.

I was already vaguely familiar with the army warrant officer program. My cousin, Bob, had joined four months before me, and I had heard he had experienced a string of bad luck. During the primary phase of his flight training

at Fort Wolters, Texas, the large engine cooling fan that
sat vertically behind him and his instructor on the Hiller
OH-23 helicopter he was flying disintegrated in flight.
Metal pieces exploded into the cockpit like shrapnel. The
engine quit and they had to autorotate.

Autorotation is the only procedure a pilot can resort to
in such emergencies. The helicopter is flown at sixty knots,
the wind flowing up through the blades to keep them turning. It comes down quickly like an auto gyro. The landing
is accomplished by the pilot when he flares the helicopter
fifty feet above the ground. When the helicopter is ten to
twelve feet from the ground the pilot pulls in collective
pitch at the last moment using the inertia in the windmilling rotor blades to (hopefully) touch down softly.

My cousin and his instructor autorotated to an open
field. Apart from several cuts and bruises, and a slightly
bent helicopter, they managed to come out of it all right.

In the tactics phase of his flight training at Fort Rucker,
Alabama, Bob had not been so lucky. Several weeks before he was to graduate he was flying in the back of a
Huey observing the instructor and his stick buddy practic-
ing forced landings. The instructor gave the student a
forced landing at low altitude. They were at 250 feet. The
instructor called for a power recovery. The student snapped
on the throttle, but nothing happened. The engine quit.
They crash landed in a farmer's field. The aircraft was
destroyed. Bob was thrown clear from the wreckage, but
the powerful G-forces he encountered in the crash broke
his back.

When I arrived at Fort Rucker to begin my training
there I visited him in the hospital. He had been lucky. The
doctors told him he would probably walk again. Bob told
me he was going to be washed out of flight school and
would most likely be given a medical discharge out of the
army. It upset him that he would not fly again, but he was
philosophical about the turn of events. He told me that
perhaps it was a sign that he was not meant to go to Vietnam after all. Would he turn out to be the lucky one?

Naturally, the prospect of their son going off to war has
a profound effect on parents. My mom tried to deny it
until the last moments at the airport. There she broke

down. I knew at the time my mother was not an emotionally strong person and her delicate mental state did nothing to lighten my concerns at going off to war. I knew this year would test her greatly. She had experienced her first nervous breakdown following the death of her mother when I was thirteen. She had never really been the same since then. After that, my sister and I constantly looked out for the telltale signs that she was slipping away from reality again. My mother suffered several more nervous breakdowns over the years, and with each recurrence she had to be hospitalized in a mental health unit until she became emotionally stable enough to return home. She was seeing a psychiatrist regularly and her condition was diagnosed as manic depressive. I knew if I got killed in Vietnam it might send her over the edge. Her distraught reaction to my final departure did not surprise me. I had expected such a response from her. What I did not expect was how my departure would affect my real father.

My father, a tough, hard-working carpenter by trade, had always been a stranger to my sister and me. He did not talk much, but when he did it was usually to release his violent temper. We both feared him. He and Mom went through a stormy divorce when I was five after which he was awarded visitation rights through the court. My sister and I would be picked up every other weekend and taken to his house where we would then be ignored while he watched endless football games on TV and simultaneously worked on crossword puzzles. Even today he is somewhat of a mystery to me. When you don't know what quiet people are thinking it is natural to think the worst.

I knew little about my dad's military career except that he had volunteered to be a soldier during World War II. His unit had been overrun in Africa. He and eight others were the only survivors out of their company. On his return to the states he went to flight school and he became an instructor pilot in the B-25 Mitchell. My childhood memory of him dressed in his blue air force uniform with those shiny air force wings pinned on his chest will always stay with me. He looked handsome and dashing, a lot like Robert Mitchum did in his younger days. I idolized him.

I cannot recall my father telling me he loved me. He

seemed too angry a man for that. About the closest he ever came to an open display of affection was when I said good-bye to him two days before I had to leave. It happened while we were standing in his driveway when he was seeing me off. "You take care," the big man said, struggling with the awkwardness he failed to hide. After a moment of silence and of staring at one another, he stepped forward and took me in his big arms, giving me the only hug I can ever remember him giving me. His sudden affection came as a shock. When he released me and stepped back his eyes were tearing. I had never seen him cry before. I could feel a big lump forming in my throat.

Then he said, "I want you to have these." He held out his hand and placed a pair of tarnished air force wings in my palm. They were the same wings I had seen pinned on his chest sixteen years before. "They got me back safe," he said. "They're good luck. You keep 'em."

I nodded. He turned and walked into the house. I watched him close the door. To this day it remains the most tender moment I've ever shared with the man.

"What'cha staring at?" Stu asked from my right. He was peering at me over his magazine. "You look like a damn zombi. You've been lookin' at the back of that seat for five minutes now."

His voice brought me back. "Nothing," I said looking over at him. "Just thinking, that's all."

"About what?"

"A lot of things. Home. Family. What do you think the flying'll be like?"

"Wet," Bob said without looking away from the window. "Monsoon season. It'll be wetter than a seal's ass, that's for sure." He looked at me and smiled weakly.

Bob and I both had orders to go to Fourth Infantry Division somewhere near a place called Pleiku. I gained solace in knowing we would be together. Stu, on the other hand, did not have his orders yet. He had been told he would be assigned to a unit when he arrived in country.

Bob cracked his knuckles and tried to stretch his legs. "Sure be glad when we get there. My legs are startin' to cramp up."

Stu leaned over me. "If your legs are cramping up now, Lawson, wait till you strap on a Huey for eight or ten hours. You're ass'll be so sore it'll feel like it's going to fall off. That's what I've been told anyway. I've heard of guys getting fourteen to sixteen hours a day. So you'd better get used to it."

Bob looked out the window at the pitch darkness and cracked his knuckles again. "Yeah, hard to imagine."

I tried to sleep. I could not. "One in three, candidate, look around you, one in three!" kept replaying in my mind. Which of us would it be? Would it be Bob, or Stu? Would it be me?

I guess I did finally doze off. I was awakened with a jolt as the plane landed heavily on the wet runway. I rubbed my eyes. When they focused Stu was leaning over grinning at us. "Welcome to Cam Ranh Bay." He glanced at his Seiko watch. "The clock starts now, gentlemen. Only 365 days to go till we go home."

"That's a pleasant thought." Bob was peeping through cupped hands pressed against the wet window trying to see outside as the plane pulled to a stop. "Hey, I can see flares."

Stu popped another Life Saver into his mouth. "One in three. Just keep thinkin', one in three."

"You're depressing, you know that, Lindsey?" Bob said.

Stu smiled. "Won't be us. It'll be some other poor slob."

"Uh-huh," Bob said idly still peering out the window. "Here come the buses to pick us up."

The inside of the plane was buzzing with conversation now while the men stood and collected their belongings in preparation to leave. The fore and aft doors of the plane opened and a flood of hot, moist Southeast Asian air rushed through the cabin. I took a deep breath and could smell jet fuel and burning shit.

Stu stood up, grabbed his AWOL bag from under his seat, and made room for us in the crowded isle. "Come on, guys, looks like the time's come to finally see what this war's all about."

I stepped past Stu and began walking behind the line of men now bunched up and moving slowly in single file for the forward door of the plane. My pulse quickened. As I approached the exit I thought that I was finally a physical part of it. I had entered that statistical machine.

CHAPTER 2

Change of Assignment

I walked down the plane's steps single file behind the other replacements. It was dark and drizzling. The air felt like a hot, wet blanket against my skin. All of us new to a combat zone scanned the darkness anxiously, trying to anticipate the unknown. I noticed soldiers working near the rear of the plane. They were wearing waterproof ponchos and unloading silver coffins from a duce-and-a-half. They were lining them in a long row next to the plane's rear cargo hold. The men inside were going home.

Once we were on the bus Stu examined the windows and said, "What do you think the screens and bars are for?"

"Grenades," Bob answered.

"Grenades?"

"Ya ain't back on the block now, sir." I turned around to see a black sergeant seated behind us. He said, "Over here you don't know who's goin' to try and kill your ass, or when they're gonna do it."

Stu laughed nervously. "Yeah. I guess you're right."

"I'm more than right. I'll advise you not to trust any of those yellow fucks, no matter how good you think you know 'em. You're better off not trustin' nobody, and be ready for anything. Soon's you let your guard down . . . ," he paused to slit his throat with his finger, "you're history. You keep that in mind and it'll improve your chances of gettin' back to The World in one piece."

Tom turned in his seat to face the man. "You sound like you speak from experience."

"Damn right I do. This is my second goddamn tour."

18

We were taken to a large building where the officers and enlisted men were separated. We filled out paperwork, had a meal in a mess hall that was as modern as any I'd seen stateside, and were shown to the BOQ, (bachelor's officers quarters) where we would stay until we shipped out to our units.

Stu sat on the edge of his bunk and kicked off a combat boot. "If this is how the war's going to be, guys, bring it on. Did you see the size of that T-bone they brought me tonight. Damn, my mom couldn't have cooked it any better."

Tom was lying on his back in bed under a sheet. "You got to remember, Stu, this is an in-country R&R center. You'd expect it to be plush."

I added, "Yeah, Bob, but even at that I was amazed when that Spec-4 told us we were free to go scuba diving, snorkeling, or water skiing on one of four boats. Water skiing! I can't imagine. Somehow I didn't think that was possible in a war zone, particularly in Vietnam."

Stu kicked off his fatigue pants, threw off his shirt, and slid between clean sheets. "Well, keep the luxuries comin', boys, because if this is war, then who I am to write home and tell them it ain't hell."

I lay in bed and listened to the rain striking the corrugated iron roof. At times it would fall softly, its light patter nearly imperceptible. At other times it would suddenly sound as if the hootch was under a waterfall. When it rained hard the rush of water created a warm wind that whistled through the screens surrounding the plywood building. I lay awake and tried to listen for gunfire or other signs that I was indeed in a war zone. I heard nothing and soon drifted off to sleep.

"Mr. Mains! Mr. Mains!" the voice repeated. "Sir, wake up."

It was still dark and I rolled over on my back and checked the luminescent dial of my watch. 0330. "Who is it?"

"Corporal Hoskins, sir. Your orders have been changed. I've come from ops to tell you to get ready to ship out."

I tried to focus in the darkness. I could not see the

person talking to me. He flicked on a flashlight. It had a red lens. "Why do I have to get up now?" I asked, slightly irritated.

"Orders, sir."

"Orders? What orders?"

"You have to be ready to fly outta here at first light. There's a C-130 leaving for Bien Hoa at 0600."

I swung my feet out of bed and sat staring at the light. "And what's in Bien Hoa? My orders are for the Fourth Infantry Division. What happened?"

"Been changed, sir. Happens all the time. Guess they need pilots up there. You're going to the 101st Airborne Division instead. Bien Hoa's their division rear. You'll in-process there. Then they'll send you to their AO where you'll be assigned to a company."

"AO?"

"Yeah, you know, area of operation."

"Oh. And where's that?"

The voice let out a little laugh as if harboring a personal joke. "Well, sir, you're familiar with the DMZ?"

"Yes."

"Well, there's a map on the wall over there." The light beam suddenly flashed on the far wall. "If you look at the DMZ and come down about a quarter of an inch, you'll be in the ball park."

"I've had better news," I said sarcastically.

"After you have your breakfast get your gear and come to operations. Be there by 0500." The light disappeared and I listened to the sound of boots striking the floor and fading down the hall.

"What's happening?" Bob asked in a sleepy voice from the bed next to me.

"I'm shipping out."

"Shipping out? Where?"

I told him.

When he heard he said, "Holy shit!"

Bob, Stu, and I had breakfast together. The two men saw me off on a bus bound for the airfield. It was raining and their green fatigues were soaked to the skin.

Bob yelled through the wire mesh of the bus window, "Take care of yourself, ya hear?"

"I will."

"And write!"

"You bet."

Stu gave me the thumb's up sign. "We'll see you at the end of your tour. Fuck the odds. And fuck TAC officer Wilson. What's he know anyway? The three of us'll be back in the California sunshine surfin', drinkin' Coors, chasin' women, and raisin' hell in no time. You'll see."

I held up my thumb. "Roger that, Stu." The bus began to pull out. "You guys take care."

They both waved as the bus drove off. I watched them run toward the billets to get out of the rain until they disappeared. I turned around in my seat. The bus was full of men, but I suddenly felt very alone. We stopped in front of a large terminal-type building. I grabbed my duffel bag and stepped off. An air force sergeant ticked my name off a manifest on his clipboard as I walked out the door. Once in the terminal I sat down and waited. I took out my pen and paper and began to write.

Sunday 20 October 1968

Hi everyone.

I arrived in country the 17th of October and I am now at Cam Ranh Bay awaiting my plane to Bien Hoa. My orders have been changed. I am not going to the 4th Infantry Division, but to the 101st Airborne Division.

My plane trip over here took twenty-two hours. It has rained continually since I've been here. It is the monsoon season for South Vietnam. It is fairly hot, it is seventy-five degrees and it's only 0600 A.M. Whew!

Please disregard the return address on the envelope. The only reason it's there is because every letter must have one or they won't send it. Please wait until I have a permanent address before you write. Gotta go. I have to board the airplane. More later.

Love, Randy

"Your plane's in, sir." It was the air force sergeant who had ticked my name on the manifest. "Writing an 'I'm Alive' letter, are you?"

"What?"

"I'm Alive letter. You know, to let the folks back home know you're OK."

I laughed. "Yeah, I guess so."

"Just follow those men over there, sir," he pointed.

I put away my paper and pen. "Thanks, sergeant."

There were about fifty of us. We walked out onto the wet tarmac carrying our gear. I carried my duffel over my shoulder. The rain had stopped for the first time since I'd been in country. The brown camouflaged C-130 stood on the ramp with the load master marshaling men inside. The sun was just cresting the horizon under the plane's wing. I noticed Vietnamese working around the ramp. The words of the black soldier who sat behind me on the bus the first night replayed in my mind. "I'll advise you not to trust any of those yellow fucks, no matter how good you think you know 'em." I wondered.

The way we were loaded in the aircraft was appalling. I was told it was a "combat load." We sat in rows indian-style on large aluminum pallets. There were approximately ten rows of soldiers sitting cross-legged eight abreast. Our "seat belt" was a joke. It was a hemp rope that the load master passed down each row and tied to either side of the aircraft. The rope on my row hung slack in each man's lap. I figured if the aircraft crashed that every man would be cut in half. That did not worry me as much as the cargo. The aft end of the C-130 slopes up at about a thirty-degree angle. Several tons of heavy equipment and luggage were packed in it. If the ropes did not cut us in half in the crash, the tons of cargo would hurl itself forward and crush us all.

The flight to Bien Hoa was so noisy it was impossible to carry on a conversation with the man sitting next to me without screaming. Pilots are always uncomfortable flying if they are not at the controls or do not know the man who is. I was no exception. The four turboprop engines outside the thin skin of the fuselage rumbled and whined with a sound equivalent to four freight trains converging.

The pilot executed a combat approach into Bien Hoa. A combat approach for a C-130 is when the aircraft is kept out of range of small arms for as long as possible by flying at altitude until the last minute. Then the pilot literally noses the craft over and dives the huge, four-engine plane like a fighter aiming for the end of the runway. At the last possible instant, just when you're certain you're going to crash, he yanks back on the control yoke and flares the heavy plane. Its inertia causes it to plant its wheels firmly on the runway. In my mind the maneuver was a controlled crash.

Throughout the approach, I kept my eye on the cargo behind me. It was not covered with nets, only a small portion of it was secured with insignificant looking straps. Nothing else. They were an ineffectual means of securing it. I could not help but wonder how many men had been crushed by such inefficient loading. Though I could have done nothing about it had it decided to come tumbling down on us, it made me feel better to keep an eye on it anyway.

Bien Hoa was what I had envisioned a camp in Vietnam to look like. The earth everywhere had been turned into thick mud from the rains. The area I was sent to had rows of sixteen-by-thirty-two-foot hootches lined six deep. Two rows of green sandbags surrounded each hootch stacked up to the beginning of the screens that surrounded each structure. The sandbags were to protect the occupants inside from shrapnel in the event of a mortar or rocket attack. Each hootch had a tin roof with sandbags tied together and draped over it every three feet or so to help secure it in high winds. Scattered outside the rows of hootches, accessible by the front door, were dome-shaped bunkers with every square inch covered with green sandbags. A wall of perforated steel planking, PSP, filled with sandbags stood several feet in front of each entrance.

A spec-4 took me to fill out in-processing forms, then he showed me to the hootch where I would bunk while waiting to ship out with my unit. As I approached the hootch I saw a captain standing outside. I threw him a salute. He looked perplexed at my action. There was something peculiar about him. His obviously new green fatigues looked disheveled. Unmilitary.

"Morning, sir," I said holding the salute.

He finally seemed to understand what was expected of him and threw me a sloppy salute of his own. "Morning."

"You staying here, sir?"

"Yeah, second bunk on the right. There's an empty bunk next to mine. You can have it."

I placed my duffel inside the door on the plywood floor. "Thanks." I extended my hand. "Randy Mains."

"John Wayne," he said shaking hands.

"John Wayne?" I smiled. "That'll be a hard name to live up to. Specially over here."

"I know. I'm used to it, though. With any luck I won't see any combat like the real John Wayne. I just want to put in my year and get out of here." He looked nervous.

"You been here long, sir?"

"Forget the sir. It makes me uncomfortable. Call me John. I've been here a week. I'm shipping out tomorrow."

"Where you going?"

"Twenty-second surgical hospital in Quang Tri."

"You a doctor then?"

"Surgeon. Only been in the army two weeks."

That explained his unmilitary air. "Were you in ROTC?"

"Nope, just finished my internship at San Francisco General. Only dealings I've had with the army started when they drafted me two weeks ago." He looked at the black cloth wings sewn on my green fatigues. "You a pilot?"

"Yep, I fly helicopters."

His eyes widened. "Shit. That's gotta be hairy. You just arriving in country too?"

"Yep."

He shook his head. "No offense, but I thought I had it bad. I've heard some pretty depressing statistics about you guys."

I half smiled and started for the door. "Yeah, John, me too."

I spent the day exploring the camp, forming my first impressions of an environment that was to become as familiar in the year ahead as the one I'd left behind in Southern California. Helicopters buzzed overhead. Even if

I could not see them it was rare when I could not hear the continual thumping noise of their rotor blades slapping the humid air. I would come to regard this noise as the pulse of the war—the sound of its very heartbeat.

Soldiers, "grunts," as they were called, strolled around the company area. They congregated in groups. I walked by one such group seated in chairs around their hootch. A stereo played "Soul Man" at an ear-piercing level as several of them played cards or wrote "I'm Alive" letters. One black soldier was dancing and miming the words as if performing on stage. Most had their shirts off. Some wore the green floppy hats known as "boonie hats." I looked upon these men as the salt of the war, its grit and sweat. To a man, they were sorrowful looking creatures, tired and worn as if an element extracted from the soggy earth itself. They appeared to be tight knit, easily ready to joke, to play grab-ass, or to exchange banter. I imagined that the bonds would have to be strong. The life of the one always depended on the others. Regardless of my odds of facing extinction, I was glad I was a helicopter pilot and not one of them.

In the mess hall that afternoon I saw my first warrant officer helicopter pilot. My first veteran. He was eating at another wooden table talking to an infantry first lieutenant and an infantry captain. I wanted to walk over, sit next to him, and ask him a thousand questions. He looked about my age, twenty-two. The rank on his faded green Nomex flying suit was that of a CW2, chief warrant officer 2. A notebook that was attached to a string worn around his neck stuck out of his right-hand breast pocket. I had been told those notebooks were called SOIs, signal operating instructions. It contained the top secret frequencies of the units in the area where he flew.

It takes one year from graduation to make CW2. That fact told me he was either in the last month of his tour or he was on his second tour. What was important to me was that he was a veteran and he *knew* what it was like to fly in combat.

I'll always remember that face. It was smooth and young, but there was something about his appearance that did not fit with his youth. It was his eyes. They were wide,

wild eyes. Anxious. They were eyes that I could tell had
seen plenty of action. They were intense, darting, serious
eyes that kept me from walking over to the man and asking
him my trivial questions.

He looked at me once and those eyes locked with mine.
I wanted to look away, but couldn't. I felt like an insignificant piece of meat sitting there in my new fatigues,
radiating inexperience. I wanted to evaporate under his
gaze. He did not smile. The eyes did not blink. They only
stared. I tried to imagine what he was thinking. He had to
be thinking that I was someone's replacement for sure.
Maybe even his. That I had a lifetime of learning in the
year ahead that would have to be condensed into a few
months if I were to survive. And that I had my dues to
pay as he had had to pay his. There was a sadness in his
eyes, or was it pity. Or perhaps I was just imagining it?
He lifted his cup, continuing to stare at me over the lip.
He took a sip and finally looked away. Throughout the
rest of his meal I continued to watch him, but he did not
acknowledge my existence again.

That night I lay on my bunk. Several songs were drifting
through the company area, coming from loud stereos
played in the hootches surrounding mine. By the dim light
of a dangling light bulb I wrote another letter home.

Monday 21 October 1968

Dear family:

I have my permanent address, so here it is:

> *WO Randolph Mains*
> *W3161785*
> *HHC/160th Aviation Group*
> *101st Abn. Div.*
> *APO S.F. 96383.*

*I've been told I'll be stationed somewhere up north
near the ancient capital of Hue. So far I haven't seen
any action or anything. At night I can hear cannon fire.
I've been told it's from Saigon to harass the VC. I have*

*only heard one round fired from small arms since I've
been here, but nothing much. Our position seems very
secure here in Bien Hoa. There was a rumor that we
were supposed to have been rocketed last night but we
weren't. If we are rocketed we've been told to go to one
of the bunkers that are set up every hundred feet or so
in the immediate area.*

*The food isn't bad and I am treated well because I'm
an officer. I haven't been in Vietnam long and I already
feel sorry for the poor ground pounders. They've got it
tough, real tough, and I don't envy them their job.*

*Oh well, not much happening now. I am just waiting
to in-process to this unit then ship out. Will write soon.*

Love to all,
Randy.

Several days later I was put on another C-130 and flown
north to Phu Bai. The C-130 pilot performed the same
hairy approach to avoid being shot down.

I was picked up by helicopter and flown five miles
north to Camp Eagle, northern headquarters of the 101st
Airborne Division. It felt good to be flying in a helicopter
again. The side doors were open allowing the eighty-knot
wind to enter. A gunner and crew chief sat in the wells
behind me. Each had their tinted visor pulled down over
their eyes. They resembled humanoids out of a science
fiction story. Like the pilots, they wore green Nomex
flying suits, Nomex gloves, and black boots. The only
human flesh you could see was their mouth and jaw. An
M-60 machine gun sat on a steel gun mount in front of
them.

I scanned the countryside trying to take in as much
scenery as I could in the short flight. I tried to imagine
what the operational flying would be like here. Would I
be able to hack it?

Camp Eagle was a sprawling place bustling with activity. Hundreds of plywood hootches, their tin roofs gleaming in the tropical sun, were scattered in no particular
fashion. Several black plumes of smoke could be seen rising from the shit being burned outside the latrines. I was

to learn that the water table was too near the surface to bury the shit, so it had to be doused with jet fuel or gasoline and set afire. Green bunkers were strewn around at random. The perimeter of the camp from the air reminded me of pictures I had seen of prisons. Concertina wire snarled and snaked around the huge area. Claymore mines were littered in the barbed wire ready to blast any force of VC regulars who tried to storm the stronghold. Tall wooden guard towers housing 50-caliber machine guns stood high around the camp. Massive bunkers every two hundred yards added to the impression of an impenetrable fortress. Helicopters were taking off and landing at various helipads like bees buzzing around a mammoth hive.

The environs of the camp consisted of small Vietnamese villages, rolling green hills, rice paddies stretching toward the sea, and inland, to the west, the thick jungle and high mountains. I was astonished to find such beauty in a country at war.

I spent another two days in-processing at Camp Eagle and was then flown to the company I had been assigned to, Charlie Company, located seven miles north of Camp Eagle. I sat in the back of the Huey staring down at the citadel of Hue. I'd heard about the Tet offensive and the bloody battle that had taken place there eight months before. Many lives had been lost on both sides. I wondered what would happen at the same time next year?

The helicopter descended as we began our approach. The pilot turned in his armored seat and yelled, "There she is!" I looked down to where he was pointing and the bewilderment must have shown on my face.

"Don't worry," he hollered. "You'll learn to love this place after a few weeks. We're away from the division headquarters and that's good. We're left alone and can keep away from all the bullshit."

My new home was a tiny patch of mud seven kilometers northwest of the city of Hue. It looked like you could walk around the perimeter in less than fifteen minutes. Hootches, tents, and bunkers were scattered around the place. Larger, more substantial bunkers surrounded the perimeter. In the center of the complex was a small, narrow airstrip made out of perforated steel planking. Several helicopters were parked to the east. The name of the place was "LZ Sally." It was primarily a fire support base with 105 howitzers and 8-inch guns that also happened to share the turf with a helicopter company—my company, Charlie Company, home of the Blackwidows.

We landed and the pilot hovered the aircraft expertly between two six-foot-high walls. Such a structure was called a revetment. A revetment consisted of two PSP walls filled with dirt and was designed to protect the helicopter against shrapnel from incoming rockets and mortars. The pilot landed and shut down the aircraft. I hopped out and my combat boots immediately sunk up to the ankles in mud.

"Randy! Randy!"

I looked up. Joe Sulak, a buddy of mine from flight school, was quickly approaching. He wore a green baseball cap with black aviator wings sewn on the front. He had a yellow scarf wrapped around his neck and wore a .38 around his waist. The holster slapped against his leg as he walked.

Joe had become somewhat of a celebrity during the primary phase of flight training at Fort Wolters, Texas, when the helicopter he was flying experienced a tail rotor failure while lifting off from a confined area. He was flying solo in the Bell-13 when it happened. He had just cleared the trees on takeoff when the tail rotor stopped turning. With the loss of anti-torque capability, the fuselage of the machine followed Newton's third law and began to spin in the equal and opposite direction from the main rotor. By all accounts, the aircraft crashed in a boil of red dust, spinning like a carnival ride gone berserk. Another solo student observed it from the air and saw Joe emerge from the smoke and wreckage running as fast as he could. The spinning on the way down had toppled the gyros in Joe's head with the result that when he tried to run in a straight line away from the wreckage he ran in ever-decreasing circles, eventually reaching the tree line where he finally collapsed in a heap. He came out of the ordeal with not so much as a scratch.

It was good to see him again.

I yelled, "Well I'll be damned, you sawed off little Texan, how the hell are ya'?"

We embraced and slapped each other on the back. It must have been a bizarre sight. I am nearly six-foot-two-inches tall, and Joe is barely five foot seven. "It's great to see you, Randy. I arrived two days ago myself. Heard you'd been assigned to the Blackwidows. Been waitin' for you to arrive. Guess who else's here? Shonehour!" Another mate from flight school.

"Hey, that's great news. I thought I'd spend the year over here without seeing anyone from flight school."

"Shonehour and I lucked out. We had orders for the First Cav, but they sent us here instead." He turned and began to walk toward the company area. "Come on. Let me show you your tent."

I threw the duffel over my shoulder and followed him. "Tent?"

"Don't worry. The hootch you'll be living in is almost finished. The Sea Bees have been working their asses off to get the company built. You'll be staying in a tent for a few days till the last hootch is completed."

"Where you staying?"

His face lost its grin. "Shonehour and I walked into a *real* shitty situation when we got here."

"How do you mean?"

"The day we arrived one of the helicopters got shot down. Pilot, copilot, crew chief, and gunner all were killed. What a hell of a way to arrive in a new company. One of the company pilots took me to the area of the pilot who just got killed and said I could sleep in his bunk. Shonehour's sleeping in the dead copilot's bunk."

"Damn, what a way to start in a new company."

"Yeah, it was real depressing around here for awhile. The gloom over the company is just beginning to lift. No one knows my name yet. To them I'm just the fucking new guy who's sleeping in Lithwinski's bunk. They haven't even taken the man's personal effects away yet."

I asked him about the yellow scarf he wore around his neck like an ascot tucked into his Nomex flying suit. All the pilots in Second Platoon wore them, he said, and I would too as I was going to be assigned to the same platoon.

I looked down at his .38. "You look like a goddamn cowboy with that holster slung low on your hip. It suits you. Where do you think you're going, the OK corral?"

He slapped the holster. "Yeah, all the pilots wear 'em. You'll get one too. It's standard issue. This place is like a Wild West show. You may need it."

"What do you mean by that?"

"In the two days I've been here I've learned not to piss anyone off. If you do, you may go home in a box."

"What are you talking about?"

"A week ago the company top sergeant got his ass blown away. Apparently he was a real asshole. The enlisted men hated his guts. So one night one of them fragged the poor son-of-a-bitch while he was sleeping in his hootch. They're still picking pieces of flesh out of the screens."

I was shocked. "Did they catch the guy that did it?"

"Nope. The way people are acting around here you'd think the guy who blew him away had performed a public service."

"How about the flying. You been up yet?"

"Shonehour and I had our orientation flight yesterday. You're scheduled for one tomorrow. They're three pilots short so they want to get us checked out and on line as soon as possible."

Joe showed me my tent. I threw the duffel on the green cot. Then he took me to the officer's club. It was a shabby sixteen-by-thirty-two-foot hootch at the end of a row of six hootches where the second platoon pilots lived. The only difference between the club and the accommodation hootches was that it did not have windows. Joe threw open the door and led me in.

Inside, at the far end, there was a crude plywood bar. It had been lightly burnt with a torch to bring out the grain, giving it a rustic look. Behind the bar were two large refrigerators. On top was a reel-to-reel tape recorder. Two Sansui speakers hung in the far corners. To the right was an armor seat out of a Huey. A bright red flight helmet with the word "HERO" sat on a cyclic stick placed in front of the seat. There were two men seated at a small table playing cards.

"Now watch out," Joe warned. "First thing you have to do when you walk in here is step on the eagle." He pointed to the floor. Painted near the entrance was a facsimile of the patch everyone in the 101st wore on their shoulder depicting the Screaming Eagle. It was framed and covered in clear Plexiglass. He made an exaggerated stomping motion on it as he entered. "Now you do it."

The two men playing cards paused to watch me. I noticed they each had a yellow scarf around their neck. I raised my foot and stomped on the eagle. "That's it," one of them said approvingly. He stood and offered his hand. "Welcome to the Blackwidows. You must be the FNG Sulak's been talkin' about. My name's Kelly, Ned Kelly."

I shook his hand. "Randy Mains. Glad to meet you. What's an FNG, anyway?"

The other warrant stood and introduced himself. His name was Doug Carson. "FNG means fucking new guy. We've all been there. Glad to have you aboard." He sat down and the two men resumed their game.

Joe grinned. "You, Shonehour, and I are FNGs. I guess we're FNGs till we make aircraft commander. That right?"

Kelly threw two cards on the table. "Some guys'll always be FNGs in the eyes of the guys who got here before them. Gimmie two cards, Carson."

I turned to Joe. "Why do you have to stomp on the eagle like that when you walk in? Isn't it usually the other way around? Don't you normally avoid the unit crest when you walk into the club?"

Kelly looked up from his hand and answered. "Let *me* educate the FNG. You see, Mains, the Blackwidows used to be with the 188 Assault Helicopter Company as part of the First Aviation Brigade. When the 101st went airmobile we were infused with them. There are still a lot of pilots in the company who don't like the 101st. They think they're a load of gung-ho airborne ranger assholes who don't know the first fucking thing about using helicopters. So their loyalty is still with the 188th. In their eyes the 188th was a true aviation outfit. So, for those reasons, if you walk in here and don't stomp on the screamin' buzzard, you buy the drinks. Understand?''

I nodded.

"Good." He looked away from me to the man seated across from him. "Your bet, Carson."

Joe shrugged and walked to the bar. "Come on, FNG," he kidded, "let me buy you a coke."

"What about the armored chair. Looks like it's out of a Huey. What's it for?"

Joe smiled. "You'll find out soon enough."

Later, he took me to the supply tent where I was issued two green Nomex flying suits, Nomex gloves, a steel pot, a flack jacket, and all-leather boots. He advised me, "You don't want to wear those jungle boots with the green acrylic up the sides. Get rid of 'em. If you crash and there's a fire they'll burn and melt into your feet."

He took me by the armory where I was issued an M-16, ammunition, belt and holster, and a Smith and Wesson .38. At last I looked like I was ready for war.

That night I found out what the armored chair in the club was used for. After eating boiled beef and overdone potatoes in the mess tent, I walked to my tent to clean my M-16. I had it in pieces on my cot when Joe poked his head in through the flap. "Choir practice at 1930 in the club by order of the old man."

"Choir practice?"

"You'll see. I'll see you there," he said and was gone.

I had heard the guys talking in the mess tent about a combat assault the First Platoon pilots had been involved in up north. By the sound of it it had been pretty hairy.

Even before I entered the club I could hear the stereo blasting out the song "Folsom Prison Blues," by Johnny Cash. I took off my green baseball cap and stuffed it into my pocket before entering the smoke-filled hootch. Feeling conspicuous as the new guy, I made sure I stomped on the eagle after I passed through the door. I saw Joe standing at the end of the bar. He motioned me over and ordered me a Budweiser.

I could hear one of the pilots telling another about the assault that day. His ship had been shot up pretty bad. He began talking with his hands, showing the listener how he had maneuvered his aircraft, a sure sign of a war story in progress. The bartender, a black enlisted clerk named Flowers, rang the bell several times in quick succession and turned down the volume on the stereo. The officer's club fell silent. A Captain Thomas leapt up on top of the bar. "We got a hero story in the offing, gentlemen. I'm sure Lieutenant Fergison would be delighted to share it with us tonight. Right, Fergie?"

An embarrassed Fergison shook his head. He knew he'd been caught. Several other officers carried the reluctant lieutenant to the armored chair. They sat him in it, fastened the seat belt and shoulder harness, and placed the red helmet on his head, the boom microphone touching his bushy mustache.

"We're all ready," said Captain Thomas. "Let's hear the war story."

The lieutenant knew there was no getting out of it. So he began, "OK, OK, I'll begin by telling you that I got the fucking shit shot out of me today." Cheers and whistles came from the men. The bartender clanged the bell rapidly.

The lieutenant grabbed hold of the cyclic with his right hand. With his left he reached to the side and pulled up the collective pitch lever. He bent forward and continued. "Well ya see we came over the last ridge line before descending into the LZ. I was flying Chock Three in the formation. The first two ships must of woke Charlie up, cuz by the time me and Fletcher overflew the position, before dropping into the LZ, I saw muzzle flashes from the jungle. I had to break her off." He threw the stick to the left and pulled the red trigger on the hand grip as if to transmit on the radio. "Receiving fire, receiving fire, I yelled. Then a couple AK-47 rounds came up between me and Fletcher and hit the overhead circuit breaker panel." He looked over toward the bar. Fletcher, the man standing next to me, raised his glass of beer in a mock toast. The lieutenant hammed it up. "But we were lucky, gentlemen. We only took two other hits in the tail boom. Charlie missed his chance. Blackwidows Four and Eight will live to fly another day, another mission." He performed a salute. Someone handed him a beer. He raised it high and said, "To God and Country!"

Everyone raised their glasses and repeated the toast, "To God and Country!"

Someone yelled, "And here's to round-eye'd pussy."

"To round-eye'd pussy!" Every man repeated as one and we all drank to the toast.

The lieutenant took off the red helmet and unstrapped himself from the seat. He walked over to Fletcher, the man standing next to me. He threw his arm around his buddy and they clinked beer cans. In a few minutes the lieutenant was talking with his hands again, but he was not put in the chair for a second time. He was left to talk. Shortly afterwards someone bellowed, "Nineteen-thirty. Time for choir practice." Everyone knew the song by heart, that is, everyone except for me, Joe, and Tom Shonehour. But we soon learned it.

> *Oh Sally Oh Sally's a hell of a place,*
> *The organization's a fucking disgrace*
> *With captains and majors and light colonels too*
> *Who sit on their asses with nothing to do!*
>
> *They stand on the runway they scream and they shout,*
> *About many things they know nothing about*
> *For all of their bitching they might as well be*
> *A shoveling shit in the South China Sea!*

The impromptu party broke up around midnight. I made my way through the mud back to my tent and collapsed drunk into my bunk. At two-thirty in the morning, KAA-WHAM! The most almighty, bone-shaking explosion caused me to spring up straight out of my cot. My heart was about to explode in my chest. It sounded as if a mortar round had landed *inside* my tent. I half expected to see one side shredded and smoldering. In the dark, half asleep and in my green boxer shorts, I threw on my steel pot, flack jacket, and unlaced combat boots, grabbed my M-16 and a bandoleer of ammunition, and bolted from the tent, running full speed for the nearest bunker. KAAWHAM! Another explosion strong enough for me to feel the shock

wave hit my chest. I screamed out in a panic, "Incoming!
Incoming! Incoming!" and dove into the opening of a
bunker.

I waited, my chest heaving, my eyes wide, sweat pour-
ing down my brow. Shit, where is everyone? I thought.
KAAWHAM! KAAWHAM! KAAWHAM! three in a row.
Shit, goddamn, is this how I'm going to die? Before I've
even flown my first combat mission? Where is everyone?
I clutched my M-16 to my chest, my eyes searching the
darkness, waiting for Charlie's inevitable assault. I chambered a round and waited for the Vietcong to start coming
through the wire. Shit! Shit! Sheeeitt!

"Hey! FNG!" a voice yelled.

At last someone's coming? They'll know what to do,
I thought. I crouched down and scooted to the opening
of the bunker cautiously and yelled with all my being,
"Incoming! Incoming!"

"Hey, you! FNG! Shut the fuck up, will ya?"

A beam of light was approaching. I stepped further back
into the bunker. The beam suddenly shone in my face.
"What the fuck you doing?" a voice asked sarcastically.

I clutched the weapon tighter to my chest. "Incoming?" I said weakly.

"There's no fuckin' incoming," the voice said sternly.
"You gotta remember you're livin' on a fire support base.
You're hearing the eight inchers firing, that's all. Probably
a grunt unit in trouble called in artillery. The guns always
sound loudest when they shoot over our heads. Now come
on, get back to bed and quit hollerin'. You're waking everybody up."

"Who the hell can sleep through this?" I asked.

"Everybody! You'll get used to it. Now get your ass
back to your tent and go to bed."

Sheepishly, I exited the bunker and walked past the
faceless man toward my tent. I felt like an idiot. I un-
chambered the round from my weapon and took the steel
pot off my head. As I was about to duck under the flap I
heard someone say, "Goddamn, fuckin' new guys. Mother
of Mary pleeeeezzee save us all."

* * *

The following day I was given an orientation flight by the company instructor pilot, IP. We practiced approaches to a grassy area outside the perimeter of LZ Sally, and he let me get the feel of a Huey again. It was great to be back in the saddle.

I was impressed with how lush and green the landscape appeared from the air. From five hundred feet you would not know there was a war going on. Vietnamese farmers outside the perimeter ignored our presence and tended their rice paddies using water buffalo to pull their plows. On Highway-1 Vietnamese civilians scurried along like bees in a hive, attending to their daily business. Some rode Mopeds, Vespas, or bicycles, and others were on foot.

I had two training flights. One in the morning for general handling, and one in the afternoon to go over emergency procedures.

I entered the officer's club after evening chow, stomped on the likeness of the Screamin' Eagle painted on the floor like Joe had told me to do, and Spec-4 Flowers rang the bell behind the bar several times. He turned off Johnny Cash on the reel-to-reel. The noise of twenty officers talking ceased abruptly when they heard the bell. Captain Thomas stood on a chair and announced, "Gentlemen, I would like to introduce a very unique warning system freshly imported to I Corps from The World. Our company has obviously been chosen as the testing ground for this new secret weapon."

I began to feel uncomfortable. I had a feeling I knew what was coming next. Captain Thomas continued, "This new weapon has been constructed to alert troops in the field in the event of impending rocket or mortar attack. Gentlemen, I present to you the new secret weapon. His name is Warrant Officer Mains."

Most of the men cheered. Others boo'd.

"In consideration of the fact that I think we've been sent a defective model, that is, he alerts us even when he hears friendly fire—last night is a case in point—I'm sure Mr. Mains would like to make full restitution to all the officers he woke up when he malfunctioned. So would you please step up to the bar, Mr. Mains, put your money down, and buy everyone a drink for waking them up last night.''

The officers cheered and Spec-4 Flowers rang the bell. I, now extremely red faced, stepped up to the bar and plunked down my money. Captain Thomas began to sing and swung his free hand, the one not holding his beer, as if he were conducting a church choir. Everyone joined in.

Ohhhhhh
We like it here,
We like it here,
You fuckin' A we like it here.
And though we have malaria
We still maintain our area
We like it here
We like it here
You fuckin' A we like it here.

''OK, men that was good. Now to show our heart's in the right place, let's give Mr. Mains a HIM.'' Everyone joined in and chanted in unison while rocking their glasses:

Himmmmm, Himmmmmm . . . Fuck, Himmmmm!

I was beginning to feel like one of the guys already.

The next morning I was given a check ride by the company instructor pilot. I passed. After lunch I was assigned to fly copilot on my first mission with a CW2 named Crawford. I reported to the aircraft at 1300 as I'd been told to do by operations. I had her pre-flighted and was seated eagerly in the copilot's seat when Crawford arrived.

He was a tall, thin, morose individual. I found out later he had a right to be morose. He was a short timer.

He did his *own* preflight, then climbed in without saying a word to me. He checked that the gunner and crew chief were ready then strapped in and started the turbine engine. He twisted on the throttle and gave the radio call.

''Sally tower, this is Blackwidow One-One, Widow Web for departure.''

''Roger, Blackwidow One-One. Wind one-three-zero at

ten knots, altimeter three-zero-one-zero cleared for take off.''

"Blackwidow One-One, roger. On the go."

Crawford scanned the instruments, and with his left hand lifted the collective lever. The aircraft rose to a three-foot hover. He eased the ship forward out of the revetment and, satisfied the aircraft temperature and pressures were within the normal ranges, nosed her over and we took off to the south. He began a right-hand turn and climbed quickly to fifteen hundred feet now heading north.

Crawford did not as much as glance at me. Nor did he talk to me. He treated me like I was not there. I waited several minutes to see if he would brief me on the mission, or even speak to me, but he did not. Finally I pressed the floor mike button and said over the intercom, "What do you want me to do?"

There was a pause. For a moment I didn't think he was going to answer. Then he looked over at me. He had the same look in his eyes I had seen in the eyes of the CW2s in the mess hall at Bien Hoa. He pressed the trigger on the cyclic and spoke on the intercom, "Just sit there and monitor your bootlaces, that's all. And, if I'm unlucky enough to get my ass shot today, you do what you've been trained to do up to this point in your aviation career. You take the controls and get me the fuck to the hospital in Phu Bai."

We flew four hours that day. We delivered supplies and men from Camp Eagle to LZs Whip, Sledge, and Tennessee. Then we landed in several remote LZs scattered in the mountains. Some of the landing sites were more difficult than any I had ever seen. Crawford took the aircraft into hover holes so closely surrounded by hundred-foot trees that if you even sneezed it would have meant disaster. I had seen nothing like it demonstrated in flight school, and I wondered if I would ever be able to do the same. Nagging thoughts about my pedal control played on my mind. There were LZs we landed in that day that I could not have begun to negotiate. I simply did not have the skill and I knew it. At the end of the mission I hadn't touched the controls once. Crawford even shot the last approach to the Widow Web at Sally.

After we'd shut down, I told him how impressed I'd been with his flying. I told him I hoped I'd be able to fly like that one day. He ran his hand through his hair and told me I probably would learn, one day. I knew it would not be with him.

As we walked back together through the mud from the Widow Web to the company area I said to him, "I know I couldn't have landed in a lot of the places we went to today. But why didn't you let me fly at all?"

He looked at me with those piercing eyes, then his expression softened. "Nothing personal, Mains. It's just that I've got two weeks left before I stop flying. I've flown nearly one thousand combat hours over here so far. I've trained my share of pilots and I figure I've paid my dues. Ops isn't makin' me fly the hairy stuff anymore. Just ass and trash, men and equipment. I made it this far. There were a lot of times this last year I thought I wouldn't. Nothing against you, Mains. Don't get me wrong. It's just I don't want any fuck-ups. I got a wife and kid waitin' for me back home. Being killed by an FNG peter pilot with two weeks left to go would just piss me off no fucking end."

That night I lay asleep in my cot when KAABOOM! KAABOOM! KAABOOM! the thunderous noise caused me to spring up out of bed. Not wanting to cause another incident, I began to lay back down again when suddenly an urgent clanging could be heard. Then someone yelled, "Incoming! Incoming!" This time we were really under attack.

I grabbed my steel pot, flack jacket, M-16, and ammunition and ran in my underwear and unlaced boots to the bunker. It was already crowded with men huddled together.

WHOOMPH! WHOOMPH! WHOOMPH! WHOOMPH! the explosions seemed to be getting closer to our company area. Someone whispered, "Sounds like they're hittin' the arty side of the camp."

Not a word was spoken after that. We just huddled together and listened in the darkness of the bunker. Several minutes passed. The mortars stopped falling. Flares popped and hissed into the air from the perimeter and drifted lazily downward casting an eerie light over our company area. I heard someone say, ''I don't fucking believe it. You gotta be shittin' me, sir?''

This was followed by muffled laughter traveling in a wave and finally engulfed everyone in the bunker. Another flare hissed and popped illuminating the bunker's interior. I turned and saw why everyone was laughing. Several flashlights were now spotlighting our CO, Major Posey. He wore the regulation steel pot and unlaced combat boots and carried an M-16, but his principle dress was a baggy pair of Hop Along Cassidy pajamas! The man's image, that of a seasoned, hardened combat veteran, was immediately and irrevocably destroyed, and he stood there mortified. I knew there and then that this was going to be more than just a crazy war. I knew something else—I knew who would be buying the drinks in the officer's club the following night!

CHAPTER 3

November 1968

Sulak's C-Ration Grenade

The Sea Bees finished construction of the last hootch. It was a day to celebrate. As I carried my belongings from the tent to the hootch, I noticed that the narrow space between the new hootch and the one next to it already looked like a chinese laundry. I counted eight sets of household brown electrical wire running into my new home, tapping into my neighbor's electric supply to run small refrigerators, tape recorders, electric shavers, and lights. The few feet separating each hootch in the company looked like that, with wires stealing electricity from the next. The camp wiring was an electrician's nightmare. That is why power failures from the overtaxed, twenty-five kilowatt generator were frequent.

I carefully set up my area and hung the green mosquito netting over the bed—a real bed! It was nothing fancy, standard army issue, but it was not a cot, and that made all the difference. I stood back to admire my handiwork. A crude, plastic woven rug mat that I purchased from the ville outside the perimeter of Sally lay next to my bed— my effort to give the dusty place a feeling of home. The 8-×-10 picture of Michelle hung on the wall over my bed. There was only one other thing left to do to make my area home. I hung my shaving mirror on the wall at eye level, making sure it hung straight, then took a long look at myself. I studied the thin blond strands beginning to sprout from my smooth upper lip. Nearly all the pilots of Charlie Company sported mustaches. It seemed to be part of the image of a helicopter pilot over here. I ran my fingers over the stubble looking forward to the day I could cultivate this scraggly embarrassment into a real mustache. I stared into the mirror. Clear blue eyes stared back. Untroubled eyes. Soft, questioning eyes. Eyes that had not yet seen combat. I wondered if, over the year, they would develop the nervous look I had seen in the eyes of the CW2 in Bien Hoa, or in Crawford's eyes now. Short timer's eyes. Darting, expectant, cautious veteran's eyes. I wondered. I adjusted the yellow scarf around my neck, brushed a lock of short, light-brown hair back into place, then stood back from the mirror to admire once again my new area. It was small, about twelve feet square, but it was tidy and neat. I was pleased.

KABOOM! KABOOM! the eight-inch guns fired. I could feel the shock waves slam into my body as the two volleys of fifty-six pounds of explosives went off. My mirror crashed in pieces on the floor along with the shaving gear that I had arranged so carefully on a wooden shelf. I was glad to see that at least Michelle's picture had remained in place.

I shared the new hootch with a pilot named Les Ramson. He was a gun freak. I was convinced he owned every conceivable make of weapon that had ever been brought into Vietnam. He even had a gangster-style Thompson submachine gun with a fifty-round barrel clip. He kept his entire weapon collection piled one on top of the other under his bunk. He delighted in showing it to me whenever I had the misfortune to be cornered by him. He had been in country for six months. He was a heavy, bearded man with suspicious eyes and a body as solid as a fireplug.

Ramson was one of the maintenance officers. He never flew operational missions, never got shot at, and only flew aircraft fresh out of maintenance. He shared the duties with two other maintenance officers, Captain Paulson and Junior. The men had nicknamed the young captain Junior because having lied about his age when he joined the service he became, at the time, the youngest captain in the U.S. Army. Junior hated this nickname but, because he never flew combat missions, unlike the rest of the company pilots, he knew he was considered to be a bit of a wimp and felt he had shaky grounds for insisting that we call him captain. He was occasionally addressed as "Captain Junior" which made him even more angry. Somehow being called Junior was less offensive to him, but he let only the pilots who flew combat call him that. Junior tried to order Ramson to call him sir because Ramson was a warrant officer, never flew combat missions, and was only a maintenance officer like himself, and therefore had no reason *not* to call him sir. But when Junior approached him on the subject and ordered him to call him sir, Ramson reminded Junior that he had an arsenal stashed under his bunk and hinted that one of his many weapons could just "accidentally" go off in the direction of Junior's hootch one night. The threat so alarmed Junior that he had to be content with just the enlisted men saluting him and calling him sir. I always felt that they did this out of compassion rather than respect for the man.

On their maintenance test flights Ramson, Paulson, and Junior made it a habit to fly the newly serviced aircraft directly above Sally. That served two purposes: One, they could be relatively sure they would never be shot at and two, if anything went wrong mechanically they would not risk going down in hostile territory. By the very nature of their cushy job one would have expected them to have no worries. Not so. All three men were extremely paranoid individuals. Les Ramson was the worst.

On one occasion, after flying five hours as copilot on an ass-and-trash mission out of Camp Eagle, I was walking to the shower wearing nothing but a pair of thongs and holding my towel in one hand and a bar of soap in the other. I noticed Ramson digging frantically with an entrenching tool in the mud outside our new hootch. "What'cha doing?"

He didn't stop digging but answered, "Taking out insurance."

"Insurance?"

"Don't you read the newspapers?"

"Of course. Whenever I can get my hands on one, that is. They're pretty rare to come by over here. But what does that have to do with you digging a hole next to our hootch?"

He threw a pile of dirt and mud over his shoulder. "You know who Jean Dixon is?"

"Yeah sure, she's the lady who claims she can see into the future. She makes predictions."

"That's right. And do you know what she is predicting now?"

"Nope."

He stopped digging long enough to look up at me. "She says that Charlie Company of the 101st Airborne Division, that's us by the way, is going to be overrun by sappers and wiped out within the next month. This here soon-to-be underground bunker is my insurance. When it happens I'll crawl through a trap door that I'll have under the mat next to my bunk. I'll have a tunnel leading to this underground bunker, and I'll live through it while the rest of you get wiped out."

"That's real considerate of you, Ramson." I looked at the one-foot-deep hole he'd already dug. "How big you going to make it, anyway?"

"About four feet square and four feet deep. Then I'll cover it with PSP and dirt. I'll have several cases of C-rations and a case of beer to sustain me till I can make my escape."

"Good luck." I turned and resumed my walk to the showers.

He yelled, "If you help me you can share it when the time comes."

"No thanks, I'll take my chances."

Around 2200 that night Joe Sulak, Tom Shonehour, and I watched, from atop a bunker in our company area, green tracers firing into our perimeter on the northern side of the compound. They appeared to float in the sable night as they penetrated Sally's northern perimeter. We could barely hear the popping from the enemy weapons that fired them. Red tracer rounds, ours, fired back. A Cobra gunship flew overhead and fired a red stream of tracers that flowed like a red ribbon making its way from the ship's miniguns to the berm. We could hear the whirr of the electric motor of the gatling gun firing bullets at three thousand rounds per minute. Was this the night it would happen? We half expected to see sappers running through our area throwing satchel charges into each hootch and blowing them all up. Maybe Jean Dixon had something. The next day there were five pilots helping Les Ramson dig his bunker.

I wrote another letter home.

6 November 1968

Dear Mom:

Got your letters today. They arrived in country the 30th and I got them the 6th. I was sure glad to receive them. I also received a letter from Greg and Michelle. Greg said a big north swell hit the coast and there were waves as high as twelve feet at the pier. Michelle sounds fine. She's busy in college. I don't have much to say except I expected more to be going on over here.

The flying is almost like flying in the States except we fly higher and faster. There is some pretty country over here. Green, lush mountains lie to the west. Along the coast, in the flat lands, rice paddies dot the land like patchwork. I find it enjoyable flying, believe it or not. I'll save the war stories for when I get home. I have flown twenty hours so far. All I do is fly. When I am not flying I am either in the officer's club or working on my living quarters.

We are living out in the boondocks. There are semi-permanent buildings here we call hootches, but nothing fancy. No running water. Fifty-five-gallon drums over the showers are filled with water trucked in from a nearby river. I haven't taken a hot shower since I have been here. You know me, that's hard to take. But the temperature is so hot here anyway you have to take one or two showers a day to feel good.

Boy, I tell you, being a pilot is the only way to live over here and we are well-respected by the ground troops and with due cause.

All aviators must wear a .38 caliber revolver. It is really neat. You can always tell an army helicopter pilot over here by his holster on his hip like a cowboy. I'll send you a picture of me soon.

When I fly I wear a ballistic flight helmet and a chest protector that fits over me like a life preserver: a bulletproof vest. Also the pilot seats are bulletproof, so I am pretty well-protected.

I'm glad Andrea is improving in first grade and that Nancy's enjoying her secretarial job at Road and Track magazine. Tell them both "hi" for me. I miss them.

Mom, for Christmas I'll have to send you some money to buy presents because I don't have access to gifts except for mail order and they wouldn't get there on time, so around the middle of December be expecting some money from me and a list of names to buy presents for.

Not much to say except when I get home a Thrifty drug store will look like a huge shopping mall to me at the end of my tour.

Please write to me when you can. Your letters mean a lot.

Randy

Lieutenant Dick Childs was a pilot who occupied the small living area across from mine. He had been assigned to the company a month before me. His secondary duty role was that of supply officer. In his scrounging patrols he was coming up with some pretty bizarre equipment. One day he crashed through the screen door of our hootch carrying two scuba tanks, and wearing a full parachute. "What do you think?" he asked me.

"What do you plan to do with scuba tanks in a combat zone? And we certainly don't need parachutes. We don't use them."

"I'll trade the scuba tanks to the Sea Bees living at the beach for jungle boots. I can swap this parachute to the air force in Da Nang for several cases of frozen steaks. Tomorrow I'm going to work on a deal to obtain a new Huey from the navy."

"A Huey! Are you out of your mind? The CO will go

nuts if you show up with a Huey. How could he justify it on the books?''

"He doesn't have to. Through my supply network I've found out that the navy has one extra Huey lying around. The naval supply officer doesn't even know where it came from. The unit's coming up for an IG inspection and they have to get rid of it, pronto, or do some pretty fancy explaining. It's already boxed up and ready to go. I can trade it to a First Cav friend of mine in II Corps who just wrote off one of theirs because they dropped it off a truck. Heads'll roll if he can't come up with a Huey to replace it. He's willing to trade anything for it.''

Dick Childs had early on earned the name ''Douche Bag'' Dick Childs amongst the other pilots because of his lousy flying ability. There was not an aircraft commander in our platoon who did not wonder how Childs had been allowed to graduate from flight school.

On one sortie his instructions were to make a landing to the airstrip at firebase Birmingham. The only obstacle for miles was a single helicopter parked to one side of the long strip. There were acres of clear space where Childs could have landed; nevertheless, he nearly managed to crash into the parked aircraft. The AC had to grab the controls to avoid a collision. Similar reports came back after each mission flown with him. The conclusion was quickly reached that he was a disaster and would surely kill someone if allowed to continue. He was not long for the Blackwidows.

The ability of the pilots to accomplish the missions under the most adverse conditions impressed me. If I were to survive I could see I would have to learn skills that involved a whole new dimension in flying that they never taught in flight school. The line between accomplishing the mission and disaster was a thin one indeed. As a new pilot to the Blackwidows, I had serious doubts that I would ever be as proficient as any of the ACs in my company. I guess that was normal. I was in awe of the precision they demonstrated when they flew in close formation and then landed perhaps up to ten ships in tight landing zones. Each

AC had learned his personal limits and knew when to push them and how far to push them and still avert disaster.

One early morning mission, however, pushed the pilots past the limits of tolerance they were able to adhere to. The incident was caused by the one weak link flying in a Second Platoon aircraft, Douche Bag Dick Childs. His error in judgment nearly cost us our lives.

Division Headquarters at Camp Eagle assigned Charlie Company the task of supplying a platoon of pilots and aircraft for ten days at a time to be stationed temporarily at Camp Evans in support of the Third Brigade's 502nd Infantry Battalion. Second Platoon drew the short straw. We were to pull the first ten days up at Evans.

We were a flight of seven Hueys flying up to Camp Evans to begin the mission. We had taken off at first light from LZ Sally. I knew the other pilots had to feel as rough as I did after a late night in the officer's club. I had managed to get only three hours sleep.

"Tighten up the formation," Chock One ordered over the UHF radio. "Weather's gettin' really shitty ahead."

The lead aircraft flew a zig-zag flight path skirting low clouds. We followed him flying between clouds as we weaved our way northward. The AC was letting me fly. I glanced over at him. His head was nodding. He was falling asleep. I added a little power and tightened it up on the fourth aircraft, trying to hold a forty-five-degree angle off my left and keeping his rotor disk on the horizon. Highway-1 was five hundred feet directly below us. I could see it through the chin bubble beneath my pedals. Suddenly everything went white. I looked up and the fourth aircraft in front of me had disappeared. Vanished. The lead aircraft had flown into the clouds. The radio suddenly exploded. "One, this is Two, we lost you, breaking right!"

"Three, breaking left."

I lost visual on Chock Four. I maintained heading and lowered collective to descend. The aircraft commander woke up at this stage. "What the fu . . . ? I got it," he snatched the controls from me.

"You got it. They flew into the clouds." I told him.

"Jesus fuck." Then he broadcast, "This is Chock Five. I've lost everyone."

"Chock Six doin' a one-eighty."

"Chock Seven breaking left. Descending."

"Seven, this is Six. Got you. Following you out."

"Roger."

"Two this is Three lost you. Can't see. Leveling out. Leveling out."

"Roger."

"This is Chock One. We broke out. Base of the clouds is at three hundred feet."

"This is Two, looking. Still in the shit."

"Four where are you?"

"Still in the clouds descending."

Suddenly out of the gray I saw an aircraft red anticollision light streak from the upper right hand of our windshield and dive in front of us at a forty-five-degree angle. It startled me and I pulled my head back. The machine filled the window. I knew we were going to collide in midair. The aircraft commander hauled back on the cyclic, the aircraft's nose pitched up, but too late. The diving helicopter was gone as quickly as it had appeared. If we were going to hit it there was nothing he could do about it. But by an amazing piece of luck we missed it by what must have been a few feet.

Moments later reports came in that everyone was out of the clouds and each ship radioed that they were flying separately to Camp Evans.

When everyone had landed and shut down Crawford jumped out of his aircraft and stomped over to the Chock One aircraft and opened the AC's door. He threw back the sliding armored plating and pulled him out with both hands by his collar.

"What the holy fuck do you think you were doin' back there? You almost fucking got us all killed."

"Sorry, goddamn, let go you crazy fuck. I wasn't flyin', my peter pilot was." When Crawford looked over at the copilot a weakly smiling Douche Bag Dick Childs was staring back at him.

"Fucking you!" He screamed, and pulled the AC out further by the collar till he had him leaning out of the aircraft nearly horizontal, nose to nose. "If I'm flying in your formation again I don't want this fucking disaster of a pilot to touch the goddamn controls. You got that? I'm too fucking short for this kind of shit. Understood?''

"Yeah, yeah, I understand. Let go. I already chewed his ass out. He won't do it again, not as long as I'm the AC.''

"Well, see that he doesn't." He threw the man back in his armored seat, spun on his heels, and stormed off towards our living area.

It made no difference that our AO was covered with menacing low clouds, drizzle, and at times heavy rain. The war ground on. There were still soldiers in the jungle to support, men to shuttle around to the fire-support bases, and supplies, ammunition, food, and mail to deliver. There were combat assaults to perform and wounded soldiers to fly back from the field.

One morning Second Platoon was given a mission to airlift a company of troops into an area near LZ Barbara eighteen miles northwest of Sally. We were to pick up the troops attached to the Third Brigade in an open staging area near Camp Evans. We flew in drizzling rain, in a staggered left formation, at fifteen hundred feet, out of the range of small arms fire, until the command, "Take up trail formation," came over the UHF radio from Ned Kelly who was flying Chock One. I was flying copilot in Chock Two and moved the controls to slip in behind Ned Kelly.

"Not too close to Kelly's tail rotor," the AC cautioned. I pulled back. "Good, now keep his main rotor on the horizon. That way you'll be sure to avoid his turbulence.''

Kelly began the approach. I could see lines of soldiers waiting for our arrival in the large staging area south of Camp Evans. Purple smoke rose in the downpour. There were ten lines of soldiers, one for each ship in our formation. I aimed for the second line of men. I kept the main rotor of Kelly's ship on the horizon all the way to the ground and planted the skids in the mud. Six heavily laden, combat-ready troops carrying M-16s, with steel pots on their heads and bulky rucksacks on their backs, scurried aboard.

"We're loaded, sir," the crew chief said.

The tail aircraft radioed, "You're up, Lead.''

Kelly transmitted, "Yellow Lead's lifting."

I mirrored Kelly's takeoff and followed him into the high mountains. I tried to make my control movements smooth knowing eight other aircraft were following behind. The area where we were to drop the troops was a ridge line south of LZ Barbara.

"Yellow Flight, this is Yellow Lead. String it out. This'll be a single-ship LZ."

All the ships acknowledged.

I had a lot of respect for Ned Kelly. In the few weeks I had known him he seemed to be a born leader. I had flown with him two days before and he had let me do a lot of the flying—more than any of my previous ACs had allowed. After takeoff from a fire-support base where we had dropped off one thousand pounds of C-rations I laid the aircraft over into a fifty-degree bank and turned back to Camp Eagle. After the turn I looked at Kelly with a silly grin on my face. He was not amused. "You probably didn't notice you pulled fifty pounds of torque in the turn." He grabbed the controls from my hands. "I got it. If you want to try another one of those fucking *hero* turns again, try it in someone else's aircraft. Don't tear the ass out of mine, understand?"

I could feel the crew chief's eyes drilling through the back of my helmet from his place in the gun well. In my enthusiasm in the turn I knew I had bruised his baby. "Yes, I understand. I'm sorry."

"Forget it. Just don't do it again." Kelly told me.

I felt lousy. I had blown the trust I had worked so hard to earn that day in one single unprofessional maneuver. Typical of an FNG, I thought.

I watched Kelly maneuver his ship up a deep jungle valley, setting up for his final approach to the LZ under radio guidance from the FAC, forward air controller, circling above at four thousand feet in a single-engine Bird Dog fixed-wing. About a mile from the LZ I could see the white phosphorous smoke rising up out of the trees from the artillery prep. Then two fast movers, F-4 Phantom jets, swept down and dropped a sortie of napalm on either side of the zone. White smoke and flames tumbled over and through the jungle. When we were on quarter-mile final two Cobra gunships fired pairs of 2.75-inch rockets into the jungle on either side of Kelly's ship. Then something happened. On short final, Kelly's chopper seemed to stop flying and fell out of the air. It looked as if he was going to go into the trees at first, but he flared violently before he semi-crash landed, planting his skids heavily on the edge of the ridge line with the nose pointing 45 degrees in the air. The machine appeared to be frozen in this position for a moment, as if stuck there, then the tail spun around wildly 180 degrees. Now the nose of the helicopter was pointed straight down the mountain and the chopper fell away from the cliff and toward the trees. He dragged the machine's skids through the treetops as the helicopter accelerated down the mountain. I was convinced he was going in. He banked sharply towards a gully, dove down it, disappearing for a moment in the trees, regained his flying speed, and started a climb. The aircraft's skids were bent in the middle at an odd angle. Other than that, the machine looked OK.

"Had a bit of a problem," he transmitted. "I'll be taking the ship back to Sally. Watch the approach. There's a hell of a downdraft on that ridge line."

"Bit of a problem!" my AC repeated. "He almost fucking bought the farm! Kelly always was the master of understatement."

The aircraft commander took the controls from me and shot a steeper-than-normal approach into the LZ in anticipation of the turbulence Kelly had warned us about. We encountered no turbulence. He took it in on the second sortie, just in case. Smooth as glass. He let me take it in on the third, fourth, and fifth sorties. None of the ships had felt the reported turbulence.

Ned Kelly bought the rounds in the club that night, but no one made him sit in the hero's chair to tell his war story. It was obvious he was pretty shaken up. No one said anything to him. Most of us believed he had just plain fucked-up the approach. He had blown it and he knew it. The worst thing that can happen to a pilot's ego is to have his confidence shaken. Ned Kelly was real quiet that night and proceeded to get very, very drunk.

Around 2300 the drizzle turned into a steady rain. At times it rained so hard that the sound of rushing water and the monsoon wind almost drowned out the drunken singing emanating from the officer's club. It rained all night. It rained so hard I could barely hear the 105 howitzers firing through the night from the artillery side of the camp.

The following morning Les Ramson was distraught because his four-foot-square-by-one-foot-deep unfinished bunker was now an overflowing quagmire of muddy water.

I sat down after breakfast and wrote a letter home.

9 November 1968

Dear Mom:

I received your letter inviting me to Andrea's sixth birthday party. Thanks, but I'm afraid I'll have to take a rain check. Give her a big birthday hug and kiss for me.

The monsoons started here today. They are actually late for this time of year. They usually end around March. The old timers say I won't fly as much in the next six months as I will probably fly when the monsoon season is over.

Not much happening. We were going to fly on a big CA, combat assault, but it got rained out. There were going to be thirty-two B-52's dropping bombs on the area, then Air Force jets were going to drop napalm, then helicopter gunships were going to prep the LZ with rockets. Finally we were to fly in the troops and their supplies but it got called off because of the weather.

The other pilots in the company are great. I tell you, flying over here is the only way to fight a war. We receive a lot of respect from the ground troops because they rely so heavily on us for transportation and for all their resupply.

I am taking some pictures and will send you some when I have taken a whole roll and get them developed which takes quite some time because we have to send our film to Hawaii for processing.

I'd really hate to be a ground pounder over here. It's

raining buckets now. I can't imagine what it's like for them in the jungle right now. They have it tougher than anyone.

More later.
Randy

A week of waiting and watching and listening to the rain falling from the dirty Southeast Asian sky became monotonous and boring in the extreme. At times it rained so hard that you were unable to see fifty feet across the company area. Everything outside the company hootches was a quagmire—deep swimming pools of muddy water. All my clothes and flight suits, after being washed by my hootch maid, came back damp and smelling of a campfire. The only means of drying laundry in the monsoon season was over an open fire in the ville.

The Blackwidows flew little that week. I flew twice as copilot up to Camp Eagle. The pilots were getting itchy. The afternoon of the eighth day the rain subsided into a fine drizzle. Our black ops NCO, Sergeant Peoples, banged on the door of my hootch.

"Come in."

He entered breathing hard. He'd obviously been running. His poncho dripped onto my plywood floor. "Mr. Mains, you'll be flying with Bob Coulshaw in fifteen minutes. The weather's clearing in the mountains and Brigade wants you to try to get mail to the guys up at LZ Veghel."

I looked out the screen to check the weather outside. Billowing, black cumulous clouds were rolling in from the mountains. "You sure, Peoples? Looks pretty nasty out there to me."

"I'm just passin' orders, sir. If it looks bad you can always turn round. Brigade requested you just give it a try, that's all."

Mail was a great morale booster. Next best thing to R&R or leaving Vietnam for good. I put on my green baseball cap, my holster and .38, and grabbed my flack jacket. I tucked the yellow scarf into the collar of my No-mex flight suit. I suddenly had this overwhelming feeling I was acting a part in a Hollywood movie, similar to those of my daydreams when I "flew" the old B-25 at Van Nuys airport ten years before. "Why not," I said. "Sounds like a good cause. Beats hell out of sittin' around here."

"That it does, sir. Mr. Coulshaw's on his way to the chopper now. You'll be takin' ship 786. Said he'd meet you out there."

The weather was miserable. We had to scud run at near treetop level to avoid the low, menacing overcast. Coulshaw guided the craft up valleys, across saddles, up more valleys, around mountains. Because we were so low I could not accurately pinpoint our position on the map. I hoped Coulshaw knew where we were. Luckily, he did.

"There she is up there," he said with a thick southern drawl, pointing. We circled in a jungle valley of drizzling rain. Below, triple-canopy jungle. Above, a solid, black cloud layer that I watched move back and forth over the LZ we were going to try to land on. According to the map we were surrounded by mountains several thousand feet higher than where we were at the moment. When I looked outside, I could not see them because they were shrouded in black clouds.

The FM radio came to life. "We have you visual, Blackwidow One-Four. Pad's clear. You can come on in."

"Roger, Kentucky Jumper. We'll give it a try."

Coulshaw began his approach. On short final the clouds rolled over the pad obscuring it. He had to bank away sharply, descend, and circle again. We circled and waited until the cloud rolled off the pad. Coulshaw tried it again. This time we made it. The grunts, most of them shirtless and muddy, ran up to us and pulled off the two sacks of mail. They were beaming and gave us the thumbs up. One of them came up to my window, stood on the skid, gave me the thumbs up sign and mouthed, "Thanks!"

The clouds were rolling down on us and threatened to cover the pad again. We had to get out quick. Coulshaw picked the craft up to a hover, kicked left pedal, and dove down the mountain the way we had come in. He headed toward the saddle in the mountain. It was just open, the cloud covering on either side making our escape route look like a narrow tunnel. If we hurried it looked as if we would barely squeeze through. The FM radio came to life again.

"Blackwidow One-Four, we forgot to throw our outgoing mail on board. Could you come back and pick it up?"

Coulshaw did not answer. He threw the machine into a steep right bank and headed back to the pad. I thought that if he had been flying with Ned Kelly he would have been chastised for making a *hero* turn. But in this case it was called for. We were racing against time.

The pad was obscured by cloud. Coulshaw transmitted, "Kentucky Jumper, we'll circle for a few minutes. If your pad doesn't clear, we'll have to throw it away and return to base. Weather's rat shit, copy?"

"We copy, Blackwidow One-Four. Thanks."

We circled. The clouds tumbled lower. We circled some more. The clouds began to force us lower still. I noticed our escape hole in the mountain saddle was covered in cloud. We were boxed in. Trapped. Surrounded by clouds that were descending upon us rapidly. The rain began to increase. That's when I saw the muzzle flashes. I shouted on the intercom to Coulshaw, "We're taking fire. Two o'clock low!"

"Shit!" Coulshaw banked hard away from the ridge line. The horizon went vertical.

I heard something hit the ship. Coulshaw pulled in collective and everything outside went white, then dark gray. I got on the gauges. The attitude indicator showed a fifty-degree turn to the right. Our angle of bank was increasing.

"Attitude!" I yelled. Coulshaw corrected.

Where are those damn mountains, I thought.

The airspeed began to drop from eighty knots to forty. Coulshaw was pulling back on the cyclic stick. "Check airspeed," I said, trying to hide the fear in my voice. The angle of bank began to increase again. Fuck. Can't see the goddamn mountains. "Check your turn!"

The wings on the instrument fell back slowly to a thirty-degree bank. We both knew we had to keep turning in a tight circle to avoid the mountains and climb up out of the valley. I looked outside. It looked like someone had painted all the windows dirty gray. I expected to see the jungle suddenly come rushing at us before the crash. It was raining hard. Somewhere out there were mountains. Coulshaw was fighting just to keep the craft from going inverted—a fatal maneuver in a Huey. I thought about my tactical instrument ticket and the joke about the hole punched in the right-hand corner. Fuck, bayonet training. Some joke. Goddamn, this is fucking serious! Calm down. Calm down. I repeated to myself.

"Airspeed," I said over the intercom. It was down to twenty knots. The altimeter read thirty-one hundred feet. "Forward cyclic. Check airspeed!"

"Gotta keep turning right," Coulshaw said. "Check the gauges and keep me straight."

"Roger. You're doin' OK. You're doin' OK." He was fighting for control.

"Take a breath. Power. Pull in fifty pounds of torque." He did.

We climbed in the soup at twelve hundred feet-per-minute in a right-hand turn. "Airspeed looks good. Relax. Keep it comin' right. Keep it comin' right. That's it. That's it. Lookin' good. Angle of bank looks good. We're winnin', buddy, we're winnin'. Four thousand feet. Lookin' good. At six thousand feet you can head zero-four-five degrees to the coast. I'll call for a radar approach. Looks good, sixty knots. Should be clear of the peaks now. You can level the wings. That's it, good."

Minutes later we broke out of the clouds at nine thousand feet heading 045 degrees. Coulshaw was wet with sweat. So was I. The sun shone brightly now that we were above the goo. "Now we got to get back down through that shit. Fuck me!" Coulshaw said.

"You want me to fly the approach?" I asked.

"No, just monitor my flying. You did good. And work the radios."

"Roger."

I dialed in the frequency. "Phu Bai approach, this is Blackwidow One-Four. We're VFR on top at nine thousand feet heading zero-four-five degrees. Request radar handling for a GCA."

"Roger, Blackwidow One-Four, are you transponder equipped?"

We had the control head, but not the guts. The transponder, an electronic aid to identify our blip on the controller's radar screen, had been removed to save on weight. "We have negative transponder." I told him.

"Roger, for radar identification, turn right to zero-nine-zero degrees."

"Roger, right zero-nine-zero degrees." Coulshaw flew the new heading.

"I have you ten miles northwest of Phu Bai, Blackwidow One-Four. On present heading you may descend to three thousand feet."

I repeated the instructions then said to Coulshaw, "Well, here we go. Here's your last chance to take out your tactical ticket and see blue sky."

He smiled at the joke and seemed to relax. "Nah, we can get down without it." He lowered the collective and began a descent.

Neither of us brought it up at the time, but we both knew that a week ago a Phu Bai GCA controller had radar-vectored a twin-engine, fixed-wing aircraft into a mountain. Eight people had been killed. We descended into wet goo again putting all our trust in the controller, hoping he would not make the same fatal mistake. Coulshaw had settled down and we descended straight ahead to three thousand feet without a hitch.

"Blackwidow One-Four level at three thousand." I radioed.

"Roger, turn left now to three-three-zero degrees and descend to fifteen hundred feet."

"Roger, copy."

Coulshaw turned and leveled out on the new heading. It began to rain heavily now, getting very dark. Even if we did break out of the clouds we probably would not be able to see the runway.

"Phu Bai, we're level at fifteen hundred."

"Roger, turn left to one-five-zero degrees and descend to one thousand feet."

I read back the clearance. Soon we were on the new course. "Blackwidow One-Four turn left to intercept inbound course for the runway. No need to acknowledge further transmissions. You are approaching glide path, turn left five degrees to intercept runway center line. That's it you're on course. Begin descent now to intercept glide path . . ."

The controller talked us down the approach path giving us instructions to make small heading and altitude corrections. It was like being talked down blind. We broke out of the clouds at two hundred feet in a torrential rain shower. We flew the approach to the runway like an airplane. When we turned off the runway for the taxi way I radioed, "Thanks, Phu Bai. We owe you one. What's your name?"

"Spec-5 Needham, sir."

"Well Spec-5 Needham, we'd like to buy you a drink."

"Thank you, sir. I'd like that."

We spent the night in Phu Bai. We tried to track down Spec-5 Needham without success. We went to the officer's club at Delta Company, our sister company, the gun platoon, and bought the men there drinks instead. That night I offered a silent toast to my instrument instructors who had taught me more than I had realized. Their training had saved my life today. This was one time when bayonet training had paid off. I also drank to another event. I was not a "cherry" any more. I had taken my first round. The crew chief had found two bullet holes, one in the fin near the tail rotor and one in the tailboom. We had been lucky today. I prayed my luck would continue.

The next day Coulshaw and I flew back to Sally following Highway-1 at one hundred feet in the rain. We landed in the mud at the Widow Web and, because of bad weather, I did not fly for another two days.

"Pilots grounded for any reason are a king-size pain-in-the-ass," Sergeant Peoples lamented one drizzly day in the operations tent. "If they ain't flyin' all they do is think up ways to get in trouble. Shit, I wish this fuckin' rain'd stop. Then you guys would quit playin' grab-ass and get out of my fuckin' hair."

He did have a point. Douglas Julian Carson III was a pilot in my platoon. I had met him the first day I arrived at Sally. He had been playing cards with Ned Kelly in the O-club. Carson was respected as a pilot. He had a good control touch and he always accomplished the mission and flew the machine back in one piece. As an individual however he was just slightly less than a pompous asshole. He had a college degree from Northwestern University and, although he never claimed to be better than the rest of us, he carried an air of superiority that grated heavily on everyone's nerves.

On this particular day his new tape player, an Akai 1800 SD reel-to-reel with an 8-track cartridge in the side, had arrived. He was listening to Bach through the new headphones. It was mid-afternoon and six of us were in his hootch playing cards. It was raining outside. Ned Kelly suddenly came up with a scheme for a little fun.

"None of you look up from your cards," he told us.

"Huh?" We all looked up from our cards.

"Assholes, I said don't look up. Keep looking at your cards and listen." We all looked back at our cards. Kelly continued. "We're gonna get Carson."

"How?" Five men leaned forward.

"Sit back and try to act natural. Shit don't let him know we're schemin' on him."

All of us sat upright and looked at our cards again. "That's better." Kelly checked his watch. "About now's the time we usually get mortared or rocketed if it's going to happen, right?" We nodded. Kelly looked over at Carson. Carson smiled, happy with his music. Kelly turned back toward us. "He can't hear us with the headphones on, so when I count to three, we all look up toward the roof, like we hear incoming. Wait a second, then make for the door as if you're makin' for the bunker."

"I get it," Joe said smiling broadly. "Then we stand outside and watch the fun."

"You caught my drift. OK, you guys ready?"

We answered with our eyes.

"OK, one . . . two . . . now!"

We all looked to the heavens. Genuine Oscar-winning horror turned our faces into hideous masks. We dropped our cards and scrambled for the door, nearly falling over one another to exit the doomed hootch. The card table got knocked over in the rush, cards fluttered to the floor.

The last guy flew outside. The screen door slammed and we stood to one side of the entrance in the rain and waited. A second, maybe two, went by. Douglas Julian Carson III exploded through the door of the hootch with a stride that would have made Jesse Owens envious. Behind him trailed his brand new Akai 1800 SD reel-to-reel bouncing along the plywood floor, still attached to the headphones on Carson's head. The door slammed behind him, trapping the cord before the tape deck could be dragged outside into the rain. The sudden jolt nearly pulled the man's ears off and it yanked his head backward; the Coss headphones recoiled like a slingshot and slammed against the screen door of the hootch.

Carson's face went crimson. "Fucking assholes!" he hollered. "Uncouth, uncultured, bastards, each and every one of you!" But his accusing words were drowned out by the deluge of water falling from the sky and the hysterical laughter from the six of us doubled over, stomping our boots in the mud.

My platoon was again sent up to support the Third Brigade at Camp Evans which was to begin another ten-day detachment. On the seventh day of our ten-day stint, our CO sent a message that we were to fly back to Sally to attend a "hail and farewell" party to be held that evening. Major Posey told us we were to fly back up to Camp Evans following the festivities the same night. When I arrived at Sally there was a letter from home waiting for me. I answered it the following day.

24 November 1968

Dear Mom:

I received your letter with the pictures of Andrea's birthday party. They sure turned out good. I showed them around to the other pilots and they got a kick out of them.

Dad wrote me a letter. He didn't say much, just told me to take care and that he was thinking about me. It's starting to rain every day now. I guess the rainy season is here to stay. It makes flying tough and a real challenge to accomplish the day's mission. If it rains "too bloody hard" we don't even go on missions.

The Joey Bishop USO show came to LZ Sally but I missed it because our platoon has been on detachment, stationed up at Camp Evans eight miles north. I heard it was a good show.

We had a hail and farewell party last night to welcome officers coming into the company, me and two other flight school buddies of mine, and for officers who are leaving. Boy, did everyone get smashed. It was hard to find two sober enough pilots to fly us back to Camp Evans where we are staying for ten days. It was a riot. We were all singing and carrying on, tripping, etc., on our way out to the helicopter after the party. Boy, did our company have hangovers the next day. I had to fly at 0630 the following morning so I was in a real hurt.

Not much else. Thanks for the pictures and keep writing.

Randy.

I pulled the pictures out of the envelope and looked at them for the hundredth time. The top picture was of Mom and my stepdad in the backyard, preparing to barbecue steaks on a hibachi he had recently flown back from Japan. There was another picture of my seventeen-year-old sister, Nancy, clowning around in one of my army uniforms. In front of her stood little Andrea waving an American flag on a stick. My favorite was one of Andrea with her hair in blonde pigtails tied with red ribbons to match her red birthday dress. She was beaming from behind a white birthday cake with six pink candles on top, surrounded by a crowd of other kids her age. Behind her a small boy was pulling the hair of one of Andrea's friends. The little girl was grimacing and appeared to be trying to fight back. The picture had been taken in our dining room. The surroundings looked so clean. Sterile. Civilized. I had only been in country six weeks and already it was getting harder to visualize life in the real world. It was so foreign to what I saw around me here.

When I went into the village outside Sally I would see kids two years younger than my little sister smoking home-made cigarettes and hustling Coca Cola or, even worse, trying to sell me the favors of their older sisters. Through-out their short lifetime all they had known was war. Their day-to-day objective was aimed at one goal: to survive to see the next. I could not imagine my little sister in similar circumstances. It was quite unthinkable. I liked to think that was why I was over here—to prevent her from one day having to know the ravages of war on home soil. Or was it? I could already foresee it would be difficult to explain what I had experienced here when, and if, I re-turned home. But I had no idea at the time how difficult. That my modest part in this fight for freedom would be in vain did not enter my imagination. At the time it was equally unimaginable that my countrymen would not want to know, or care, about the sacrifices I was making in the war—sacrifices similar to those my father and stepfather had made during World War II, or both my grandfathers had made in the First World War.

Dismissing the feelings of homesickness and isolation brought on by the pictures, I put them back in the enve-lope, stuffed it in the top pocket of my Nomex flight suit, threw on my green baseball cap, and walked through the mud to the mess tent for morning chow.

I flew eight-and-a-half hours that day as Ned Kelly's peter pilot. We flew ass-and-trash to several fire-support bases ten clicks east of the A-Shau Valley. He let me do a lot of the flying. I finally felt I was starting to get the hang of landing in some medium-tight landing zones without overcontrolling the aircraft. My pedal control was settling down and I was not fishtailing the Huey's tail all over the place. I felt pleased with my performance.

Walking back from the Camp Evans revetment area to our hootches Kelly remarked, "You're improving, new guy."

"Thanks." His remark meant a lot. I valued the man's assessment of my flying ability.

"In over eight hours of flying you didn't pull one of your hero turns. My crew chief was waiting for it. He told me he'd kill you if you tried it again. But you didn't. You showed restraint. He said he may even let you fly *his* aircraft again if you keep it up."

"Thanks a lot, Kelly. I'll try to keep that in mind."

The other pilots from our platoon returned from their missions, had chow, and settled into an evening of playing cards or writing letters. Those not on flare pilot standby were able to drink a few beers.

At 2230 Joe Sulak, Tom Shonehour, Stony Rutherford and I decided to turn in for the night. We shared an underground bunker that Stony had discovered when we first came to Camp Evans. It was twenty meters from the hootch where the others from our platoon slept.

Stony Rutherford was one of the married pilots in the Blackwidows. I had noticed a certain air of conservatism about many of the married men in our company. I guess it was to be expected. They carried the added burden that if they got killed or wounded it would destroy a future that they had mapped out with their wives. Fair enough. No one could blame them. There were exceptions of course, but generally one could tell the married from the single pilots by this attitude to the job. Single pilots possessed a spirit both in and out of the cockpit that bordered on juvenile or even reckless. We were unencumbered by the added responsibilities of wife and children that weighed heavily on the shoulders of the married pilots. The single pilots lived from one day to the next, just getting the job done. The married pilots lived for the date of their DEROS. Although we all aimed to get through the war alive and back to The World, it seemed the single guys were more willing to take chances along the way. But taking risks was just not part of Stony Rutherford's life style. Stony made no bones about letting everyone know this war business was not for him. He carried the added cross of having a round, innocent-looking baby face, rather like a cherub out of a Rubens painting.

Stony had flown more than five hundred hours and had not yet made aircraft commander. A pilot with normal aspirations makes AC after flying three hundred combat hours. Stony had been in country for more than six months and was still a peter pilot. He made it clear he had no inclination to make AC. Besides, none of the ACs had recommended him for command of his own ship anyway. That suited him. He was content to be a professional co-pilot throughout his tour and have someone else make all the decisions for him.

Because of Stony's nervousness and lack of ambition, he became an easy target for pranks and practical jokes. This particular night was no exception.

The four of us were in the underground bunker preparing for bed when the idea came to Joe, Tom, and me after Stony had remarked, ''This underground bunker is a hell of a lot safer than that open hootch the other guys are staying in. Hell, sappers could just come marching through and blow their shit away in a heartbeat.''

Wearing only green boxer shorts and shower shoes, I was tossing a bayonet at an eighteen-inch support post that stood in the middle of the small bunker. ''But Stony, there's only one way in and out of here. Up those wooden steps,'' I pointed in the dim light with the bayonet. ''Probably the last thing we'd hear before we got our shit blown to kingdom come is the grenade, or satchel charge, or whatever bouncing down those steps.''

Stony immediately got that familiar worried look on his round face. He looked at the steps leading into the underground bunker. ''Yeah, but they're really hard to see from ground level. Especially at night. During a sapper attack the dinks usually run like hell to get in and out as fast as they can. They're looking for easy targets, places like the hootch up there where the rest of the guys are staying. Naw, I think this is the safest place at Camp Evans.''

I tossed the bayonet. It tumbled through the air and its point stuck deep into the splintered wood. I walked over and pulled it out. ''A grenade goes off in here, Stony, the four of us'd be splattered against those PSP walls like hamburger meat in a blender.''

Joe looked up from writing a letter. ''We'd be done for, that's for sure, Stony.''

Tom added, ''They'd need to scrape the remains off

these metal walls with a spatula. Wouldn't be enough to send home in a matchbox.''

Stony said defensively, "Charlie'd never find this place in the dark.''

Tom shrugged. "Maybe yes, but then again maybe no. One thing's for sure, with the steep angle of those steps and the length of them, it'd take just about four seconds for anything tossed down to tumble in here and explode just as it hit the dirt floor.''

"I have to use the latrine,'' Rutherford said abruptly scurrying up the steps in his green boxer shorts. Joe and Tom shot me amused glances. We talked in low tones and quickly made our plans. We heard Rutherford's voice again.

"Holy shit! Hey you guys get up here. Looks like Evans's being overrun!''

Tom, Joe, and I scrambled single file up the steps. The other pilots living in the hootch nearby had brought their folding chairs outside to watch the fire fight on the perimeter. Two Cobra gunships were firing rockets and miniguns at the perimeter. Flares were being launched. They hissed and then popped over the battlefield illuminating the VC caught in the wire. We watched for half an hour, got bored, then decided to go to bed.

Rutherford, Joe, Tom, and I lay in our bunks. The darkness in the bunker was so thick you could have cut it. We could still hear the whirr of the Cobra's miniguns and the occasional hiss and pop of flares being launched.

In the darkness Joe said to Rutherford, "Don't worry, Stony, if sappers do get through tonight all you'll hear before the big bang is the sound of the explosive device bouncing down those wooden steps. That's all. Good night.''

"Good night.'' Tom said.

"Good night.'' I echoed.

"Good night!'' Stony exclaimed. "How in hell can you guys go to sleep knowing we may be pulverized down here?''

"But you said yourself we're safe,'' Tom reminded him in a consoling tone. "And that's good enough for me.''

"You'll never hear the explosion,'' Joe said. "Just the

sound of metal bouncing against wood, Stony. That'll be the last you'll hear.''

''Thanks a fucking lot, Joe!''

Five minutes passed. In the solid darkness, Joe sneaked from his bunk, as he had told Shonehour and me he would do, and silently made his way to the base of the steps. He carried with him a full can of ham and lima beans from our C-ration case. He tossed it up the short flight of stairs. It fell with a dull thud and bounced back down the steps sounding, just as we'd hoped, like an M-67 fragmentation grenade tumbling in on us.

Rutherford began to scream, ''Holy Shiiiitt!'' He dove from his bunk knocking Joe on his ass in the darkness, and scurried up the steps hollering at the top of his lungs, ''Sappers, goddamn, sappers everybody, sappers, sappers!''

It was a solid week before Stony would utter one civil word to either Joe, Tom, or me. For the remaining five months that we had to support the 502nd up at Camp Evans, there was an empty bunk in our personal bunker. From that night on Stony Rutherford elected to stay with the other pilots in the open and vulnerable hootch.

CHAPTER 4

December 1968

Merry Christmas, Ernest James

Most of the pilots had flown more than nine hours today. There was a mood of hearty camaraderie in the club at Sally following a particularly successful mission. Several of our ships had taken hits, but we had all made it back alive. Luckily, no one had even been wounded. Twenty aircraft had been involved in airlifting men and equipment, operating out of Firebase Bastogne, into the various landing zones in the jungle. It had been a muggy, sweltering day. The LZs had been tight and difficult. The officers were ready to party.

At 2130 Ops Sergeant Peoples walked through the back door of the officer's club surveying the smoke-filled room. He found the CO and yelled to him over the loud music, "A platoon of grunts two klicks west of Evans is in contact, sir. The flare ship stationed up there from First Platoon has expended all its flares. Brigade's requesting we fly up another ship ASAP to lend assistance!"

"It's raining like hell out there, Peoples. You sure they can get up to fifteen hundred feet to drop flares in this weather?"

"Other crew managed it, sir."

"Guess you're right. Send the flare crew then."

"Can't. Pilot's sick. He ate some bad C-rats or somethin'. He's doubled up on his cot in the flare tent. When he's not throwin' up he's runnin' to the shit house. You'll have to send someone else."

"Are there any other ACs available?"

"They're all in here, sir. Rest of the company ACs are stationed up at Evans."

The CO looked around the small room. He motioned for Spec-4 Flowers to turn down the reel-to-reel. "Good Lovin" by the Young Rascals was reduced to conversational level. The men fell silent.

"The flare pilot's ill," the CO announced. "Who's sober enough to volunteer to fly a flare mission up at Evans?"

Several hands flew up. "Watkins, Fisher, you're both elected."

The two men did not look very sober to me.

Joe, standing next to me, said, "The old man's sending *them*?"

I shook my head. "Guess the rules are different in combat. A few beers, so what?"

The two men exited the hootch into the rain. Spec-4 Flowers turned up the volume on the tape recorder. "We Gotta Get out of This Place" by the Animals, the theme song for every American GI based in Vietnam, now vibrated from the sixty-watt Sansui speakers on the wall. All the officers joined in the chorus.

Barely fifteen minutes later the two warrant officers sent to fly the flare mission barged through the door of the officer's club. Their unexpected entrance silenced the room. They were soaked through and caked with red mud. They looked like two NFL players after a game in the rain and mud. The first man, Watkins, yelled, "Woooeeee!" and jumped in the air to plant both feet on the likeness of the Screaming Eagle on the floor. Fisher did the same. Watkins's Nomex was torn off at the shoulder. He had a trail of blood trickling down his forehead, over his nose, and down his chin. He plopped down in the armored seat, pulled the shoulder straps over him, strapped in, donned the red *hero* helmet, and began to tell his story. "First of all, where the fuckin' hell's my beer?"

Someone handed him a Budweiser. He popped the top, pressed the can to his lips, threw his head back, chugged it down, squashed it in his hand, threw it to the plywood floor, and then announced, "Gentlemen, drinks are on me. Fisher and I are *fucking* lucky to be alive tonight, and I'm here to tell you we're going to celebrate."

Someone yelled, "What're you guys doing back here?

What happened? Your aircraft red-xed or couldn't you find it in the rain?'' The club filled with laughter.

Watkins's thin, muddied face molded into a satanic grin. He reached into the deep pocket of his green Nomex. He pulled out the hand grip of a Huey's cyclic. "This is what's left of the fucking flare aircraft. We crashed right outside the perimeter. Couldn't see the concertina wire for all the fucking rain on the windshield. Caught the skids on the wire on take off and we went ass over tits and speared into the mud, nose first. The aircraft thrashed itself to pieces. Fish and I climbed out of the wreckage, said fuck it, and came in here for a beer.''

Everyone raised their glasses and cheered.

Joe leaned over and said in my ear, "They're all fuckin' nuts.''

"No shit.''

Several days passed. The rain finally stopped. The weather cleared somewhat and nearly every pilot in the company flew from first light till dark to catch up on re-supplying the firebases and units in the AO and shifting men and equipment before the next heavy rains began.

On December 6 our platoon had all ten ships shut down and lined up on the PSP landing strip at Sally waiting for troops to arrive so we could fly them into the field. I sat on the floor of the Huey with a note pad on my lap and wrote a letter home.

6 December 1968

Hi:

I received your Christmas care package of goodies last night. Thank you very much. You couldn't have picked better stuff to put into it. It's the best thing that's happened to me since I got here. The surfer magazine and the MAD magazines are great. The chocolate chip cookies and brownies traveled well also.

There isn't much to tell you about what has been happening. I still really like the flying over here. I flew nine hours yesterday.

The other night while flying from Camp Evans to Camp Eagle I did something different. We had several pilots on board so I asked the aircraft commander if I could fly as door gunner for a change. The gunner said he did not mind so I did. Anyway, we started to receive fire over Hue, which is normal. I asked the pilot if I could fire back and he said OK. It was really neat to see my tracer bullets disappear into the night. I suppressed the fire on the ground, though. Who knows if I got the guy or not. All I know is that I stopped him from firing at us. One tracer round missed our tailboom by three to ten feet.

That's about it for excitement.

Tell Nancy that we do have a radio station over here but we hear the songs that were popular several months ago back home.

Not much else. Will write soon. Hope you received the money I sent for Christmas presents for everyone.

Love,

Randy

The following day I was assigned to fly copilot with Ned Kelly on a trip to Da Nang for a PX run. I was thrilled to finally have my turn to go. I hoped to buy a reel-to-reel tape player for my small living area. That would really make it home, I thought. If the sound of whopping rotor blades was the pulse of the war, music was its life blood. Most of the pilots owned tape recorders to play their own particular brand of music. It helped them maintain their sanity.

We flew south along the coast of Vietnam and over the Hai Van Pass. Kelly told me that several months before a convoy got wiped out there. "Used to happen regularly," he told me over the intercom. "There was a time it was one of the most dangerous stretches of road in Vietnam."

Once over the pass we descended and flew at fifty feet and eighty knots over the beach at Da Nang. We had to fly at that altitude to stay below the approach path of the Da Nang air base, one of the busiest in Vietnam.

It was about seven-thirty in the morning when we flew over the shanty town of Da Nang. There were small fishing boats anchored in the muddy harbor. A makeshift city spread along the beach and crept inland. The crudely constructed dwellings made of plywood, tin, and scraps of cardboard looked as if they would be destroyed by one stiff monsoon breeze. Vietnamese men and women lined the beach, squatting and waving at us as we flew overhead. Some wore the familiar conical woven straw hat. Most wore black pajamas.

"Know what their doin' down there?" Kelly asked.

"Smiling and waving," I answered, thinking his question odd.

"Look closer."

I did. "Smiling and waving," I answered again. "They seem happy to see us."

"Boy, you are some FNG." Kelly said shaking his head. "They're taking a morning George. Giving birth to another VC. They're taking a morning shit!"

I looked down at them out the chin bubble. He was right. Lined in a row for as far up the beach as I could see were people along the water's edge shitting into the Gulf of Tonkin. "They wouldn't get away with that in Huntington Beach. I can tell you that much," I said jokingly.

"Jesus, this isn't Huntington Beach, if you haven't noticed." He pointed ahead. "That's Monkey Mountain in the distance there," Kelly referred to Marble Mountain, a tit of a hill sticking up out of flatlands a short distance from the blue-brown sea.

"There're still VC living in the caves up there. Every once in a while they lob a mortar or two into the marine compound at the base of the mountain just to keep 'em on their toes."

"Why doesn't someone go up and clean 'em out? Shouldn't be too hard to do."

"You'd think it'd be easy but it isn't. Every so often the marines launch an assault up the hill. Several months back the Army Special Forces sent ten Green Berets up the hill. None of them ever came back. The VC and NVA are like cockroaches. You can't get rid of the fuckers. So they're just plain ignored.''

"Tenacious little devils, aren't they?''

"You don't know the half of it, new guy. As a race of people they got more wanna than we ever thought of having.''

"Wanna?''

"Yeah, wanna. They wanna win this war a hell of a lot worse than we do. This is their land not ours. They got a vested interest in it where we don't. We're just tourists. How long you been here anyway, new guy?''

"I don't know. Eight weeks I guess.''

"How about you, Murphy?'' he asked his crew chief.

"Nine-and-a-half months, sir,'' he said from the right-hand gun well.

"And Jackson, how about you?'' he asked the gunner.

"I'm so short I gotta reach up to touch bottom, sir. I'm what you call a two-digit midget. Twenty-seven days and a wake up and I'm fucking outta here.''

"And I've been here seven months,'' Kelly said. "We keep counting, every one of us, and we won't stop counting till our year's up and we can fly back to The World on that freedom bird and try to forget about this godforsaken shit hole.''

"Amen, sir!'' Jackson agreed.

"That's the *big* difference between this war and the war our fathers fought,'' Kelly continued. "If we were told we couldn't come home till it was over, you can bet your ass we'd end it quick. We'd defoliate the jungles, have the Sea Bees level this fucking country, pave it with black top, and turn it into one huge parking lot for Bangkok.''

"Now you're talkin', sir,'' the crew chief said enthusiastically.

"There's a huge difference between them and us,'' Kelly continued. "We're just visitors in this war, clock watchers waiting for the day when we can go home.''

I thought back to what Stu had said before we got off the aircraft in Cam Ranh Bay. "The clock starts now, gentlemen,'' he'd said. "Only 365 days to go till we go home.''

"That's why we're going to lose this fucking war,''

Kelly said shaking his head. "Cuz it's not *our* war. Never has been. It's the enemy's. And they got a hell of a lot more motivation and wanna to win than we ever thought the little fuckers had."

It was the first time any of the pilots had shared such a negative view with me. I was young, apolitical. Patriotic, yes. Political no. It never occurred to me that the American military machine could be overcome. Never. Especially by a backward country where the people used water buffalo to plow their fields and squatted on the beach to shit into the sea. I thought little about what Kelly had said. He had to be wrong. It was inconceivable to me that America, with all its wealth, military might, and righteousness could ever lose such a war.

We landed the aircraft at the pad near the PX and walked the half a klick up a dusty road to the huge, warehouse-type building. Duce-and-a-half trucks, some full of soldiers, others heaped with supplies, and many jeeps rumbled past, each covering us in their cloud of dust. Because Da Nang was a built up area, modern and civilized compared to the primitive living conditions at Sally and Evans, I felt out of place in baggy green Nomex, yellow scarf, and holstered .38. This must have been how the early cowboys felt when they returned to a relatively civilized town after weeks on the trail. I had my first inkling that some of my newness was beginning to wear off. I may have been an FNG in the eyes of most of the guys back at Sally, but the grunts and other troops I passed on the street wouldn't know the difference. Knowing this made me stand a bit taller as I walked into the large, air-conditioned building.

The PX was cavernous, filled to the gunnels with every imaginable type of booze, liqueur, 35-mm camera, civilian clothing, food, candy, wrist watch, jewelry, stereo system, tape recorder, and reel-to-reel tape player. And everything was unbelievably cheap.

I bought a reel-to-reel, two twenty-five-watt Coral speakers, ten tapes, several bottles of booze, and some stateside cookies. The brownies my family had sent in the Christmas care package had arrived as hard as bricks, and the chocolate chip cookies were powdered dust and pulverized chocolate bits. I had not told my family in my letter home that the food items had arrived damaged.

Ned Kelly let me fly his ship back to Sally, even letting me hover it into the tight revetment. I was definitely putting the polish on my control touch. After we shut down I rushed my tape player back to the hootch, plugged it in, and put on the newly purchased Moody Blues "In Search of the Lost Chord" tape. When I heard the noise that came out I was shocked. The voices were low and distorted sounding as if the performers had each consumed a bottle of Valium before the recording session. "I've been ripped off!" I exclaimed.

Les Ramson was sitting on his bunk cleaning a British Sterling machine gun. "No, you haven't. Your recorder's set on different cycles. It's probably made for fifty cycles." He walked over and made an adjustment on the back. "There, now give her a try." It sounded perfect. My area was now complete.

That night I was scheduled to be flare copilot. That meant the aircraft commander and I had to sleep in the flare tent outside of operations where we would stand by in the event of a call out. I took my tape player with me.

"What'cha gonna do with that?" the AC, Mick Shubert, asked.

"What? My new tape player? Bought it today on the PX run to Da Nang. Figured we could use some music."

"Where you going to plug it in?"

I surveyed the tent. One naked bulb hung on a wire over our heads. I pointed, "Up there."

Shubert sat on his cot with arms crossed. "This I gotta see."

I reached into the chest pocket of my flight suit and pulled out a screw-in type socket which had two plug receptacles on either side. I had scrounged it from the supply officer, Douche Bag Dick Childs. With Shubert holding my flashlight I stood on a chair and unscrewed the light bulb, screwed in the socket, and put the light bulb back in.

"What about the plug on your reel-to-reel," he asked. "The prongs are round. The ones in the socket up there are flat."

I pulled out my Buck knife, opened it and said, "Watch."

I cut off the plug and stripped the rubber insulation off the two wires. Shubert said, "You're sure going to a lot of trouble just for a little music."

"You bet. But it'll be worth it. You'll see." I stood on the wobbly chair holding the cord with the two bare wires. "Ten seconds from now we'll have music." I reached up to plug the bare wires into the light socket.

Shubert told me later that before I tripped off the 25-K generator, plunging the whole of Charlie Company into total darkness, he swears he actually saw an arc of electricity, like a bolt of lightning, pass from my left hand, around each ear like a brilliant halo, to my right hand, completing the circuit. That was the moment I yelled, "Hollleeyyy Fuuuckkkkk!" and was thrown off the chair and bounced, with a resounding thud, onto the dirt floor. At the same time all the lights and electrical appliances in the company went dead.

I vaguely remember picking myself up off the ground and hearing shouts in the darkness from the company area, "Hey, hell, who the fuck tripped off the goddamn generator!" The next night I had to buy the rounds yet again in the officer's club and be rewarded with a "Himmmmmmmm Himmmmmmmm, Fuck Himmmmmmm!" from the guys for "creating an electrical disturbance, a hard ground fault" in the flare pilot's tent. I was in no uncertain terms told to stay the hell away from any form of electronic tampering. No further warning was necessary. I could just picture the headlines: "Local Man Electrocuted in Vicious Skirmish with Enemy Tape Recorder. News Shocks Parents of Vietnam Vet!"

I was extremely grateful to be alive.

Of the ten aircraft commanders in my platoon it was generally agreed upon by the other peter pilots that Bernie Nivens was the most difficult AC to fly with. He was a high-strung individual—tall, lanky, and extremely nervous. He had a right to be. He was a "magnet ass." Bernie Nivens had been shot down twice, and if hits were to be taken, Magnet Ass Bernie Nivens seemed to attract bullets like a black suit attracts lint.

Bernie had acquired another name, Wishy-Washy Bernie Nivens. He was so afraid of his lousy luck that he figured if he flew his helicopter "by the book," as he had been taught in flight school, he would lessen the risk of getting shot down or taking hits. So, when you flew as his peter pilot, Wishy-Washy would rabbit on incessantly about the proper flight-school procedures to be followed. On takeoff he would insist that you pull no more than 2 percent engine N1 above hover power. After takeoff the rate of climb had to be exactly five hundred feet-per-minute flown at precisely sixty knots. Upon reaching cruising altitude he would tell you how to level off. "Lead with forward cyclic till ten knots below eighty knots, *then* you can reduce power. You've got to practice flying by the book. We were taught those techniques for a reason."

On approach he would insist on the normal flight-school sight picture of between twelve and fifteen degrees, then he would talk you all the way down as if you were a ten-hour pre-solo student. Eight hours in the cockpit with Wishy-Washy seemed like eight days. After flying with him it quickly became obvious *why* he was a magnet ass. Putting into practice the techniques we had learned in flight school was a sure way, even in my inexperienced viewpoint, of making you a sitting duck in combat. Over here it was necessary to learn a whole new method of flying in order to make it through your year alive. Bernie Nivens had earned the name wishy-washy because whenever he was shot at, the flight-school techniques he preached so religiously went right out the window, and flying for survival took over. It was without a doubt his flight-school flying that put him into the sitting-duck type of situations in the first place.

I was flying with Wishy-Washy one day over the mountains northwest of Camp Evans. We were inserting men into a secure landing zone at the foot of Firebase Barbara. We had taken five sorties of four men each into the same LZ without incident. He was letting me fly at the time.

"Sixty knots on the climb out, Mains," he tapped the glass on the airspeed indicator. "Not fifty-five, not sixty-five. Sixty. Try to fly the machine with precision."

We'd been flying for more than three hours. I was hot

and sweaty and so particularly tired of his grandma attitude that I did something a peter pilot should never do; I
voiced a strong opinion of my own. "Some of the other
ACs might not agree with your techniques, Bernie. I've
flown with them all and one thing I've noticed is that they
fly defensively to lessen their exposure to enemy fire. Flying like we were taught in flight school is just asking for
it."

Bernie's face went red. "You telling me how to fly?"

"No. I'm just telling you what I've observed, that's all."

"The rest of the guys are cowboys. They tear the shit
out of their machines. You fly like I tell you and when you
get a ship of your own you'll treat her well and she'll
always get you back safely."

"Or not at all," I said automatically without thinking.

"I've been over here nearly nine months and I'm still
alive."

"I'd say you've been lucky, Bernie. You've never received the million-dollar bullet that'll fuck up your day."

"And you, a new guy, are going to tell me how to stay
alive longer?"

"I'm just telling you what I've observed in my flying
with the other ACs. It's my prerogative to adopt the style
of flying that I think is going to keep me alive. That's all
that concerns me. Your style, Bernie, I'm afraid will only
serve to get me sent home in a box."

Bernie went scarlet. He grabbed the controls away from
me. "I've got it."

"You've got it."

"If that's the way you feel and you think you already
know all there is to know about flying over here there's no
reason for me to try and teach you."

I wished that I'd never entered into this conversation.
Why couldn't I have just kept my mouth shut. Another
case of my alligator mouth overriding my hummingbird
ass!

Bernie flew a textbook sixty-knot approach beginning
at fifteen hundred feet into the landing zone surrounded
by high jungle. I actually squirmed in my seat as we continued the slow descent. The other pilots would have flown
in at treetop level and, on occasion, they would have var-

ied their approach path if the wind direction, velocity, and obstacles permitted it. Not Bernie. I felt we were like a huge, green clay pigeon suspended in the air, inviting someone to take a potshot at us. Charlie must have had the same idea. How could he resist such an easy target? At two hundred feet on final approach, the ridge line on my side of the aircraft lit up with green tracer rounds flying in our direction. The crew chief began firing his M-60. Several grunts in the back began firing their weapons too. At that point Bernie's flight-school technique ceased abruptly and survival flying took over. He threw the aircraft hard left and dove at the trees but not before we took several hits. I scrunched down. My rectum clamped down so tightly I thought it would pinch the seat. I waited for one of the bullets to rip into my body, silently cursing Bernie for getting us into this mess.

"Receiving fire! Receiving fire!" Bernie transmitted over the fox mike radio to the ground unit we were supporting.

"Roger, Blackwidow Two-Seven. We saw where the fire came from. We're sending men to the location to neutralize the position, over."

"Well, do that. I'm heading back to Evans to check out the bird. . . . Shit!"

Just then the oil pressure light on the master caution panel illuminated. The gauge was slowly falling to zero. Bernie radioed on the ground unit. "Parachute Runner, Parachute Runner, this is Blackwidow Two-Seven. We're heading for Barbara. Oil pressure's falling. A bullet must have hit an oil line."

"Roger, Blackwidow Two-Seven. Copy. Good luck."

We would need all the luck we could get. Bernie leaned forward in his seat and pushed the cyclic over, banking the craft, then leveled out on a beeline course for LZ Barbara, the only landing pad for miles. The firebase was just two klicks away. God, please let us make it, I thought.

Mountainous, triple-canopy jungle passed under us. And probably the enemy. An engine failure here would surely mean our lives. If the crash didn't kill us the enemy certainly would. If we were caught we would probably be strung upside-down by our ankles and skinned alive. Then, they would cut off our penises and stuff them into our mouths before our guys could find us. The NVA and VC loved to get their hands on helicopter pilots. I had heard enough stories to know I didn't ever want to get shot down.

By now Bernie's conservative flight-school techniques had vanished. We were now flying at 115 knots. The machine shook and vibrated as it neared VNE, velocity never to exceed. I checked the gauges. The needle of the engine oil pressure gauge was reading zero. The temperature needle was now rising steadily above the red line. Hang in there. Don't quit, don't quit, I said to myself, as if my thoughts could somehow keep the engine running long enough to make it to the pad.

Bernie did a good job of getting us down. He executed a power-on autorotation planting the skids on the PSP pad. Once down safely he immediately rolled off the throttle. I breathed a heavy sigh of relief. When the blades had stopped we got out and inspected the damage. Bernie had done it again. He had taken five hits, four in the tail boom and one in the engine oil tank causing the oil to gush out. The aircraft was checked by a maintenance team flown out from Sally, repaired, and flown out the same day.

When I arrived back at Sally I made a beeline of my own. I marched into ops and requested that I *not* be scheduled to fly with Wishy-Washy again. My request was granted.

A new first lieutenant joined the Blackwidows. His name was Ernest James. He was a blond-haired, sparkling blue-eyed kid fresh out of flight school and bubbling with enthusiasm. He couldn't wait to fly his first combat mission. Ernest looked even younger than Junior although he claimed he was several years older.

Ernest was a first lieutenant so he fell into the category of RLO, or real live officer, as all commissioned officers were labeled by the warrant officers. It was unusual to find a RLO who was humble, soft spoken, and unpretentious, but Ernest was. I liked him from the first day I met him which was a week-and-a-half ago.

Most of the pilots in Charlie Company thought Ernest was crazy to actually *want* to fly combat missions, but

Ernest did want to experience combat in the worst way. I was one of the few pilots who understood what he felt.

Because Ernest was a senior lieutenant in the company the CO made him operations officer. That virtually grounded Ernest, which nearly broke his heart. Ernest and I formed an immediate and fast friendship. On one of the many evenings he came by my hootch for a few beers he asked me, ''Randy, what is it really like to fly in combat?''

''You need to ask some of the more experienced pilots, Ernest. I've only flown about 150 hours since I've been in country. I'm hardly the guy to talk to.''

''Yeah, but the experience is still fresh for you, Randy. It's still new, exciting, exhilarating. You aren't burned out yet like some of the other guys I've asked. Come on, tell me what's it like.''

''Hell, Ernest, you know if anyone hears me telling you war stories I'll be buying rounds in the club and made to sit in the hero's chair forever.'' Ernest just smiled and gave me a pleading look with his baby blues. ''OK, OK, Ernest, you win.'' I collected my thoughts, then began, ''You know the old adage about flying don't you? Hours and hours of sheer boredom punctuated by moments of stark-raving terror.''

''Yeah,'' he said hanging on my words like I was some guru speaking great truths. His blue eyes were sparkling.

''Yeah . . . well, it's like that. You fly ass-and-trash in and out of landing zones and fire support bases for hours at a time. You may have been in and out of an area twenty maybe thirty times. Then there's the one time you fly over the same area you've flown over all day and you start taking fire. You get on the radio and start screaming for arty, your asshole gets so puckered you couldn't drive a needle up it with a sledgehammer. That's the moment of terror.''

''What about the CAs. They've got to be hairy.''

''In a way yes, in others, no. In combat assaults there are aircraft everywhere. The LZs have been heavily prepped by B-52 strikes, then by artillery. Then the ARA gunships prep it with rockets and there are usually fast movers stationed at twenty-thousand feet with napalm if the situation really gets heavy.''

"Aren't you afraid of getting shot when you're in those LZs surrounded by thick jungle where Charlie may be waiting for you?"

"Goddamn right I'm afraid!" I pointed between my eyes. "I get a feeling right here every time I go in. Like someone's pressing on it with their thumb. Like there's a big, red bull's-eye painted here and that's where the AK round will find its mark. But thank God our exposure's limited. We come in low over the trees and we're a target for maybe thirty seconds max. That thirty seconds is the time it takes to fly over the trees, land, drop off the troops, and take off again. As a peter pilot I'm too damn busy hovering over the controls in case the AC gets blown away to think about much else. I can always feel the bull's-eye pressure on my forehead though. I think it's just me. But it seems like it's over before it's begun. Once one or two sorties of troops have been inserted the LZ is usually secured."

Ernest punched his palm with his fist. "Damn, Randy, I want to do that."

"Can't you convince the old man to let you fly?"

"Nope, he says he needs me here. It's so damn frustrating."

There was a moment of awkward silence. Then Ernest asked, "Can I hear my song?"

"Sure, Ernest." I reached over, put the tape on the reel-to-reel, and turned it on. The hootch was empty, as the other officers were in the club, so I turned up the volume. The song was "Love is Blue" by Ronnie Aldrich and his Orchestra. It was Ernest's favorite, and he would often stop by to have me play it for him. In the dim light of the hootch Ernest and I sat silently listening to the beautiful melody with its rising crescendo of violins. When it had ended, Ernest stood up to leave, and I walked him to the screen door.

"Thanks, Randy. That song always gives me goose bumps." At that moment a flare sailed into the air on the perimeter then popped, illuminating his boyish face. Tears were clouding his sparkling blue eyes.

"You're always welcome, Ernest. You'll get your day in the cockpit. You'll see."

He shrugged and smiled. "Wish it'd be soon. God, I want to fly."

"I know, Ernest. Believe me, I know."

A week later Ernest James received orders promoting him to captain which put the final seal on his ambitions to fly. He could see himself spending the remainder of the war flying a desk as operations officer. Even more reason to chug-a-lug the "Blushing Asshole" sitting in front of him on the bar.

The bartender of the officer's club, Spec-4 Flowers, had devised the drink one night for an officer who had just been promoted. His creation consisted of a shot from every bottle of booze behind the bar *plus* a touch of grenadine to give it the pink color which gave rise to its name. It was in the finest tradition of the United States Army that newly promoted officers had to drink for their new bars. On this occasion, the commanding officer, Major Posey, dropped the shiny new captain's bars into the brimming mug and handed it to Ernest. Ernest looked into the mug suspiciously. The record number of Blushing Assholes consumed by an individual who then made it back to his hootch under his own power was five. It was one of the warrants in First Platoon who had made CW2. He drank them in quick succession and was found the following afternoon *under* his hootch moaning like a man who had been fragged by a hand grenade.

"Drink, Captain James," the CO commanded.

Ernest raised the glass to his lips, closed his eyes, and the men chanted, "GO! GO! GO! GO! GO! GO!" as he gulped down the volatile liquid. He finished and slammed the empty mug down on the bar. He turned to face the crowd displaying the new captain's bars clenched tightly between straight white teeth. Everyone cheered.

The next morning Ernest was reported missing from his hootch. After a short search by the company clerk he was found unconscious, half standing, half leaning against the corrugated iron fence surrounding the outside urinal, one leg stuffed up to the thigh in an overflowing piss tube. After only three Blushing Assholes that is how Ernest spent his first night as a newly appointed young captain.

23 December 1968

Merry Christmas everyone! I flew to Da Nang today on my second PX run so I was able to stock up for Christmas. I bought an imperial quart of Bacardi rum for $1.40, a bottle of Old Granddad bourbon and a quart of Smirnoff vodka for the same price.

The supply officer lives in my hootch and I have been made Assistant Supply Officer so we have the best hootch in the company. Being an officer has its advantages. With my tape player we have almost all the comforts of home here. Well, almost. I haven't seen a round-eyed girl since I've been in country. When I do I'll probably pass out.

The rains are here to stay. We've been told by operations that we may get hit by a typhoon tonight. Guess we'll be grounded for a while. Keep writing, your letters mean more to me than you'll ever know.

Love, Randy

I lay on my bunk in the darkness surrounded by the thin green mosquito net. I thought about Michelle as I'd done so many nights these last months. What would she be doing right now? Who would she be with over the holidays? Would the company of her family be enough for her or would she need to find someone else? I threw the unwelcome thought from my mind. She had been good about writing to me, as she'd been when I was in flight school. So supportive. I closed my eyes trying to picture how she looked the night before I left. That special night when she had cradled my head in her lap and stroked my face with her long nails. The vision came back. I could almost capture her lovely scent again. God, how I missed her. Especially now, at this time of year. The holidays always made one so melancholy. I rolled over on my stomach and pulled my pillow close to my face imagining I was holding her. I ached with longing. What was she doing now? Did she miss me as much as I missed her? God, these questions!

Thinking of Michelle in this way brought to mind a girl I'd met during my flight school days. It happened in August, a month-and-a-half before graduation. Bob Lawson, Stu Lindsey, and I had earned a three-day pass, a break from flight training. We had completed our advanced instrument check rides and had all passed. Our next phase of training was to transition into the Huey. To celebrate, we had decided to spend our three days on the beach at Panama City, Florida.

Stu owned a 1964 Volkswagon Bus he had driven out from California. It was painted green and white and covered all over with huge, colored stick-on flowers. It was one of those outrageous buses common during the late sixties in California, but rarely seen in Alabama. We had attended a "Paul Revere and the Raiders" concert several weeks before in Montgomery, Alabama, and, at the conclusion of the concert, as we were driving out of the parking lot, we were pursued by a herd of groupies who thought the psychedelic bus with California plates had to contain members of the band.

Now we had three days off. Three days! When we drove through the main gate at Fort Rucker the feeling of freedom was something sweet and tangible. Bob was riding shotgun. He pulled out a six-pack of Colt-45 and popped the top on one of the cans, spraying malt liquor everywhere. "Whoa!" he yelled. "Here, Stu, time to party."

Stu was driving. He took the can. "Waaaahoooo! Three glorious days in the sun." He took a long drink. "Damn, that tastes good. Look out ladies here come the horny bastards from California."

"I'll drink to that," Bob said tossing a can back to me then popping one open for himself and taking a long drink.

"You'll drink to anything, Bob," I said.

"True, my friend, so true." He shoved a tape in the 8-track, "Country Joe and the Fish." The three of us considered this our theme song and we sang along with it:

For it's one, two, three what are we fightin' for?
Don't ask me I don't give a damn.
Next stop is Vietnam!
For it's five, six, seven open up your pearly gates.
There ain't no time to wonder why,
WOOO HOOOO we're all gonna die!

We had driven about a six-pack's distance and were working on number two when Bob suddenly said excitedly, "Stu, pull over, pull over!"

"What, hell, what's the trouble?"

"No trouble, just saw something. Stop. Pull over, will ya?"

Stu pulled off on the shoulder of the two-lane road. "What is it?"

Bob smiled. "Watermelon!"

"Watermelon?"

Bob flung open the passenger door, jumped out and ran toward a field seventy-five yards away. He leapt over a barbed wire fence, walked several yards, and bent over. When he stood upright he held a plump green melon over his head. That's when we heard the two gun shots.

"Holy fuck!" Stu exclaimed. "He's gettin' shot at."

We watched Bob spin around to look behind him. A farmer with a shotgun had suddenly appeared and was in hot pursuit. Bob tucked the melon under his arm like a halfback and began to run.

"Hurry up you dumb fuck!" Stu screamed. "Run! Run! Run!"

Bob looked as if he possessed superhuman abilities when he placed his free hand on a fence post and vaulted the barbed wire fence, his body going horizontal, still holding onto the melon. When his feet hit the ground he did not break stride and ran toward the bus. Stu popped the clutch. We began to roll.

"Come on, get in, get in!"

Bob caught up and ran alongside, threw in the melon, and dove in. We left the roadside in a cloud of dust.

"You crazy fuck," Stu scolded. "You damn near got your ass shot full of rock salt."

Bob was puffing hard and turned to look out the window at the farmer shaking his fist. He turned back and picked up the plump melon. "Yeah, but look at this beauty. It was worth it. Damn, I need another beer. Whew! Good experience for Nam, huh? Bet I'm the first of the three of us to get shot at."

I popped the top and handed Bob a beer. "Now that's one distinction you can keep!"

* * *

I met Lorraine on the beach in front of the Fountainbleu Hotel. In retrospect, I suppose she met me. Stu and Bob were horsing around in the sea while I was lying on my towel, soaking up the sun, when she walked up and asked me the time. She plopped down next to me and we talked. She was from Atlanta and spoke with a southern accent that could melt butter. She was twenty-one and attractive, with short, curly brown hair that framed a delicate face with bright blue eyes. She worked as a secretary for an insurance firm in Atlanta and told me this was her first visit to Panama City.

During our conversation she looked down at my left hand. "Is that a service ring you're wearing?"

"Yes. It's a flight school ring."

She reached out and lifted my hand to take a closer look. It looked like a college ring, solid white gold with a large blue stone. "Sixty-eight twenty-three?"

"That's my class number. I'm due to graduate September twenty-third. The sixty-eight means this year."

"What's WORWAC mean?"

"Warrant Officer Rotary Wing Aviator Course."

"So you're training to be a pilot, are you?"

"Yep. Helicopters."

"You going off to Vietnam then?"

"Most likely."

She lowered my hand to my towel and smiled. "You doing anything tonight?"

Her forward question took me by surprise. "No, I . . . I haven't anything planned."

"I would really like to see you again, if that's all right. Would you like to meet somewhere later?"

This was too good to be true. I would have been certifiably crazy to have said no. "How about dinner?"

She smiled more with her eyes than with her delicate mouth. "Yes, I'd really like that."

We set a time and a place. I later made some excuse to remove myself from the company of Bob and Stu. I knew they would probably want to come if I told them I was meeting someone. I took a taxi and met Lorraine at a prearranged spot. After we shared a few drinks and dinner, we went at her suggestion for a walk on the beach.

The conditions were perfect for romance. In the moonlight, feeling the warm breeze on sunburned skin and the still-warm, squeaky-white sand under bare feet, I took her into my arms and kissed her gently on the mouth. That unleashed a passion in her which took me completely by surprise. It was almost animal-like, as if she had been keeping her emotions pent-up inside and they finally had come flooding out. As we held one another she kissed my neck, face, and lips and pulled me tightly against her slight frame. The heat between our two bodies was electric, and it was now no secret that her charms had me in full arousal. She embraced me pulling me even closer as if trying to fuse our bodies together, as if she would never let me go. She planted small, sweet kisses on my neck until her soft lips were next to my ear, then she whispered, "Randy, I love you."

Her words came as a shock. This was all happening too fast. I never considered myself particularly attractive to women. All through high school and my short time in college the girls hardly noticed me. I hadn't even lost my virginity until I was nineteen. Nineteen! I knew I lacked the kind of animal magnetism some men have that makes women fall at their feet, but that seemed to be what Lorraine was doing now. I had made it a rule that I would never tell a girl I loved her unless I meant it. The words were too special to be used so lightly. I had told only one girl I loved her. That was Sarah, the girl with whom I had lost my virginity. At the age of nineteen, after knowing her for only three months, I had asked her to marry me when I turned twenty-one, and at the time she had said yes. Sadly, six months later, she met someone else, her future husband, and we split up. I met Michelle six months later. I had not even told Michelle I loved her. I thought I loved her, but after Sarah, I was not sure.

Now this vibrant, attractive woman I held in my arms in the soft moonlight and truly desired had told me she loved me after knowing me for less than seven hours. How could I handle it? I did what any other all-American young man would have done in a similar situation. I took her to the nearest hotel room I could find and we made love all night long.

I was able to get free the next weekend and I met Lorraine again in Panama City as we had agreed. She had rented a hotel room and was waiting for me. When I look back on our two days together I wonder why our passion did not set fire to the bed. It was on Sunday afternoon, as we walked along the beach by the water's edge, that I learned why I was so special to her.

I checked my watch. "In about thirty minutes I've got to start heading back. I've got to be back at Fort Rucker by six o'clock."

She began to cry and embraced me. "God, Randy, I missed you last week. All I could do was sit at my desk and think of you. I was useless to anyone."

I raised her chin with my finger to look into her eyes. "And I missed you, Lorraine." I paused for a moment to look down at her and gather my thoughts. "There's something troubling me though."

A look of concern came over her face. "What is it?"

"Well . . . I guess it's the suddenness of our relationship. I've got to admit, I'm more than a little confused by it all."

"You mean, that I could tell you I love you without really getting to know you. Is that why you're confused?"

"Something like that. Yes."

"But I do love you, Randy. I love you in a very special way."

"Special way?"

"Yes." She bit at her lower lip as if she were having difficulty with the words. "I must tell you. I hope you won't be angry with me."

"Angry? Why would I be angry? I may be confused about my emotions, but I can't imagine what you could say to make me angry."

"OK, here goes then. Randy . . . I'm . . . I'm married."

I stepped backward. "Married! But you don't wear a wedding ring."

"I stopped wearing it several months ago. Please don't

hate me. Listen to what I have to say. Then maybe you'll understand."

I tried to compose myself. "Go on."

"You see, my husband is serving in Vietnam. He's a sergeant over there. In the army. He's been there for eight months. We had a good relationship when he left. Up until several months ago he used to write me letters telling me how much he loved me and missed me."

"Up until a few months ago? You mean he doesn't write you anymore?"

"Yes, he writes. That's the problem. When he writes he also sends me pictures."

"Pictures? What kind of pictures?"

She shook her head without speaking as if trying to fight off her desire to begin crying again. "When he writes he sends pictures of dead people, Vietnamese. Dismembered bodies. Charred men, women, and children. He's been affected by what he's seen over there. It's just so foreign to me. I want to understand, but I can't relate to what he's experiencing in Vietnam. I really do want to understand, to be supportive. How can I when he sends me those awful pictures. It's like he's a totally different person from the man I married." She began to sob.

I pulled her into my arms and held her close to me. She cried into my chest. I stroked her hair. "I think I understand now, Lorraine. It's OK. God, I'm so sorry." I kissed her head and held her tightly. After that weekend I never saw her again.

KAABOOM! KAABOOM! the artillery battery firing into the mountains brought me back. Would someone be consoling Michelle while I was over here? Was she in someone else's arms right now? Would I change as drastically as Lorraine's husband had changed before his year was up? I tried to drive these negative thoughts from my mind, but they kept flooding back.

I rolled over on my back and stared into the darkness where I knew my green mosquito net hung eighteen inches from my nose. I listened to the rain beginning to fall lightly on the tin roof. I welcomed the nightly rain. The sound would drown out my actions. I tried to imagine Michelle with me now. I tried to conjure up her lightly perfumed aroma, but the tropical air was too thick and wet to capture it. Her face was in front of me now, suspended, as if my head were on her lap again and I was looking up at her. I brought my hand under the dank sheet and let my fingers trail slowly down my moist chest, imagining it was she who was caressing my body. I held onto her image and slowly worked my hand lower. Quietly, slowly, I held her sweetly in my mind and began to relieve myself in the only way I could.

Choir practice was called and all officers were to be in the club on Christmas Eve by 2030. We were told it was a "command performance" which meant we couldn't get out of it. Major Posey ordered all officers to attend to sing Christmas carols.

Spec-4 Flowers had set up an overhead projector and the words for "The Twelve Days of Christmas" were displayed on the movie screen, a four-by-four-foot piece of plywood painted white and nailed to the wall. A captain from First Platoon, with a pockmarked face and a fine baritone voice, stood next to the screen with a wooden pointer, and we followed his lead.

On the first day of Christmas my true love gave to me:
A hand job in the left seat!
On the second day of Christmas my true love gave to me:
Two tits a dripping and a hand job in the left seat!
On the third day of Christmas my true love gave to me:
Three twats a twitchin, two tits a drippin, and a hand job in the left seat!
On the fourth day of Christmas my true love gave to me:
Four maidens a fucking, three twats a twitchin, two tits a drippin, and a hand job in the left seat!
On the fifth day of Christmas my true love gave to me:

Five Shanker Sores!

*Four maidens a fucking, three twats a twitchin', two tits
a drippin', and a hand job in the left seat!*

And the song continued, the words becoming more foul
with each verse. For some reason the filthy language and
hint of sacrilege didn't offend anyone. No one protested
or complained. Foul language was part and parcel of the
experience in Vietnam. It was accepted without question.
Each officer sang with gusto, trying to outdo the man singing next to him. We sang with commitment, as if we were
singing directly to God. We wanted our voices to be heard
all the way to the DMZ. To Saigon. To Hanoi! Our passion
for singing somehow proved our firm commitment to be
there instead of back in The World with family and loved
ones. I suppose our singing warded off a type of depression, too, that if allowed to surface would most certainly
destroy morale. I remember saying to Joe in between
songs, "We'll probably get struck dead by lightning when
we return to our hootches tonight. God's gotta be really
pissed off with these songs we're singing on his son's
birthday."

"Ha! Lightning never. Mortars, rockets, maybe. That's
how God'll pay us back if he's really pissed off at us. He
can't be too fond of us anyway or we wouldn't be in this
hell hole in the first fucking place. But lightning? There's
no way he'd waste that old trick on us." Joe pulled out
his Zippo lighter and showed it to me. "This is the way I
look at my relationship with the big man upstairs."

I took it and read it. On one side was the raised 101st
Airborne crest with the Screaming Eagle. I turned it over.
Engraved on the back it said:

I KNOW I'M GOING TO HEAVEN
BECAUSE I'VE SPENT MY TIME IN HELL.

I threw it back to him. "You gotta be kidding, Joe. I can't
imagine you thinking that melodramatic crap."

"It's a memento. A present, that's all. One of the grunts
gave it to me today after we pulled his unit out of the
jungle. He'd been out there for a month. He gave it to me
as a Christmas gift after we landed back at Eagle." Joe lit

a cigarette, blew out the smoke, and put the lighter back into his pocket.

I left the club just before midnight. I was the first person back to our hootch. I was getting ready to turn in when where was a knock at the plywood door. It was Ernest. He had brought two beers with him. He wanted to hear "Love Is Blue" on my tape player before going to bed. He sat on my bunk and I played it for him. He listened with a distant smile on his young face. When it finished he lifted his Budweiser in a toast, "To combat flying."

"To combat flying," I toasted back and took a long drink.

"To round-eye'd pussy," he said with a wink.

"To round-eye'd pussy, Ernest." I drank.

He finished the drink then cradled the can in his lap. Looking down at it, he idly ran his finger around the lip of the can. He looked at me again and raised the can. "Merry Christmas, Randy Mains," he said looking at me with his features set. Sincerity filled his blue eyes.

"And Merry Christmas to you, Ernest James." We clicked our cans then drank to the toast.

"KABOOM, KAABOOOMMM! the eight-inch guns exploded making me jump and dribble my beer. "Not too damn merry for some poor bastards out there," I said wiping my chin.

"Or for us stationed here at Sally. Not really," Ernest said solemnly.

I tried hard to fight back the image of my family and the Christmas decorations I knew would be scattered around the house. The colored lights strung around the roof outside. The decorated tree in the living room, its fresh pine scent filling the house. I tried to push back the recollections of Andrea's excitement in the expectation of Santa Claus sliding down our chimney. I suddenly felt deeply depressed. "Yeah, Ernest," I said softly. "You're dead right. Not really a merry Christmas here is it?" I tossed back the rest of the beer and pulled out the cardboard box from under my bunk. The care package my family had sent. "Christmas brownie?"

"From The World? How could I refuse?"

I handed Ernest one of the small brown bricks. He examined it and tried to take a bite. He finally gave up, leaned over, and rapped it hard against the floor. It left a mark in the dusty plywood. He looked up at me in bewilderment. I began to giggle. So did he. Our giggles turned into deep belly laughs until tears rolled down our cheeks and fell onto the floor to mix with the Vietnamese dust. In the background we could hear singing drifting from the club.

And though we have malaria!
We still maintain our area!
We like it here, we like it here!
You fucking A we like it here!

CHAPTER 5

January 1969

Cobras in the Shit House

My humanities professor in college informed our class one day that ancient man thought the sky was continually ablaze and that night was a huge black animal skin draped over the sky. Holes in that skin covering the flaming sky explained the appearance of the twinkling stars.

Tonight in the moonless sky the stars looked like dazzling flecks of shimmering silver reflecting the fire behind them. I had never seen the stars so brilliant.

Joe, Tom, and I sat in the dirt with our bare feet dangling in a drainage trench that ran outside the pilots' hootch at Camp Evans. Tom and I leaned in toward Joe who was sitting between us and the three of us continued to sing:

From the park you hear the happy sounds of the carousel,
You can almost taste the hot dogs and french fries they sell,
Unnn-derrr the bo-o-oard walk. Down by the sea-ee-ee-ee, yeah.
On a blanket with my babeee, that's where I'll beee!

The three of us spotted it at the same time. It was a white speck in the sky, a light, larger than any star. It appeared from the horizon, rose like a rocket, then hovered in midair, like an object at the apex of its trajectory. Then it began to descend. It appeared as if it was coming right at us. Without speaking the three of us dove into the shallow trench. We poked our heads up and watched it. It seemed to grow larger, about twice the size of any star.

Then, to our utter amazement, it rocketed straight up, accelerating as it rose until it simply disappeared. Vanished. To this day we have no idea what it was. We discussed it for five minutes and could not come up with a plausible explanation. It *was* New Year's Eve. Maybe it had something to do with that? Or was it a UFO? In a combat zone one could expect to see anything. Not wanting to appear fanciful we decided to treat the matter as the mystery it was.

"What a fuckin' place to spend New Year's Eve," Joe lamented, his Texas accent thicker than usual. He checked the luminescent dial of his Seiko. "One minute to midnight. Hoo-fucking-ray! You two think I'm going to give you a New Year's kiss, you're out of your fucking minds."

"Cheer up, Joe, and just watch the perimeter, OK?" Shonehour directed.

We did not have to wait long for the show to begin. Suddenly perimeter flares rocketed overhead like fireworks and popped all around us. Machine guns fired red tracers into the air. Grenades and M-79 grenade launchers fired, WHOOMP! WHOOMP! WHOOMP! exploding into the perimeter. Each bunker on the berm opened up to celebrate our New Year. Then the 105-mm howitzers fired accompanied in sync with the loud eight-inch guns. KAAWHAM! KAABOOM! KAAWHAM! KAABOOM! KAAWHAM! KAAABOOMMM! What a show! It was the loudest, if not the most unusual, New Year's Eve I had ever seen rung in.

4 January 1969

Dear Mom:

Received your letters today. Our platoon has been living up at Camp Evans for the last ten days and I haven't had a chance to pick up any of my mail at Sally for a while. Sounds like your Christmas was a good one. Hope you guys got what you wanted. I haven't been doing anything special, just flying a lot. I have received letters from almost everyone before Christmas so I am doing a lot of letter writing. I have flown over two hundred combat hours now. As much time as I got through all of flight school.

I don't have much to say. I just wanted to write and tell you I'm fine and that I'm thinking about everyone. Write again soon.

Love, Randy.

That was a typical I'm alive letter. Nothing important to say except to give the family a date to look at in order to let them know that on that day their son was alive.

At that time I received a letter from my mom which made me extremely angry. In it, she told me how my stepfather had pulled strings to get the son of a family friend into the California Air National Guard. My stepfather had done this because the boy had a promising career playing baseball for a Los Angeles team and did not want to ruin his career chances by going off to war. No one could blame him.

I was angry because I too had asked my stepfather to get me into the guard when I was in my first year at college. I figured it would keep the draft board off me long enough to attain my four-year college education so that one day I could transfer into the real air force and fly jets. But he refused my request, maintaining it would be better character building to make it in this world without his help.

Ned Kelly approached me at the bar in the officers' club and asked, "You got any objection to flying copilot on an FOB mission with me tomorrow?"

I had heard a little bit about the Forward Observation Base missions. They were veiled in secrecy and were reported to be the hairiest missions the Blackwidows flew. "You think I'm ready?"

"You, Joe, and Tom are the most senior peter pilots we've got." He allowed himself a small smile then quickly stifled it. "Guess we have no choice. You want to volunteer, or don't you?"

"Sure. Ok, why not?"

"Good, then have my aircraft pre-flighted by 0515. We've got a 0530 crank time."

I threw him a mock salute and clicked my boot heels together. "Roger, captain."

He shook his head, "When you going to stop being such a fuckin' new guy."

I laughed. "Probably the day you get on that freedom bird to take you back to The World, Kelly. Hey, can I buy you a beer?"

He checked his watch. "Naw. Gotta get up in six hours. Tomorrow'll be a long day. I'm gonna turn in. I suggest you do the same. I don't want a half-drunk peter pilot flying with me tomorrow. On FOB missions you need all your faculties. You'll see what I mean tomorrow. Good night," he said and left the club. He seemed unusually serious to me. I figured he knew what he was talking about. Following his example, I also finished my beer and left the club to turn in.

It was dark when we took off from the Widow Web at Sally. We were a flight of two Hueys and we flew loose trail formation at fifteen hundred feet following Highway-1 to Mai Loc. Joe was flying copilot with Bob Coulshaw. We landed at Mai Loc as the arc of the sun began to peek over the horizon.

Mai Loc was the Forward Observation Base for the Fifth Special Forces Green Berets. I had only flown this far north once or twice before. Mai Loc was a barren, rectangular patch of dirt covered with a maze of radio antennae, a few tents, and several hootches. The compound was surrounded with a high barbed wire fence and scattered bunkers.

We parked the two helicopters on the PSP pads inside the wire fence and the four of us joined up and began walking toward operations. Kelly said, "You guys go ahead. I'll catch up. Gotta give birth to another VC," and he made his way to a small latrine.

Joe, Bob Coulshaw, and I were about to duck under the flap leading into the operations tent when we heard the most godawful scream. We turned and saw Ned Kelly scrambling from the latrine. His Nomex was wrapped around his ankles, and he fell to the dirt kicking. "Moth-erfucking, shit, goddamn, Jesus, shit-fuck . . . ahhhh!"

We rushed over. Coulshaw asked first, "What the hell you up to, Kelly? You look like you been chased by a gator. Damn, I've never seen you move so damn fast be-fore."

Kelly sprang to his feet and jerked his pants up, tucking in the top of his Nomex shirt and looking back at the latrine with wide, wild eyes. "There's a fuckin' goddamn big-ass snake in there. I'm not shittin' you guys. And not just any kind of snake." He was breathing hard, obviously still scared to death.

"What happened?"

"Just as I sat down on the two holer, just got my ass down, I saw a movement off to my right. Then I see this flat brown and gray head pop up out of the other hole and it's starin' at me face to face. It was a goddamn cobra, that's what it was. Scared the goddamn livin' shit out of me, Jesus." He shivered.

Joe laughed. "Well if it scared the livin' shit out of you then I guess you won't be needing to go back in there then, will ya?"

Kelly shot him a disparaging gaze. "Not fuckin' funny, Sulak, not fuckin' funny at all."

We cautiously checked out the latrine and found noth-ing. We even pulled out the cut-in-half fifty-five-gallon drum that collected the shit. Nothing. Kelly's snake had gone. Vanished. Simply disappeared. We gave Kelly a hard time about his "mythological" snake and told him that he had been seeing things, that he was probably suffering from severe combat fatigue. If secrets were to be known, I am certain that there was not one of us from that day on that did not check out the Mai Loc shitter thoroughly be-fore planting our thin, white bottoms down over the black plywood hole!

We walked into the operations tent and were introduced to a friendly special forces sergeant. The man had no neck and two thick arms festooned with tattoos. He offered us coffee and led us into another room for our briefing. I will never forget the impact of that briefing. It was the first time I had heard that Americans were flying reconnaissance teams into Laos.

The sergeant threw back a green tarp covering a map on an easel depicting regions north of the DMZ and an area sixty miles west of Vietnam's western border. Over the map were bold black letters that read SECRET.

"Gentlemen," he began in a raspy voice. "We've got one six-man recon team out at the moment consisting of four Americans and two ARVN scouts." He pointed to a red dot on the map about forty miles into Laos. "If you have to extract them, it'll have to be by Mcguire rig. There are no natural LZs I'm afraid. Nothing but triple-canopy jungle."

Kelly took a drag of his cigarette, blew out the smoke and asked, "Any signs of the NVA?"

The sergeant pointed to a spot north of the red dot. "They think there's a company here. That's where they were headed. Their mission is as per our SOP. They're not to get into contact unless it's a matter of life or death." The sergeant looked at me and Joe then at Kelly, "New pilots, huh?"

Kelly closed his eyes and nodded. "Afraid so."

The sergeant made the next speech for the benefit of us. "The only people who know about what we do here is the President of the United States, me, the team of course, and you, the pilots. That is why this is strictly a volunteer mission. We don't accept married personnel. The risk is too great. Under the current political climate I'm afraid if you go down over the fence," he pointed out the border on the map with a thick stubby finger, ". . . and we can't get to you, the United States government will disavow any knowledge of your whereabouts and you will be listed as missing in action. Is that understood, gentlemen?"

I felt a thick lump form in my throat. I stared back into the cold eyes of the unsmiling special forces sergeant. I did not speak. Neither did Joe. We both just nodded our heads, agreeing to the crazy conditions.

After breakfast in the mess hall we spent the day sweating in the sunshine with our shirts off and pitching horse shoes outside the ops tent. Joe and Ned Kelly tied their yellow neck scarves around their heads in a thick head-band to keep the sweat from dripping into their eyes.

Just before lunch the ops sergeant came running out from the tent. "The team's been compromised. They're being chased. Here." He handed Coulshaw and Kelly each a slip of paper. "Those are the coordinates, frequency, and call sign. Can you go get them?"

Everything went into fast motion. My heart began to race. I threw on my Nomex shirt and dashed for the air-craft. Kelly started the engine quickly and in no time we were a flight of two heading west. I pulled out the map and circled the coordinates. Khe Sahn, where nearly a year ago the marines got their asses handed to them during the Tet Offensive of 1968, passed five klicks to the south of our flight path. A sudden sickening thought came to mind. Tet was twenty-five days away. Sally was only seven klicks from Hue, site of some of the bloodiest fighting in the history of the war. Shit! I pushed the thought from my mind. One day at a time I told myself.

The huge vertical face of Co Rock rose out of the jungle ahead. It was on the Laotian side of the border—the high-est geographical feature for miles. Co Rock looked out of place, as if it had been shoved upward by some primeval swelling causing it to tower like a natural fortress high above the surrounding terrain and thick jungle. Its sheer, brown face was scarred and had been blasted barren by megatons of ordinance from countless air and artillery strikes. Huge artillery pieces had once been positioned on Co Rock by the enemy. During the bloody battle of Khe Sahn railroad cars with the guns mounted on them were rolled out of caves located on the face of the ominous looking peak. The enemy had fired down on the men at Khe Sahn, pulverizing them unmercifully. From this stra-tegic position, I could see it would have been like shooting rats in a barrel.

Kelly positioned us north of Co Rock and flew a com-pass heading of 265 degrees. I followed our course with my finger on the map. Kelly did not need to look at it.

Twenty minutes into Laos, Kelly pulled out the piece of paper the sergeant had given him and read the team's call sign. He transmitted on the FM radio, "Lively Runner,

Lively Runner, this is Blackwidow One-Two. Do you read, over?"

Silence.

Kelly tried again.

This time a faint whispered reply came back. I could barely make it out. "We read you, Blackwidow One-Two. We've managed to give the enemy the slip. There's a company of NVA five klicks to the north of us. We think they've sent a platoon in pursuit. Wait . . . we hear you. We hear you. Popping smoke."

"Roger," Kelly acknowledged. He leaned over in his seat. "Murphy, Jackson."

"Yes sir?"

"Keep your eyes pealed. Jackson fire only if I tell you."

"Roger that, sir."

"Follow me close, FNG. Although we make a hell of a lot of noise hovering over the jungle the enemy can't tell where the noise's coming from. But in case he gets lucky," Kelly paused to look over at me, "Our skids'll only be a few feet from the treetops. There won't be but a fraction of a second for you to take the controls from me if I get hit. So don't fuck it up."

"Roger."

"I have the smoke, sir," Murphy said. "It's purple. One-thirty low."

"Got it," Kelly said. He dumped the collective and kicked the machine out of trim, causing us to fall out of the sky like a greased refrigerator. Kelly radioed, "Got your purple smoke, Lively Runner. Be over your location in three-zero seconds."

The reply was a little louder than a whisper now, "Roger, Blackwidow. Confirm purple smoke. We're ready for you."

"Get the ammo boxes ready, Murphy," Kelly ordered to the crew chief.

"Roger that, sir." He climbed out of his position behind his M-60 and knelt on the floor of the Huey next to the three steel boxes.

The three Mcguire rig ropes were tied on individual tie down rings located on the Huey's metal floor. They were individually coiled neatly inside their own ammunition box. The heavy ammo box acted as ballast. Once the air-craft is in a stable hover over the trees, on command the boxes are thrown from the aircraft. The line unravels as the box falls and breaks through the trees and branches and finally finds its way to the jungle floor where the team members are waiting. At the business end of each rope is a canvas swing-type arrangement. That is where the man sits. An adjustable loop is positioned on the rope at about eye level for a man to slip his wrist through as a safety precaution. That way if he falls out of the seat while air-borne, or becomes unconscious for any reason, he will at least hang by his wrist and not fall to his death.

Kelly stopped the dizzying descent, leveled out, and set up a short final approach to the area over the green carpet below where I could see the last of the purple smoke fil-tering up through the trees. Kelly hovered the machine five feet above the trees. "OK, throw em out!" he com-manded.

The crew chief shoved out the three boxes. Suddenly I could hear the clacking of machine-gun fire below. Kelly held the hover. There was no talking on the radio, just that damn sporadic clacking of machine-gun fire. My hands and feet were a breath's distance away from the controls. Time seemed frozen.

"I see them, sir," yelled the crew chief. "They're grab-bing the ropes."

Come on, come on, come on! I thought. More clacking of small-arms fire below. I waited for the bullets to hit the ship. There was nowhere to go if we got hit. Just a sea of green, a flat jungle carpet for as far as I could see. What the fuck am I doing here? I thanked my stars I was not flying with Magnet Ass Bernie Nivens. My heart began to beat harder, louder, until the radio crackled.

"OK, we're on, Blackwidow. Let's dee-dee."—which is shorthand for the Vietnamese term "didi" meaning to run.

Kelly pulled in a handful of collective. We rose quicker than I thought we would. Twenty-five, fifty, sixty, eighty, one hundred feet and still climbing. I could see that the trick was to come up exactly straight or else you would drag the three men dangling on the ends of the 150-foot ropes through the trees.

"They're clear of the trees, sir," the crew chief yelled. "Let's do like the man said. Let's dee-dee!"

Coulshaw radioed, "Blackwidow One-Four on short final."

"Roger."

Kelly nosed the chopper over, gained sixty knots, and we climbed slowly to two thousand feet above the jungle. I turned in my armored seat to look back. Murphy was lying on his stomach with a quarter of his body hanging out the open cargo door. A shock of blond hair whipped in the sixty-knot wind from under his green flight helmet.

"They've locked arms and legs, sir," he reported. "They're not spinnin'. They look stable to me. I can see Mr. Coulshaw's ship hovering over the place we just left."

"Thanks," Kelly said. He seemed to relax.

The FM radio crackled, "Blackwidow One-Four we're on! Go, Go, Go!" I could hear continuous, heavy small-arms firing in the background of the team leader's radio transmission.

"Roger, lifting."

Coulshaw was about five klicks behind us when we arrived over LZ Vandergrift, a marine airstrip ten klicks south of Mai Loc. I never thought I would consider Vietnam friendly territory, but after flying over Laos, I certainly did.

Kelly brought the ship to a two-hundred-foot hover over the PSP airstrip. The crew chief directed him in by laying on his stomach again and talking Kelly down slowly. Any forward movement could cause the three men suspended on the long ropes under the aircraft to get hurt. Kelly lowered them down flawlessly. Once they were safely on the ground we landed next to them and they scampered aboard. We had lifted out one American and two Vietnamese scouts.

We watched Coulshaw and Joe make their approach. It looked odd with three men on the long, thin strings dangling so far below the aircraft. Coulshaw slowed his machine and came to a two-hundred-foot hover. I could make out the figures now. But something did not look right. In fact the scene looked terribly wrong. Two of the figures were slumped over and hanging out of their canvas seats. The third man was struggling to hold on to them. They were held in only by their arms, literally hanging there by their wrists through the loop on the rope, and twirling slightly as Coulshaw slowly descended. When they reached the metal landing strip only one man stood initially, but as his weight settled he grabbed his leg and collapsed. The other two looked like rag dolls as they slumped in a heap on the PSP airstrip.

The surviving soldier later told us that the enemy platoon had caught up with them as they were being pulled up through the trees. They had stood on the jungle floor and fired up at them as they ascended, wounding all three. The other two young Americans had been alive for several miles, but had died en route.

We flew the two dead men and the wounded soldier to the 22nd surgical hospital in Quang Tri. After taking the survivors back to Mai Loc we were released to fly back to Sally after dark. We arrived at the Widow Web by 1930 and by 2000 it was raining again.

We had chow in the mess tent. It consisted of boiled beef, stewed potatoes, cabbage, and green Kool-Aid; we called it "green death" because of the metallic taste from the large aluminum pot in which it was mixed. For dessert we were served the familiar yellow custard, which I left uneaten on the wooden table. Then I ran for the club, trying not to get too drenched in the tropical downpour.

I stood with Joe at the end of the bar drinking a Budweiser and discussing the events of the day. Captain Ernest James entered, ordered a Blushing Asshole from Spec-4 Flowers, and cornered me at the bar. He had heard about our mission into Laos and he wanted me to tell him all about it.

"Not here, Ernest," I told him quietly. "Come by the hootch later."

He nodded then winked. "Gotcha, Randy," and he threw down the Blushing Asshole and ordered another.

"Slow down on those, Ernest, or you'll never make it to the hootch."

"I'm getting used to these now. I'm in training to break the record."

"Just remember what happened last time," Joe reminded him. "Or you'll end up spending the night sleeping vertical with your leg stuck in a piss tube again."

"That'll never happen. I was just out of practice, that's all. I can beat five Blushing Assholes and still make it back to my hootch under my own power." Spec-4 Flowers handed him another of the pink-colored drinks. "Thanks." He raised his glass. "To your good health, gentlemen."

"To flying combat, Ernest."

"To flying combat!" He said enthusiastically, then chugged half the contents.

Ernest never made it to the hootch to hear about the Mai Loc mission. He was found the next morning by Les Ramson. Ramson was awakened at 0600 by what he thought was a wild boar outside the hootch. That's what he claimed anyway. Armed with a 9mm pistol that he pulled out from under his bed, he stomped outside angrily to investigate the racket. To his surprise he found Ernest, fully clothed, sitting upright in the unfinished bunker. His back was propped up against the muddy bank, arms thrown to each side as if he were relaxing in a bathtub of brown water one-foot deep. His head was thrown back, mouth gaping open, his drunken snores sounding exactly like a series of small pig snorts.

The Blackwidows were assigned the task of supporting the marines stationed up at Quang Tri, located north of Camp Evans and south of Dong Ha. We were to fly in support of the marine "super grunts," as they were called.

Quang Tri was a large-sized base with an airstrip long enough to accommodate C-130s. There was a squadron of marine helicopters based there—mostly Charlie and Echo model gunships and many tandem rotor CH-46s, the smaller brother to the army's CH-47 Chinook. There were also several Korean War vintage radial-engine H-34 helicopters. And there was a fixed-wing contingent of twin-engine OV-10s and small, single-engine Bird Dogs.

Other than the overloaded gunships the marines operated, they did not have in their inventory a small troop-carrying helicopter to insert and extract the six- and eight-man super grunt teams, so they called on the army to supply them with two. The Blackwidows were the army helicopter company closest to Quang Tri, so we were instructed by division headquarters to carry out this task.

The super grunts were the marine's equivalent to the army's Special Forces Green Berets. To the best of my knowledge they did not perform recon missions over the border.

We were met on the airfield by a marine major and his number two in charge, a tall, lanky captain with ears like wing nuts who spoke with a thick southern drawl. While the major made the introductions the captain stood on the skids and inspected the cockpit of one of our ships. "Sheeeeitt!" he exclaimed, scratching his head. "You fellas hardly got any instruments. Not even a tacan. How do you find your way around the country without a tacan?"

I looked at Kelly and he looked at me. We both shrugged. Kelly said, "We use maps."

"Maps?" The captain said unable to hide the amazement in his voice. "You mean you boys fly around the country in all kinds of weather by usin' simple pilotage?"

"Yeah, sure. Don't you?"

"Hell, no! We ground an aircraft if the tacan's not working. I certainly wouldn't consider taking one without it, would you, sir?"

The major chuckled. "Our SOP says we don't. But we probably do things a bit differently from our army cousins here."

"Sheeeeeit," the captain said again, stepping off the skid by the cockpit. "You wouldn't catch me flying round here without a tacan, that's for damn sure."

Kelly pointed to his eyes. "These are the best navigation tools you can have. They seldom go unserviceable. You can trust them a damn sight more than some electronic nav aid. And the ADF, forget it. You fly the needle on it thinking it's taking you where you want to go, and odds are Charlie has a station set up cross the border somewhere with the same frequency to draw you to him; then he'll shoot your ass down when you make your let-down. No, sir, my two eyes are the best navigation aid I've got and the only nav aid I'll trust.''

The skinny captain shook his head. ''Sheeeit. Not me. You army pilots are even crazier than the stories I heard about ya'll.''

The major slapped my back. ''And they're good pilots, Captain. Damn good, and we're damn lucky to have 'em on our team. Gentlemen, if you'll follow me, I'll show you the club and where you'll be staying.''

The marines treated us like royalty. That night we ate lobster in the mess hall. Lobster! It was an amusing sight to watch because many of the officers had obviously never eaten lobster before. It had been boiled like a big shrimp and was served in the shell, so it was left up to the individual to crack it open. The marines, being marines, attacked the crustacean with knives and forks, and several even tore at the shells with bare hands, gnawing on the shell with their teeth to get at the sweet meat. One officer stabbed at his lobster with a fork, shooting it off his plate and knocking over his water glass.

When I was nineteen I'd had a job working in the kitchen at The Village Inn on Balboa Island, and I had been taught how to prepare lobster by the chef there. I laid the sharp knife along the length of the shell down the center and pushed down with my palm making a neat cut. Then, using my thumbs, I peeled the shell back from the incision, exposing the tender meat.

The lieutenant sitting across from me hollered, ''Hey everyone, watch how the army guy does it. He's got class, unlike the rest of you slobs.''

His comment was followed by rude remarks and friendly cat calls. Soon everyone was following my example.

That evening we were taken to the club and we were not allowed to buy a drink. It was not long before we were singing a host of songs that we had never heard before.

Oh! . . . My husband's a brick layer,
a brick layer
a brick layer
My husband's a brick layer
a brick layer is he.

All day he lays bricks
he lays bricks
he lays bricks
and at night he comes home and lays me!

Oh hey gig-a-gig
fuck a little pig
faaaalllowww the moon!

Faaaalllowww the moon!

Faaaalllowww the moon!

Hey gig-a-gig
fuck a little pig
faaaalllowww the moon
faaaalllowww the moon and you'll see!

A first lieutenant with whom we had been drinking took Kelly and me to his room later to show us an unregistered Colt .45 he kept there.

"You said you can get booze for $1.40 a bottle?" he asked me drunkenly.

"Yep." I answered back drunkenly.

"Here." He thrust the loaded .45 at me. "You can have it then. Just bring me a bottle of Smirnoff next time you come up."

"That's all you want for it? A bottle of Smirnoff?"

"That's all."

I extended my hand, "You got a deal."

He shook my hand smiling. "Deal."

Kelly and I wove our way along the perimeter in the dark in the direction of the hootch where we would be staying. Suddenly Kelly froze in his tracks and said, "Quiet. There's movement in the wire."

We both stopped and crouched down. I cocked my newly acquired .45. I strained to listen. Singing was drifting from the club. I squinted to see in the darkness. There was a quarter of a moon, but it was covered by thin clouds. I could just make out figures making their way towards us. There were three about fifty yards away and they moved silently.

I whispered, "What do we do?"

Kelly had the .38 out of his holster. "Be quiet and wait."

I was sobering up quickly. The figures were dressed in black and getting closer. I took aim with the .45. Kelly sighted down his .38. As the figures neared I could hear my heartbeat pounding in my ear drums. It seemed so loud that I was afraid the closing figures would hear it. I put pressure on the trigger. The outlines got to within twenty-five yards. Kelly scared the hell out of me when he yelled, "Halt! Who goes there?"

I was ready to pull the trigger when I heard a frantic, "Don't shoot, don't shoot. We're friendly. For God's sake don't shoot!"

"Who are you?" Kelly asked.

I heard one of them say with a Brooklyn accent, "I told you this was a dumb fuckin' idea, Zimwald. You shoulda listened to me, goddamn it."

"Put your hands over your heads and move up slowly," Kelly ordered, still leveling his weapon at them.

"OK, OK, but for Christsake don't fuckin' shoot!"

The three figures stood erect with hands in the air and approached us. I could now tell they were too tall to be the enemy and I began to breathe easier.

Kelly and I stood there as the three men dressed in black pajamas approached. One even wore a conical Vietnamese hat. Kelly asked, "What the fuck you jokers doing out there? You looking to get yourselves killed?"

"Just having some fun," one answered.

We were now face to face. "Just having some fun?" I exclaimed. "You almost got yourselves blown away. Is this how marines have fun? Sneaking around in the dark through barbed wire on their own perimeter?"

"We do it all the time," one answered. "It's kind of a game."

"Game!" Kelly holstered his weapon. "You're fucking nuts, all three of you. Get the hell out of here before I report you to your commanding officer. And for fuck sake don't do it again."

"Right, sir," they said and scurried off.

"Fucking marines," Kelly said. "Got about as much sense as a fucking ice cube."

"That may be stretching it, Ned, don't you think?"

He chuckled. "You're learning, FNG, you're definitely learning." And with that we went off to find our hootch and turn in.

28 January 1969

Dear Howard,

I received your letter the 20th but I've been unable to answer because I've been with my platoon up at Quang Tri seven miles south of the DMZ flying for the Marines. So far I have logged 260 combat hours, (six air medals) and I'm due to make Aircraft Commander in forty more flight hours if the other aircraft commanders in my platoon think I'm ready. TET is coming up, the Vietnamese lunar New Year, and it seems to be on everyone's mind. Remember the big TET offensive last year in Hue? Well, everyone's gearing up for that.

The flying over here is exciting to say the least. To make it even more interesting, I volunteer for the missions flying for the Special Forces up north. Sometimes we make our own excitement. For instance about three weeks ago I was flying as copilot on our way back to LZ Sally from Quang Tri.

The weather was below minimums with a slight drizzle. Following the road low level we flew over the Hue Bridge which crosses the Perfume River. We decided to fly under it at ninety knots. We didn't do it once, but twice. It was a crazy thing to do, I know, but it seemed the thing to do at the time. I know it was a battalion first. It reminds me of the story you told me once of buzzing your company area in your B-24 in North Africa which resulted in blowing out all the windows in the mess hall. Anyway, there's not much else. I think of you all and can't wait to come home. Only eight more months to go.

Randy

Thinking about it now I guess we pilots were as crazy as the marines Kelly and I had caught sneaking through the wire up at Quang Tri. As if life wasn't fraught with enough danger we had to go out and look for ways to try and kill ourselves.

When Jeff Leach and I flew under the Hue bridge we had hit the skids on the water as we passed under. I held my breath both times we did it, and I'll admit I was nervous. Not scared, just nervous, but I should have been scared. It was a stupid thing to do. The clearance was minimal. If I had to guess, it was maybe twenty feet from rotor head to the bottom of the steel bridge. You might say we had as much sense as an ice cube. Probably less.

In the club that night I told Joe and Tom Shonehour about our escapade. Several days later Shonehour came up to me with a gleam in his eye.

"Leach and I did it too," he told me beaming.

"Did what?"

"Flew under the bridge. God, was it great!" He had a pronounced spring in his step when he walked off.

When Leach and I had flown under the bridge the weather had been extremely poor. It had been drizzling with a three-hundred-foot overcast. Visibility had been down to a half mile. When Shonehour and Leach did it the sun was shining in a blue, cloudless sky. There was one other small detail about their exhibition. A one star general from brigade, several full colonels, and two photographers, one from *Time* and one representing *Newsweek,* were crossing the bridge at the time.

The photographers, seasoned war correspondents experienced at capturing a shot in the heat of combat at a moment's notice, managed to frame Leach's aircraft perfectly as it passed below them. The general had the photos enlarged and intelligence evaluate them to nail down which company the ship belonged to and who had been flying. On receiving the report the general's first reaction was to court-martial Shonehour and Leach. The *Newsweek* and *Time* photographers, however, wanted to run the photo as a cover story back in the U.S. A lot of rhetoric took place in headquarters at Camp Eagle. Many strings were pulled to keep the story out of the press. In the end Shonehour and Leach were grounded for two weeks and both men hit with an Article-15 plus a stiff fine. Needless to say, no one flew under the Hue bridge again—and got caught, that is.

CHAPTER 6

February 1969

General Patton and the Buffalo BBQ

Charlie Company's executive officer, Captain Curly, entered the mess tent and glanced across to where I was drinking coffee at one of the wooden tables. He walked over checking his clipboard, "Mains, you'll be officer of the guard on the seventeenth."

I thought for a moment. "But that's Tet, sir."

"Well *now* we know you know how to read a calendar," he said sarcastically.

"No, I mean, after last year wouldn't you feel safer with an RLO infantry officer acting as officer of the guard? Hue is just a few klicks up the road. You *do* remember what went on up there last year at this time?"

Captain Curly was a short man with a bald head. He ran his hand over his barren pate then said, "You questioning my judgment, Mr. Mains?"

"Of course not, sir. It's just that . . ."

"Just that what?"

"Well, just that I've never been officer of the guard before. I'm just a pilot. Last year a division of NVA occupied Hue. A division! Every year during Tet there has been some sort of action. So I just thought . . ."

"Well don't think, Mr. Mains. Just do it. You'll have a land line to the ops tent and you'll have comms with the other five bunkers you'll be in charge of. If you have a problem you can call ops and they'll alert the company."

"That could be too late, sir. I really think . . ."

"There you go thinking again." His eyes rolled back then drilled into me. "Just do it, understand?"

"Yes, sir. I understand."

* * *

For several days before my duty I stood next to the huge metal CONEX container that was our mail room and watched how the other officers of the guard went about inspecting the troops.

When the day arrived I stood in front of three rows of five men at 1715 sharp. All fifteen men were standing to attention in front of the ops tent. I wore my steel helmet with camouflaged cover, my gleaming pistol strapped snugly into its spit-shined holster and a flack jacket over freshly pressed fatigues. My boots glistened under bloused pant legs. I felt like General Patton! I looked right and left and called, "All right men, Attentennnnshunnn! Preeee-seeent-arrmmmms."

I walked down the line inspecting the troops individually, mimicking what I'd seen the other officers do. I never considered myself to be a hard ass. Not by any stretch of the imagination. But considering the importance of the date I thought it would be reasonable to expect the men to meet some pretty high standards. My life as well as the lives of the troops on guard duty with me and the men in Charlie Company were my ultimate responsibility. So I figured I had better take the job seriously.

I inspected each man, checking his overall appearance, but I was mainly concerned with the cleanliness of his weapon. It might, after all, be the weapon to fire the bullet that would kill the VC that was about to kill me.

I took the weapon from the first man standing at attention in front of me, opened the breech, placed my thumb in the chamber, and sighted down the barrel. I was shocked. I looked at the man. "You plan on growing potatoes in there, corporal?"

He looked surprised. "No, sir."

I handed the weapon back to him. "Do you realize what the date is today and what is significant about it?"

"Yes, sir."

"You plan to shoot dirt clods at the enemy if he decides to come through the perimeter tonight, or do you plan to use real bullets?"

"Bullets, sir." he said, looking at me oddly.

"I doubt a bullet could furrow through all the dirt plugging up that barrel. I suggest you go back to your hootch and clean that weapon. I want to see reflections of the reflections when I look down there next time. Understand?''

''Yes, sir!''

''Dismissed.'' He ran off toward the enlisted men's hootches.

By the end of the inspection I had sent three others back to clean their weapons.

It was customary to select the soldier who stood out from the rest for outstanding appearance and possession of the cleanest weapon. The man I chose was dismissed and excused from having to pull guard duty. Such a person was called a supernumerary. I then gave the remaining men the password for the challenge response, ''flying leopard,'' and read the standing orders from a notebook taken from Ops. By 1800 we were all secure in our bunkers waiting for the sun to go down.

I examined the inside of my bunker into which thin, black wires snaked their way from the perimeter, through the tangle of concertina wire. The wires led to detonators on the claymore mines and FU Gas barrels. I peered out the small slit between the sandbags and could see the green claymores stuck in the ground. Their arched faces pointed in the direction from which the enemy would be coming. Claymores are anti-personnel mines. They contain a one-pound charge of C-4 plastic explosive and, when detonated, scatter six hundred steel balls toward the enemy. Ten clackers, the small, hand-held firing mechanisms for the claymores, sat in line next to the telephone on a crude wooden table in the center of the bunker. The firing devices for the four, fifty-five-gallon FU Gas, or jellied gasoline, barrels, buried in the ground outside our stretch of the perimeter, also sat on the table. There were twenty steel ammo boxes of M-16 ammunition, twenty fragmentation grenades, and I counted more than one hundred rounds of 40mm ammunition for the single-shot M-79 grenade launcher I would use as the first line of defense. Also on the table, in its own wooden box, I found a starlight scope.

I performed a commo check with ops and the men in

the other bunkers. I told them that I would be firing the M-79 indiscriminately into the berm throughout the night and not to be alarmed. The M-79 had a sound easily distinguished from anything the enemy had, so our men knew that if they heard it it would just be me. We were well prepared, except for one very important detail—I was a pilot, not an infantry officer.

Along with the two men assigned to my bunker I sat on top of the sandbags and watched the sun sink slowly beneath the horizon. In the distance I could see lights switch on and glow in the ancient city of Hue. As twilight gave way to blackness, I tried to check my runaway imagination which was straining to produce columns of dark-clothed bodies creeping through the wire toward us.

I scanned the perimeter as I had been taught to do in basic training. "Don't let your eyes fix on one spot," the drill instructor at Fort Polk had said. "Continue to scan keeping the head and eyes moving. Always moving. That's the way to pick up any movement." I placed the M-79 grenade launcher in my lap and brought the starlight scope to my eyes. The eerie, green sparkling picture showed a perimeter free of invaders.

"See anything, sir?" asked the corporal who sat next to me.

I handed the starlight scope over to him. "Nah. Nothing."

"You think we'll get hit tonight?"

"Can't be certain," I said trying not to dwell on the possibility. "But any poor soul that tries it can count on this: If I see anything out there tonight, anything at all, you can bet it's going to look like World War III cuz I'm going to throw everything we've got at him."

"I'm behind you, sir."

"Me too," the third man, a sergeant from supply, said.

I continued to scan the perimeter through the starlight scope. Every ten to fifteen minutes I loaded the grenade launcher with a round that looked like an overgrown .45 shell, and I shot it into the perimeter. THUNK . . . KA-WOOMPH! If there was anyone out there planning on getting through I would let him know there was some crazy bastard indiscriminately lobbing grenades, and maybe he would stop and think twice about it.

At 2000 hours I decided to check on the men on the other five bunkers, calling them first on the land line to tell them to expect me. I grabbed my M-16 and struck off. About forty minutes later, after I had talked with the men on the first four bunkers, I was about fifty meters from the rear of the last bunker when I heard a round being chambered.

"Halt, Halt, or I swear to God I'll shoot!" the voice had a quivering panic in it that scared the hell out of me.

"It's me. Don't shoot, it's the officer of the guard."

"Flying . . ." he said, uttering the first word of the challenge. "What's . . . what's the second password then? Say it. Say it or I'll shoot!"

I could feel the familiar pressure between my eyes, the invisible bull's eye. Imagine being shot by one of your own men. "Leopard!" I hollered. "Leopard, leopard!"

"OK. You can approach. But walk slowly."

I approached very slowly. When I could make out the figure of the man I could see his weapon pointed at my face. "Relax, relax, it's me. Mr. Mains."

The barrel of the weapon dropped. "OK, sir. I . . . I just had to make sure, that's all."

I climbed up next to him on the bunker and sat down. He was alone. The other two men were inside. We began to talk. I found out he had been in country for only two weeks. He'd arrived in Charlie Company only four days ago and he was scared, really scared. I tried to put him at ease. "The way I figure it, Charlie Company couldn't be safer tonight."

"Whaddaya mean? You said yourself *every* Tet something happens."

"Yeah, I know I did say that, but we're so damn prepared tonight there's a good chance nothing will happen at all. I don't know about you, but I don't plan on letting anyone even get in the neighborhood of LZ Sally, let alone through the perimeter. You got your M-79 handy?"

He grunted at my last statement, handed me the M-79, and scanned the berm.

I chambered a round. "What's your name anyway?"

"Private Billingsley, sir."

I aimed the weapon upward toward the perimeter and fired. THUNK . . . KAWOOMPH! "What's your MOS, Billingsley?"

"Company clerk."

I opened the breech and extracted the shell casing. "Where you from in the states?"

"Montana."

"You got a girl back there?"

His voice perked up. "Yes, sir. We're engaged to be married."

"Congratulations."

"Thanks," his voice trailed off. "She's worried to death about me bein' over here. *She's* worried, humph. What the hell am I talking about. I'm fuckin' worried."

"That's understandable, but it's not so bad here."

"Yeah? Then why am I about to shit myself then?"

I loaded another fat round, aimed, and fired. THUNK . . . KAWOOMPH! "I'm scared too, Billingsley."

"You are, sir?"

I took out the spent shell. "Yep."

"You don't show it."

"Just cuz I hide my fear doesn't mean I'm not scared. I can't show it can I? If I did then how would that make you and the rest of the guys feel? Besides, I've found from flying you can't think straight if you're too scared. But enough of that, tell me about home."

"Well, uh, I live in the country, sir. On a small ranch my daddy and two younger brothers run. Mom's a school teacher and I got an older sister in college."

Billingsley and I talked for nearly two hours. When I hopped off the bunker to return to my own he said, "Sir?"

"Yes?"

"Thanks. I . . . I enjoyed talking to you tonight. I feel better now."

"I enjoyed it too, Billingsley. See you in the morning."

"Yes, sir. See you in the morning."

Once back at my bunker I took the starlight scope from the corporal from motor pool and scanned the perimeter. "Told you, sir. Quiet as a morgue."

"I'll be inside the bunker. Going to read the letter from home I got today. Here," I gave him the M-79. "Feel free to fire it every ten or fifteen minutes or so just to let Charlie know the crazy bastard hasn't fallen asleep."

He laughed. "Roger that, sir. I'll give you a call if I see anything."

17 February 1969

Dear Mom:

I received your letter dated February 10th. I'm so glad you got my pictures and money I sent you. I was hoping you would write and tell me you received them so I could put my mind at rest.

It sounds like the weather has been better there lately. You're finally getting some of the sunny weather southern California is famous for. I wish I was there.

It's 2345 here now and I am writing this from inside a bunker. I have a poncho draped over me to block the light of my flashlight from showing outside. I am on the southeastern perimeter of LZ Sally. I'm officer of the guard tonight and I just came back from my rounds of the other five bunkers. The men are jumpy and it helped to go talk to them. Today marks the Vietnamese lunar New Year. TET. Every TET the Vietnamese have put up a big offensive. Last year was the worst. The brass say that if nothing major happens during this crucial time, peace may be probable. I sure hope so. I keep my fingers crossed. Give my love to all.

Randy

The long night passed giving way to gray, then slowly the world outside our bunker was illuminated by a beautiful sunrise. We all breathed easier knowing that the night had passed without incident—or almost without incident.

Besides the eighty-four rounds of M-79 ammunition I had fired, Billingsley had called excitedly on the land line around 0330 to report that he had spotted movement in the wire.

"Wait one, Billingsley," I said on the land line. "I'll have a look through the starlight scope." It was overcast with no ambient light, so when I looked in the direction of his bunker through the scope I could make out only an outline. Something was definitely out there. It was big and it was moving ever so slowly.

I spoke softly into the land line receiver. "I confirm, Billingsley, I do see something out there. Now, before we take any action, here's what we'll do. I . . ."

That was all Billingsley needed to hear from me. The next instant the whole perimeter erupted into a blinding flash, KAAAWWAAAABBBRRROOOMMM! an orange, yellow, and red eruption as Billingsley detonated a barrel of jellied gasoline, Fu Gas, in front of his bunker. In the light given off by the cataclysmic explosion I could see no regiments of NVA charging. Not even a company of VC. Not a platoon of sappers. Not even one VC. What I did see was a startled water buffalo who one second was grazing, and the next became beef barbecue on the hoof.

"Nice, Billingsley," I said over the land line and hung up.

The phone in my bunker rang immediately. It was the CO. "What the holy hell's going on out there, Mains?"

I explained what had happened.

"I thought we were being overrun, shit. See that it doesn't happen again!"

"Yes, sir," I said meekly and hung up.

Several days later I was walking to afternoon chow when one of the warrants from First Platoon stuck his head out of the hootch next to mine and yelled, "Anybody here have relatives in Southern California they want to talk to?"

I could hardly believe what I'd just heard. "Yes!" I answered back.

"We got a phone patch with a guy in Long Beach. Is that close?"

"Damn, yes. My folks live in Huntington Beach."

I ran to the hootch where the MARS, or Military Affiliate Radio Station, unit was located. It had two large, square aerials mounted on the roof. It was a ham radio net. It worked by the operator contacting other hams in various parts of the states who then made phone patches via the radio link. In this case my folks would be billed only for the phone call from Long Beach to their home— about forty cents.

I rushed to the radio operator's side. He turned a big black dial on one of the many radios sitting on a workbench. "That's better. Now, what's your parents' phone number?"

I told him. The next thing I heard came as a shock. It was my sister Nancy's voice. "Hello?"

I could hear the voice of the radio operator on the other end explaining what was taking place and issuing instructions for her to say "over" when she had finished talking. I was instructed to do the same. The radio operator held the microphone up to my mouth. "Go ahead," he told me.

"Nancy? Over."

"Randy? Randy, is that you? Over."

"Yes, yes. God, I can't believe it. I'm talking to you from the hootch next door to mine. . . . Over."

"All the way from Vietnam? You're calling from Vietnam? . . . Over."

"Yes. Over."

"I can't believe it. God, Randy, we really miss you! Over."

"I really miss everyone too. Over."

"Want to talk to Mom? She's standing right here. Over."

"Put her on. Over."

There was a short pause. Then I could hear Mom's voice. "Randy? Oh Randy. We miss you, sweetie. Oh how we all miss you." There was a long pause. She did not say over. I heard Nancy telling her. ". . . Oh, sorry, over, honey."

"What are you guys doing? Over."

"Oh it's such a warm and beautiful day. You know how it can get occasionally this time of year. It's so clear. Saddleback Mountain looks like it's in our backyard. You can see for miles. Should be able to see Catalina Island clearly off the coast. You know how it gets, honey. Nancy, Andrea, and I are going to have lunch at the Jolly Roger on

Balboa Island, then after that we'll take the ferry across the bay and go to the pavilion and sit and watch the sailboats sail by. . . . Over.'' Immediately a sickening wave of depression hit me. It nearly overpowered me. I suddenly realized they were living in a world parallel to mine here. Mine, based on survival, was a day-to-day existence. Their world was so normal. God, I wanted to be there with them. How I wished I had never made this call.

"Hi brother Randy. . . ." It was my little sister, Andrea.

"Hi Andy. I wish I could be there with you. Over."

"I miss you. I love you, Randy."

"And I love you, Andrea. Over."

There was a long pause. Andrea did not know what to say next. She finally spoke, "Mom says I have to say good-bye now," she said in her happy, little-girl voice.

I could feel my eyes tear. "I miss you, Andy. Your big brother loves you. Always remember that, OK? I . . . I gotta go now. Other people are waiting to make calls too. Over." I lied.

"We love and miss you, Randy. Over," my mom said, now on the verge of tears. I could tell by her voice.

"I'll write real soon, Mom. Your letters mean more than you'll know. Please keep writing. Over."

"We will, sweetie. Gotta run now. We love you. Over."

"Love you too. Bye. Out."

The operator thanked the man in Long Beach for placing the call and signed off. I felt like I'd been kicked in the stomach.

In the dim hootch the operator looked up at me. "It's tough, huh?"

"I'll never ever do that again." I breathed out heavily. "I never could have imagined it'd be so tough."

"Most of the guys do it only once. Hell, I run this setup. I could call home nearly every day if I wanted to, but I don't. It's too damn painful. It's better to keep home and loved ones in the back of your mind. Once you hear their voices, know what they're doing, hear what the weather's like, it's fucking murder."

I felt numb. Like I had just been told I'd lost a loved one. "Thanks."

"Don't mention it."

I put on my green baseball cap and made my way to the mess hall. It took me a good three days to get over that call. It had been a big mistake.

24 February 1969

Dear Mom:

It's 0805 in the morning. The weather is real bad and we're on standby to fly so I thought I would write a few lines to you. I was supposed to take off at 0730 but there is a very low ceiling with steady drizzling rain. It is getting worse so I don't think we'll fly before 12 o'clock.

It was good to hear your voices on the phone the other day. I don't think I'll do it again though. It made me miss home way too much.

I did something interesting three days ago with three other pilots from my platoon. The four of us took a day off from operational flying and did something the Special Forces teams we fly practice as a matter of normal operations. I flew at sixty knots hanging from the bottom of a helicopter at 2000 feet attached by a 150-foot rope. Let me explain. When we fly missions up north for the Special Forces we usually have no set landing zone to pick up the team because the jungle is so dense. If the team is in trouble we have to get them out quick so we carry three ropes per helicopter tied on the floor and coiled in ammunition boxes. The setup is called a McGuire Rig. The way it's deployed is, first, we hover over the trees where the team is supposed to be then the crew chief or gunner throws them out. The heavy boxes penetrate the thick jungle and carry the ropes to the jungle floor. At the end of each 150-foot rope is a harness, like a canvas swing, that each man sits in. When all three men are secure on their separate rigs they lock arms and we pull them up vertically through the trees. Once they're clear of the jungle, we fly them twenty-five to thirty-five miles to home base with them on the ropes below us.

Four of us from our platoon, all pilots, practiced this

method of extraction from the airfield. We were picked up and flown around for ten to fifteen minutes at two thousand feet on the end of our ropes with arms and legs locked together so we wouldn't spin in the strong wind created by our forward airspeed. Don't worry, Mom, I wouldn't do it again, but it was good for us as pilots to know what the guys we're pulling out of the jungle have to go through. The experience will make us that much more careful. I'll write again soon.

Love, Randy.

Captain Curly approached me as I was walking to the showers with bar of soap in hand and dressed only in flip flops and a green towel wrapped around my waist. "Mains, you're scheduled for your aircraft commander check ride tomorrow. I guess the other ACs in your platoon are getting damn desperate if they have to recommend the likes of you." His stern look melted into a smile. He was one of those men who looked funny smiling. "Good luck."

"Thank you, sir."

Joe Sulak and Tom Shonehour had been recommended to be ACs too. If we passed we would be assigned our own personal aircraft. Then it would be up to us to train the new peter pilots unfortunate enough to fly along with us.

Tom and Joe flew their check rides a day ahead of me. They both passed the combination oral examination and the 1½-hour check ride without incident. My check ride, on the other hand, nearly got me killed.

I was scheduled to fly with the senior company IP, a CW2 named Chuck Decker. He gave me the oral exam in the operations tent. I noticed right away he had short-timer pilot's eyes—intense, darting, suspicious. While we walked out to the Widow Web to our aircraft he told me, "I got less than two weeks of this shit to go, Mains." He was one of those guys who did not look at you when he spoke. "I already got my orders. I'm going to Rucker where 150 hour students will be trying to kill my ass. So I want you to keep it in mind that this'll be a straightforward check

ride, nothing fancy. It'll be as I've briefed you in ops.
Nothing more. Any questions?''

"No. Don't think so."

"Good."

The first hour went well. We were flying south of Sally
just outside the perimeter, making our landings to a grassy
area away from the rice paddies and Vietnamese ville. I
made the takeoff after making a running landing with a
simulated fixed-pitch tail rotor failure.

"That was fine, Mains. Now take it around and I'll give
you a hydraulic failure on downwind. I want you to perform the emergency procedure and land the aircraft as you
would in a real emergency."

"Roger."

A hydraulic failure in the Huey is no major event if
handled properly. It is like losing the power steering in
your car. The controls become extremely stiff and difficult
to move, but you can get down OK if you make a running
landing as does an airplane.

We were on climb out passing through two hundred feet
when Decker reached over to turn off the hydraulic switch.
It was a special kind of switch that had to be lifted up and
pulled back over a small barrier to turn it off. In this way
it could not easily be inadvertently switched off. I now
had no hydraulic pressure to assist me. I moved the jerky
controls. Decker was looking out his side window as if
disinterested.

I recited the emergency procedure. "First, I'll adjust to
a comfortable airspeed between sixty and seventy knots.
I'll recycle the switch. If that doesn't restore the hydraulics I'll reach up to the hydraulic circuit breaker. Pull it
out, if no power's restored push it in . . . what the . . . ?''

I noticed the engine N2 RPM decreasing. I instinctively
tried to lower the collective to enter autorotation. I mus-
cled it down. As I did I quickly scanned the instruments.
Compressor RPM decreasing. Two hundred fifty feet of
altitude. Descending quickly.

Simultaneously Decker's head swung to look in the
cockpit. Thinking I was just an FNG trying my best to
kill him he said, "What're you doin'?"

"Engine's quit! Switch on the hydraulics!"

He visibly jumped in his seat and quickly switched on the hydraulics. I aimed the ship for a dry rice paddy. He transmitted, "Mayday, Mayday, Mayday, this is Blackwidow Three-Three engine failure southern perimeter of LZ Sally!"

He just got the mayday call out when we passed through fifty feet and I hauled back on the cyclic stick, raising the nose of the chopper and putting us into a flare. We stopped descending as the airspeed washed off quickly. At twenty knots the machine began to sink again as we ran out of airspeed to trade off for height. At ten feet I yanked up on the collective pitch lever on my left to use the inertia in the wide blades to cushion our descent. I pushed forward on the cyclic. The aircraft leveled. I used the remaining collective pitch to cushion our landing. The craft skidded over the soft dirt for ten feet and we came to an abrupt stop. The blades coasted down slowly above us. We had been lucky. We landed in the middle of the rice paddy and missed the four dirt banks surrounding us.

The blades coasted to a slow, steady run-down and Decker looked at me with wide, disbelieving eyes. "What the fuck happened?"

"Engine quit, that's what happened. I think I know why it quit. Put your hand on the hydraulic switch again."

He reached over taking the switch between gloved thumb and forefinger. "Look there. Look at the cuff of your flight glove."

"Well I'll be fucked," he said.

We almost were. Behind the hydraulic switch sat the fuel switch. It was an "up and over" type of switch like the hydraulic switch in front of it. When he turned off the hydraulic switch the cuff of his flight glove had caught the fuel switch and turned it off also.

Two helicopter gunships landed next to us in a boil of dust. "Blackwidow Three-Three. You OK?"

"Roger," Decker radioed on guard frequency. "Wait one." He turned on the fuel switch and said to me on intercom, "Try to start her up."

I did. The fuel ignited and the turbine engine whined to life again.

"We'll be fine. Thanks for coming."

"Roger. Glad to be of assistance," and they lifted off.

I twisted on the throttle to bring the RPM up to flight range. "Want to continue?"

"Are you nuts? Like I said earlier, I'm too short for this shit. Take us back to the Widow Web." It was the first time that day the man smiled. "Congratulations, Mains. You passed. I have to admit that was some check ride. Yes siree," he chuckled to himself shaking his head. "That was one *hell* of a check ride."

CHAPTER 7

March 1969

"Dear Mom: Your Son's a Star!"

If I had not been looking forward to Tet because of the frightening stories I had heard about the events of the preceding year, I was looking forward even less to the A-Shau Valley assault being planned by the 101st.

The year before the First Cav had lost fifty-eight helicopters the first day they flew into the A-Shau. Some of our old hands who had been peter pilots at the time said it was a real bloodbath. One of the pilots had a reel-to-reel tape recording of the radio traffic taped by an enterprising pilot on that day. A group of us listened to it in the officer's club one night. The screaming and horrendous radio chatter recorded from the three aircraft radios blaring at once did not fail to raise the hair on the backs of our necks.

Worse than the actual assault was the waiting to go in. The operation was plagued with delays. We sat through two three-hour briefings in our mess hall which detailed at length the assault on the A-Shau. When the day finally arrived for the first assault, and we were all psyched up for it, the mission was called off. This happened again several weeks later. We psyched ourselves up like football players going into the Super Bowl, then at the last minute we were told, "Sorry, game's been canceled." The day-to-day waiting was becoming unbearable, and we all would have preferred just to get it over and done with. On both occasions bad weather had stopped us from carrying out the massive airlift of troops.

Even more worrying was the obvious lack of security surrounding the upcoming mission. We had waited so long that the details of the mission had doubtless been compromised to the enemy. This was brought home to me by an incident that took place after the third briefing, held in the mess hall, detailing the A-Shau Valley assault.

The following morning I rolled out of bed at 0500 ready to go on the mission only to be informed by ops that it had been scrubbed, yet again! When I got back from an early breakfast my hootch maid, Thu Yung, (pronounced too young) was making up my bunk. She stood upright. "Oh, Mr. Mains. You here?" She said with genuine surprise in her voice. "What happen? You not go A-Shau today?"

Her words horrified me. I marched over to operations and cornered Ernest James. "What kind of security is it when even the hootch maids know when we're going to assault the A-Shau? You remember what happened last year. You can bet if our hootch maids know, Charlie knows. And if he knows he'll just be sitting in the jungle waiting for us, and we'll see an even bigger bloodbath than the First Cav saw last year!"

Ernest only shrugged, unable to offer any consolation. He did talk to Major Posey who ordered that from then on all Vietnamese employed in the mess hall would be required to leave the building during briefings. Big deal!

The mission had become so compromised even shopkeepers in the village as well as the hootch maids were calling in debts and giving no further credit. Naturally they wanted to be paid in full in the likely event that the man owing them did not return from the massive assault.

I had been told that the A-Shau assault would be a huge media event. The first aircraft to land would contain the camera crews from the major networks plus several photo journalists. After our first briefing in the mess hall three weeks before I'd written to tell my family to look for the 101st in the *Los Angeles Times* and on the six o'clock news.

16 March 1969

Dear Mom:

Received your letter yesterday night dated 8 March. You said you were going to watch for our company in

*the newspapers. We postponed going into the A-Shau
Valley until further notice because of weather.*

Well, my company has moved. We have moved from
LZ Sally to Phu Bai now. Phu Bai is about seven miles
south of Hue and it's really neat here. There is a big
airstrip where C-130s and 707s can land. LZ Sally was
a very small place, actually very vulnerable to attack.
Here in Phu Bai, though, it is really built up with a big
PX and hospital nearby.

Our hootches here are longer than the sixteen-by-
thirty-two-foot hootches we lived in at Sally and we can
build our areas any way we want them. My area's coming along. I have some mats down on the floor and a
shelter over my bed to hold my belongings on top. I
made a desk and I have a beaded curtain covering my
doorway. I bought a chest of drawers from the gook
village. We have a 30-k generator in the company but it
is not hooked up yet. Should be tonight, though.

I confiscated a black light and bought one of those
fluorescent paintings from one of the villages to hang on
the plywood wall. My tape recorder is set over my bunk
with my speakers on the opposite wall. I'm listening to
Peter, Paul and Mary's ''Leavin' on a Jet Plane'' right
now. God, I can't wait. Because we're based in Phu Bai
I should receive my mail a day sooner because the airstrip is here.

In February a new battalion arrived in Vietnam from
the States to support the 101st, but will not become operational until April. It's an army experiment to see if
an aviation unit can be fully trained and combat-ready
for instant insertion into Vietnam. There is a good
chance that I will be infused into it because I'll have
just enough time left in country to fly with them and
teach the new pilots how to fly over here. Seven warrant
officers and eight regular officers are supposed to be
infused from our company. I hope I don't because in
our battalion we have all experienced people. But in
their battalion everyone is new and I can see that will
be a problem. I'll let you know what happens.

I really like our new location here at Phu Bai because

it's more like civilization, whereas at Sally we were kind of alone. Not much else for now. Will write again soon.

Love, Randy.

P.S. I've found out that I'm going on R&R to Bangkok the 19th of April. I will be over the hump then. Can't wait!

The idea of training a unit in the states and expecting it to measure up to the standards of a seasoned combat unit in Vietnam was absurd. Our company commander, however, saw this as a wonderful opportunity to get rid of what he termed, "the assholes and the incompetents of Charlie Company."

Using the same logic, the commanders in the 158th saw a golden opportunity to rid themselves of their assholes and incompetents. So on the day the swap took place the Blackwidows received six men instead of the fifteen we had expected. In my opinion only two of the officers we received fell into either category. The two undesirables were Captain Buck Phillips and a man we immediately nick-named "Captain Crunch" after the character in the breakfast cereal. Of course the 158th were similarly served by the Blackwidows, but with a significant difference. The men we sent them were *experienced* incompetents or assholes of which Douche Bag Dick Childs was one.

Captain Crunch flew for a month or two with a manner so abusive and cocky that he managed to alienate all his fellow pilots. To gain more control over the men he assigned himself to operations with Captain Ernest James. Captain Crunch was bearable only as long as you could avoid talking to him. As a pilot warrant officer you did not have to talk to him. You could simply tell him to "f—off" and he usually did. The enlisted men, on the other hand, could not be so direct without getting into a lot of trouble. Captain Crunch soon became so unpopular with the enlisted men that his hootch would get CS'd with the vomit-inducing gas at least one night a week. So common did the occurrence become that his five hootch mates kept their gas masks on a nail over their bunks, and whenever another CS canister was thrown into the hootch they simply donned their masks and walked outside, grumbling until the gas cleared.

It was, however, Buck Phillips, the second undesirable, who was to become the biggest problem for me. He would be the one to try, along with Major Torq, the new company commander, to get me drummed out of the United States Army. But I am getting ahead of myself.

At about the same time that the 158th arrived in country I started to notice a drastic change in the attitude of the new pilots coming to the Blackwidows. Their outlook on the war seemed distant. Removed. Uncaring. I felt they were less motivated than Joe, Tom, or I had been nearly five months ago. They lacked the enthusiasm of my predecessors to get the job done.

These FNGs told us how public support for the war back home was waning—that there was a strong public opposition movement that was gaining momentum urging the United States to pull out. Public opinion claimed that we were doing more harm than good in Vietnam, that the American war machine was indiscriminately killing and maiming innocent victims of a war they themselves did not want. The opposition claimed that we Americans were prolonging and propagating the war for the good of the politicians and not for the good of the people we were trying to help. The reports were confusing. It was difficult to believe public sentiment could switch so radically, that Americans back home were not supporting their fighting men overseas as they had during World Wars I and II and the more recent Korean War. The thought was beyond my comprehension and went against everything I was brought up to believe in, so I simply chose not to believe it.

18 March 1969

Dear Mom:

Hi.
Not too much to write about, but while I was free I thought I would write a letter to you.

I have been working pretty hard on my living area, which is a chore. We have to wire our hootches and build our area ourselves. It's a full-time job, I tell you.

Phu Bai is all right, boy. All we need now is our generator and we'll be up-tight. My tape player is all set up and ready for action.

The only thing I am sweating out is the possibility of getting infused into the new battalion. If I do, I'll have to move from here to Camp Eagle and start all over again. Ugh!

I hope Andrea is feeling better after her fight with the flu. Poor kid.

I am now flying as an AC, Aircraft Commander, and it is making my time pass super quick because of the added responsibility. Enclosed are several copies of my AC orders. Please keep them in a safe place for me. I must have them for my next duty station.

Not much happening over here. Yesterday I flew eight hours. By the way, I have some pictures, forty-five of them, to send to you guys. They turned out real good. When I get a chance I'll send them in a small album like I did last time.

Until my next letter, take care of one another.

Love, Randy

On the evening of 21 March 1969, all the ACs and peter pilots in Charlie Company were informed that the A-Shau Valley assault would begin at 0500 the next morning. The mission would take place as per our previous briefings. I went to bed early though the news caused me to sleep only fitfully that night.

At the scheduled time, twenty Hueys cranked up in the dark and departed the Widow Web for the staging area at LZ Birmingham. We shut down in a long row on the left side of the oiled-dirt airstrip and waited.

Some of the men drank coffee, some wrote letters home, others opened cans of C-rations and ate the bland contents, while still others tried to catch a few minutes of sleep. The six soldiers assigned to each ship sat by the machines and waited. We all waited for the order to get airborne and insert the first wave of troops.

I was aircraft commander of the number two aircraft.
The number one helicopter, Wishy-Washy's ship, carried
the most important cargo of all: the news media. The commander in the C&C, command and control, aircraft who
had been flying over the valley at five thousand feet since
first light radioed back and said the ground fog had finally
burned off and gave the order to begin the assault.

Captain Crunch, Bernie's copilot, ran to the center of
the strip. He held his arm over his head and made several
sweeping circles. "OK, crank 'em up. We're going in."

We flew low level, two flights of ten, over sharp ridge
lines and small valleys, guided on the radio by the commander, Eagle Six, flying in the C&C bird. The closer we
got to the valley, the more nervous I became. The tape
recording of last year's assault I had heard in the club
replayed in my mind. Would Charlie be waiting for us this
time? I wondered.

"You're two klicks from the first LZ Yellow Lead," the
C&C commander radioed from above. "You'll be landing
to the area on the valley floor as briefed."

"Roger," Wishy-Washy Bernie Nivens answered. His
voice sounded two octaves higher than usual.

I flew echelon right on Bernie's ship, concentrating on
keeping his rotor disk on the jungle horizon. I kept glancing at the news cameras aimed at me from the open door
of Bernie's chopper. Great! I thought. If we do get hit,
shot down, or blown to pieces the event will be captured
for posterity and shown on the six-o'clock news for all my
friends and family to see. I vividly remember that photographer with the probing lens filming us . . . waiting to film
the action . . . waiting for that Pulitzer prize-winning shot.
Waiting . . . I silently cursed him.

We flew over the last ridge line and began a smooth
descent. This is where Bernie's flight-school flying paid
off. Flight Lead in a formation had to fly precisely by the
numbers or else the formation would quickly disintegrate.
Any error in angle or bank or airspeed or descents or
climbs that were too quick or too slow became magnified
one-hundred-fold in a flight of ten.

The southern valley floor had been well prepped with

previous B-52 strikes, arty, naval artillery, and ARA. The LZ loomed in the distance. It looked scarred and torn, dotted with huge craters filled with muddy water. I could see twisted foliage and angular roots sticking up in the humid air from felled trees, blasted out of their individual patch of moist earth by tons of ordnance.

"You're one klick out, Yellow Lead. Good luck."

"Roger Eagle Six. Break . . . Yellow Flight this is Yellow Lead. We're beginning the approach. Pick your spots."

The aircraft commander flying the ship behind us radioed, "Goddamn, Chock Two, this is Three. A burst of tracers just flew up between us. It looked like your ship was covered. Shit. Did the guns see where it came from?"

A gun team leader answered. "Roger, Chock Three, this is Gunslinger Four-Zero, we saw it. We're rolling in hot."

"Charlie was shooting at us," my peter pilot said. "Did we get hit?"

The crew chief answered. "I think I heard something hit the tail."

I concentrated on the approach and said, "Keep your eyes on the gauges. Stay close on the controls. We'll check it out when we land somewhere safe."

"Roger that," the peter pilot answered.

The primeval real estate on our port and starboard sides erupted in small flashes followed by dirt blasting high into the air. The ARA Cobras dove from the sky paralleling our course and continued firing their rockets. I surveyed the long landing zone and tried to judge where Bernie was going to land. I picked a spot near a large crater and committed myself to it.

I could see the quick puffs of white smoke from the M-60s on Bernie's ship firing on both sides. "Open fire." I commanded.

The loud clatter of our own M-60s drowned my thoughts as I guided the aircraft down, aiming at a spot to the upwind side of the bomb crater. The troops waited anxiously at the door until our skids hit the ground. Then they leapt out.

"We're clear, sir."

I knew that it would be several seconds until Chock Ten would be on the ground. The waiting was unnerving. "Come on, come on, come on!" I surveyed the area expecting enemy gunfire at any moment and the chaos that follows, as it had happened last year. The enemy B-40s, 51 caliber, the familiar clatter of AK-47 machine-gun fire, the green tracer rounds. Where was he? Where was the enemy? Nothing.

Chock Ten finally radioed, "You're up Yellow Lead."

"Roger, lifting."

Ten helicopters took off as one. I could hear Eagle Six talking to White Lead in the second wave of ten behind us. They were beginning their approach. I waited for the words "Receiving fire, receiving fire." Again nothing. Was the enemy just playing with us? Was he going to wait for the second assault, third, or fourth before he let us have it?

I let the copilot fly the ship back to Birmingham where we would pick up more troops. Wishy-Washy and Captain Crunch were told on the command net to return to Camp Eagle to pick up the division PIO, Public Information Officer, now that the news media had been successfully inserted. I was told to move up from Chock Two to Chock One. I would be Flight Lead on the second lift into the A-Shau.

We landed back at Birmingham, picked up six more troops, and headed west into the mountains again. On final approach to the LZ I chose to land to the upwind end of a huge bomb crater. That way, when I flared, the aircraft's tail boom would be over the hole and could not hit the ground. It was a trick I learned as a peter pilot. A hitch in my plan became apparent however when I was on short final for the LZ. There was a news cameraman standing on the exact spot where I was going to land.

"What's that guy doing?" I said over the intercom.

It was impossible to go around with nine aircraft in trail, and I could not aim at another spot. There was no other and I was too heavy anyway. I was committed. "He'd better get the hell out of the way or else he's going to get flattened," the copilot said.

The man did not move. He kept on filming, the lens aimed at us with his eye glued to the viewfinder of his news camera. I continued the approach as if he were not there. It was a "him or us" situation. At the very last instant, when the situation seemed to be irrevocable, he must have realized I was not going to avoid him. He dove to the side of the bomb crater just as our skids planted into the soft earth. I silently cursed him.

On the third assault the Chock Two aircraft landed to my left. I glanced over and watched in horror as one of the soldiers jumped and ran from the chopper. The adrenalin must have really been pumping because the young soldier's feet were running before he hit the ground. He left the helo like a rifle shot and clambered up the side of a felled tree directly under the chopper's rotor blades. I could hear the loud "THWAK!" as the end of the metal blade hit the grunt's steel helmet. Arms and legs flailing, he did a one-and-a-half flip with a half-twist, landing in the bomb crater next to us in the middle of a huge puddle of water. Two of his buddies grabbed the unconscious soldier by the armpits and dragged him to our now empty chopper and threw him aboard.

"Chock Two, this is Lead," I radioed. "We got a medevac. You take the lead. Gotta get this guy to the hospital."

"Roger."

I took off and banked hard right in a maximum performance climb heading for the coast. I called brigade. They told me to take the man to the USS *Repose*, the hospital ship offshore. I had never landed on a ship before. I checked the SOI, hanging around my neck by a string, for the ship's frequency.

As we neared the coast I could see the white ship several miles off shore. I dialed in the frequency and called to tell them what we were bringing them.

"Roger, Blackwidow 25. This is the FDO. Flight deck officer. You're cleared to land. Ship's head is zero-eight-five, speed five knots. Apparent wind red twenty at fifteen. Report abaft the beam, over."

I looked over at my copilot. "You understand anything that guy's sayin'?"

"Nope."

"Me neither. Guess we'll figure it out when we get there." I pulled the red trigger on the cyclic stick and broadcast, "Roger, Blackwidow 25. We're coming in."

"Copy, Blackwidow 25. We have medical staff waiting."

I looked back at the Huey's floor and asked the crew chief on the intercom, "How's he look, Taylor?"

Taylor was kneeling by the man's side. "He's unconscious but breathing. His head looks like an overinflated football."

I could just make out the flight deck at the stern of the ship when we were a klick away. I could also see an American flag flying near the bridge. That was all I needed to check the wind direction. I figured that if I just treated the deck of the ship like a moving jungle ridge line and simply drove the helicopter down to it till the skids hit the steel deck I'd be all right. We landed without incident.

The crew chief jumped out to inspect the tail boom for any hits we might have taken on the first sortie into the A-Shau. Men and women in brilliant white uniforms ran out to us, crouching under the spinning rotors, to take the injured soldier away. We must have looked like something out of The Twilight Zone. They certainly appeared so to me. Here we were in our combat machine, dressed for the A-Shau Valley assault. M-60 machine guns and ammunition draped on either side of our aircraft; thick bulletproof chest protectors held in place under our shoulder straps; space-age flight helmets, the gunner and crew chief with the smoked visors pulled down making them look like beings from another solar system. And here they were in their sterile hospital uniforms, pale skin, clean fingernails, some wearing snow-white shoes, others with spit-shined low quarters. Were we part of the same war? I thought not. They took the man, carefully laid him on a stretcher, and rolled him away.

The crew chief climbed back behind his M-60. "We took one hit through the elevator, sir. Only went through the skin. Didn't hit anything else. Won't be a problem."

"Thanks, Taylor."

The radio came to life. "Blackwidow 25, ship's head is still zero-eight-five. Speed five knots. Apparent wind red twenty at thirteen. You're cleared for takeoff forward of abeam when ready."

"Blackwidow 25, roger." I looked at my copilot, shrugged, then looked up at the American flag snapping in the wind to orient myself to the wind direction.

I lifted the machine to a hover, pushed in left pedal, and took off along the left side of the ship into the wind. I banked over the blue-green Gulf of Tonkin forward of the ship's bow and leveled out to fly back to the coast, back to the war.

"Thanks, Blackwidow 25. We'll take good care of your soldier."

"Thank you, *Repose*. It's good to see a little bit of 'Real America' for a change. Talk to you later. Out."

I found out later that the soldier had suffered only a concussion and, apart from waking up with a severe headache, he was going to be all right. The steel pot he had been wearing had saved his life.

We refueled, with rotors running, at the POL at Camp Eagle and returned to Birmingham to pick up another sortie of troops. We heard that one of our aircraft from First Platoon had been hit by an RPG on the third lift while we were on the dust-off mission. It was Chock One, and the aircraft had just taken off from the valley floor when it happened. The AC, a first lieutenant named Ward, the peter pilot, a warrant officer named Kirby, a gunner named Miller, and the crew chief, Miles, all had been killed when the ship exploded in midair.

Several of the gunships from Delta Company had taken heavy hits also. One of the Cobras from ARA got shot down and crash-landed on the side of a ridge line. Luckily, no one had been seriously injured, and a Huey was able to fly in and rescue the two pilots. All in all the A-Shau assault was not the bloodbath we had expected, although it did have its moments.

Eagle Six in the C&C bird ordered four of us from Birmingham to an LZ to pick up soldiers that aircraft from the 158th, the new stateside outfit, had inserted in the wrong coordinates. The news of the mistake did not surprise us.

It was like old home week. Ned Kelly flew Chock One. Joe Sulak was the AC in Chock Two. Tom Shonehour flew Chock Three, and I was the AC in the fourth aircraft.

The landing zone was big enough to hold all four aircraft, but it was surrounded by high jungle. The four of us made the approach with gunship support. The waiting soldiers scampered aboard. It was now midday and extremely hot and humid, robbing our aircraft of precious horsepower. Ned Kelly was the first to attempt a takeoff.

Bringing his aircraft to a hover, he reported it was at the red line on power. He hovered to the end of the zone, turned around, and accelerated, nose down at a steep angle, toward the high trees. Just when it looked as if he was going to crash into them he pulled back on the cyclic, and the nose of his chopper pointed skyward, trading off airspeed for altitude. Once the aircraft was over the trees the nose dropped and he accelerated away. Tom and Joe did the same.

Because I had just refueled, my aircraft was a lot heavier than the other three ships. I tried to bring the aircraft to a hover, but it sank back down into the high elephant grass. The engine could not produce enough power. There was no way we were going to get out of there with six soldiers on board. We could not leave them. We could not take off. We were trapped. I surveyed the tree line expecting to see the enemy at any moment. I felt very alone and extremely vulnerable. The familiar bull's-eye pressure was building up between my eyes. I called on the VHF, "Send in another ship. We can't get out."

A ship from the 158th had just inserted a load of soldiers a klick away and was empty. The pilot was stateside trained with little combat experience. He was flying a brand new, powerful H-model Huey. Eagle Six directed him to land and take three of my soldiers.

He made a quick, steep approach into the LZ and landed next to me. Three soldiers from my aircraft ran over and hopped aboard, and he quickly departed. Even with only three soldiers onboard our aircraft was heavily laden, and I had to use the airspeed-trade-off-for-altitude takeoff maneuver to get out.

I learned later that the 158th pilot had had a rotor overspeed coming into the LZ and had over-torqued the machine's main transmission and drivetrain during the takeoff. The machine had to be flown back to Camp Eagle for maintenance because of his lousy piloting technique. The pilots in the Blackwidows got a chuckle out of that story.

The insertion of troops from Birmingham lasted for several hours. Later in the day we inserted soldiers into a small landing zone on a ridge line overlooking the A-Shau. It was a tight, single-ship landing zone. On the first wave we lost one of our ships. The story is best described in a letter I sent home to my stepfather.

24 March 1969

Dear Howard:

Hi. I have a few minutes to scratch a few lines to you. We took off on our mission today at 0645 but the clouds were too low and too thick to continue. We were to fly up north along the DMZ for the Special Forces. I'm back at Phu Bai now waiting for the weather to clear so I have this opportunity to write.

Our company flew into the A-shau Valley two days ago. You probably saw the assault on the news back home because NBC cameramen took movies and news photographers took stills of my ship in formation from the lead helicopter. Our company lost a helicopter on our first lift into a real tight LZ. The pilot and copilot managed to get out without a scratch. The LZ we landed in was surrounded by fifty-foot trees, blown out of the jungle by a five-hundred-pound bomb dropped from a sky crane helicopter earlier. The reason the aircraft crashed is because just before the ship could set its skids on the jungle floor the grunts started jumping out prematurely. The pilot couldn't control the helicopter as it began to rock back and forth as the soldiers leapt out. The aircraft's rotor RPM began bleeding off so he maneuvered the aircraft in a tight

*right turn to try and dive out of the LZ. In the turn his
tail boom hit a tree stump knocking out the tail rotor,
and the helicopter spun 360 degrees and crash-landed
on its side and tumbled down a mountain slope. The
crew scrambled out before it burst into flames. No one
was hurt up front. The crew chief got one of his fingers
cut off and the gunner was thrown clear and wasn't
found for twenty minutes. He was knocked unconscious. When they got to him he had a cut on his head
and possible skull fracture. Going into the A-shau Valley a cobra gunship got his hydraulics shot out. One
of our ships lost its hydraulics too.*

*On the first lift of the assault, the pilot of the ship in
trail behind me radioed and said we were covered by a
hail of green tracers. I wasn't even aware we were being
shot at. We were lucky. We only took one hit through
the elevator. Last year during the first day of the air
assault into the A-shau Valley the 1st Air Cav lost a lot
of ships! All I can say is I go on r&r in two weeks and
I'm ready.*

More later,

Randy.

I did not mention the four men we lost in the ship that
had been blown out of the sky by the RPG. I never referred to death in my letters. In order to spare their feelings I pretended it did not exist.

Charlie Company spent the rest of that week plus all of
the next in support of the troops we had inserted into the
A-Shau. All the pilots were flying eight- and nine-hour
days. As each day passed I mentally ticked off another on
my countdown for R&R. The closer the date got the more
excited I became.

Just before sunrise on March 25 Phu Bai was hit by a
barrage of rockets and mortars. It was the first time we
had been hit since Charlie Company moved from Sally. I
didn't mention the attack in any of my letters home to my
family. I needn't have bothered to spare their feelings,

however, as they would find out about the attack in the usual way—through the news media.

In due course I received a letter from home. The A-Shau Valley assault had hit the news and headlines back home. My mom sent me a picture of my helicopter going in on the first lift. When I saw it I was reminded of that photographer and his probing lens.

30 March 1969

Dear Mom:

I received your letter today with the clipping. The picture you cut out is of my helicopter flying into the A-shau. Your son's a star! Ha!

Things are looking up here at Phu Bai. We scrounged a pool table the other day and I now spend my rare time off trying to sharpen up my game. It's raining now, and 98 degrees. I'll never get used to this crazy weather. I've practically got webbed feet! I go on r&r in a few days so I'll write to you from Bangkok.

Love to all.

Randy.

31 March 1969

Dear Mom:

Received your letter today with the enclosed clipping from the newspaper describing the rocket and mortar attack that occurred here a week ago. I can't believe it made the headlines. I was eating breakfast in the mess hall when they started coming in. When the first one hit and exploded I leapt from the table and ran for the aircraft as I'd been instructed to do in the event of an attack. By the time the fourth one impacted I was in my ship, airborne and gone. That is the plan we follow in case of an attack like that. All the ACs are supposed to run to their aircraft and take off. The attack wasn't anything big though because it was mainly aimed at the south end of Phu Bai. Please don't worry. I go on r&r soon. Will write from there.

Love, Randy.

CHAPTER 8

April 1969

R&R "Back in the USSR"

When I examined the stack of letters Mom had entrusted me with that night in her apartment, I was only able to find one letter for the month of April. The date was 29 April 1969, and the letter was written on stationery from the Siam Hotel Co., Ltd., 1777 New Petchburi Road, Bangkok, Thailand, but I had sent it from Vietnam.

There are distinct memories of the R&R that easily come to mind. It would be understandable to question someone's memory after twenty years, but I can assure you that if a half-naked Thai girl chased you around your hotel room, over bed and dresser, brandishing a Buck knife and threatening to cut off one of the most favorite parts of your anatomy, you would not be able to erase a memory so terrifying.

My R&R began the morning of April 19. I watched Bien Hoa Air Base disappear below me from the window of the 707. It felt odd actually to be leaving the war behind me. It would take more than just lifting off a runway to rid my mind of the war. I knew that. But I was determined to try my hardest to push it aside. It felt strange to wear the once familiar civilian clothes I had dug out from the bottom of my footlocker back at Phu Bai. My shoes had mildewed and become stiff from disuse. It had taken half a day of scrubbing to rid them of the green mold. It had taken a full box of soap powder and three washings to rid my clothes of the pungent jungle smell. It was yet another unexpected by-product of my six months in combat that I now felt out of place wearing civvies. By this time I was far more comfortable wearing my scruffy combat boots and my loose-fitting Nomex flying suit and yellow scarf, which had been my uniform each day of the last six months.

After landing at Bangkok's Don Muang airport I was one of a herd of soldiers taken by bus to a large room in the USO building to receive a short briefing before being let loose on the city.

"Men!" the sergeant E-6 began from his podium. "Welcome to Bangkok. You will have seven days here. Before you leave this building bound for your respective hotels it is my duty to warn you that statistically you have a 60 percent chance of contracting some form of venereal disease during your stay here. VD is rife, gentlemen, so I suggest you take the necessary precautions."

Like the war stories I had heard, the stories about VD in Southeast Asia were many and sometimes lurid. It was said that certain strains were so resistant to modern antibiotics that once you caught them they were with you for life. Vietnam Rose, for example, was one of those. It was even rumored that one strain turned your penis black until it eventually atrophied and fell off! I never did manage to verify that one. But even after taking all the health risks into consideration, for some odd reason, the sergeant's advice did not sway me. It did nothing to persuade me to take "the appropriate precautions." I had decided well before leaving Vietnam that going on R&R meant, first and foremost, I was going to get laid. I was also going to get drunk, I was going to dine in as many good restaurants as I could afford, and if there was any time left over, I was even going to see the tourist sights that Bangkok had to offer. I was quite simply going to treat myself to one hell of a good time. What I would not allow was any negative thinking that might spoil my long-awaited week of R&R. I was here to forget about war and death. I had been sent here to enjoy living and forget the ugliness I'd seen. I was here to relax. It was my duty to salute smartly and do just that!

In retrospect I realize how immature I was to disregard the health warnings, but at the time I saw myself as the young warrior, halfway through his tour in a not-so-friendly war zone with the very real possibility of returning to America in a coffin staring him in the face. Or even worse, I might return home as a cripple. So I was going to blow off a lot of pent-up steam. For a week I was going to indulge in every hedonistic pleasure. I was going to do it while, biologically, everything still functioned. The way I viewed my situation, my week in Bangkok could well be my last opportunity to experience life to the fullest.

In the USO in-processing center I met two infantry first lieutenants with whom I hit it off immediately, and we decided to stick together. One of the lieutenants had had the Siam Hotel recommended to him, so after changing our "green money" to Thai baht at a military money exchange office we flagged down a taxi and instructed the driver to take us there.

The best way to describe Bangkok traffic is to compare it to the bumper cars at the fair, but without any consideration of organization or safety. The clogged streets were teaming with cars, trucks, bikes, and Vespas, each adding its contribution to the thick accumulation of foul-smelling engine exhaust. Amongst the traffic one could spot the odd darting pedestrian running for his or her life in an attempt to cross the street. It was every man for himself. The only rule I could see was that there were no rules. If one vehicle was a paint job's thickness ahead of the other, it had the right of way. There were many times the three of us thought a collision was imminent and threw our arms outward, closing our eyes for the impact, when, at the last possible instant, our driver would take the action necessary to avoid it.

The Siam Hotel turned out to be a fairly upmarket hotel for Bangkok. Not exactly up to Holiday Inn standards, but clean enough. We checked in, took our luggage to our individual rooms, and met in the lobby fifteen minutes later.

For transportation we decided to hire a taxi and driver from the hotel for the entire week. We were told that both would be at our service twenty-four hours a day and, with the cost split three ways, it seemed like a good deal.

The three of us had discussed our first plan of action. I acted as spokesman and told Sam, our Thai driver, "Sam, take us to the best massage parlor in Bangkok,'' and added, ''The one with the cleanest girls.''

''I know just where to go,'' Sam said smiling at us in the rearview mirror.

While negotiating the nerve-shattering traffic he told us the place we were headed had the reputation of being the cleanest place in Bangkok. ''The girls have a medical test every two weeks and keep a health card that is stamped after every examination. It is the best place, I can assure you,'' he told us.

The three of us knew that it would probably be an easy matter for the girls to obtain forged health cards, but figured it was in the interests of the management to at least try to keep the girls clean—that is, if they wanted future business from the weekly throng of American GIs. This was our way, anyway, to try to ensure we did not end up in the 60 percent infected bracket. Privately I figured my odds were reduced to about 50 percent.

I cannot recall the name of the establishment that Sam took us to. But I do remember the wonderful manner in which we picked our masseuse. We were truly like three small boys in a candy shop with an unlimited selection before us, insatiable appetites, and more money than good sense.

Our driver ushered us inside. As we entered, the first thing thrust into our hands was a frosty bottle of a lethal beer called Singha. I had been warned about Singha. It was said to be partly made with ether. I could believe it. After the first bottle, which barely even touched the sides of my throat because of the thirst I had developed in the sweltering heat, I was well and truly anesthetized.

An attractive lady approached us. I guessed that she was in her early thirties. She asked if we would like a massage which struck me as an odd question. Why else would we be here? We answered politely in the affirmative and she motioned with a long red fingernail. ''Come this way then, gentlemen,'' she said with a coy smile.

We came to a wall covered with a full-length curtain and were made to stand in front of it. I glanced across at my two companions. We shrugged looking at one another blankly. Then Mama San pulled a chord at one side and the curtains parted slowly. We were now looking through a one-way glass at what, in my estimation, must have been seventy-five or even a hundred Thai girls. They were sitting in a room similar to the lecture theater of my old college. We had called it "the forum." The seating was tiered, each row higher than the one in front so that one's view was unimpeded. Here the rows were curved and tiered deeply so that the feet of one girl were level with the head of the girl sitting in front of her. That way most of the girls' charms were exposed for our inspection. Each girl wore a white cotton blouse, white shorts, and high heels. Pinned on her chest was a large red button with a clearly visible number painted on it.

Mama San approached us. I remember her heavily perfumed scent. "Pick a number please, gentlemen. Take as long as you like." One of the lieutenants voiced my thoughts in mumbled tones, "Holy shit. Goddamn, I've died and gone to heaven."

I scanned each row methodically, my eyes falling on each girl to assess her individual beauty. A particular girl caught my eye almost immediately. She had long, shapely legs. Her sable hair was neatly cut short in the style of the British singer Lulu. She looked taller than the rest of the girls, and her lips turned up in a natural smile. Her dark brown eyes sparkled even from a distance. "I'll take number thirty-seven."

Mama San smiled approvingly. "You have very good taste, sir."

The two lieutenants each took their pick and the three of us were led down a dimly lit hallway to our allotted massage rooms. A girl brought us another bottle of Singha beer and I entered, taking a sip from the bottle.

Dominating the room was a well-constructed, long wooden table on which rested a padded mat. A bathtub was in one corner and a work table sat next to the "bed." Creams, oils, powders, and instruments of pleasure sat on that table. The dark wooden walls of the small room or cubical stopped three feet short of the ceiling. What was being said in the adjacent cubicle was clearly audible.

"Can you guys fucking believe this place?" came the disembodied voice of one of the lieutenants.

"No," answered the other lieutenant. "R&R's going to be out-fucking-standing."

"And I'll drink to that," I replied to both, taking a large gulp from the bottle.

The door behind me opened. Mama San entered leading in by the hand the vision that I had picked from the lineup of girls.

"This is Chu," Mama San said. "She will take very good care of you." I was very willing to believe that. I extended my hand and introduced myself. The girl smiled politely and half bowed as she timidly shook my hand.

"I will be back later," Mama San said with a smile. "You are in good hands now. Please enjoy yourself." Please enjoy myself? God, if I don't I have to be dead! I thought.

Chu was even more beautiful close up. Her olive complexion was smooth, flawless. She motioned to me to move next to the table with the padded mat and then methodically removed my clothes. I was relieved to see her take the trouble to examine me for any visible signs of a problem that could infect her. I assumed that this was normal practice with all her clients. She led me to the bath. She washed my hair, shaved me, cleaned my nails and my feet, poured warm water over me, and scrubbed me until every square centimeter of skin on my body was bright pink. She drained the tub, had me stand, and toweled my body dry. She wrapped a fresh towel around my waist and laid me on my stomach on the long table. That is when she began the massage. Her pampering, with her strong, deft fingers working deep into my muscles, sent warm tremors of pleasure through each cell of my body.

I could tell the two lieutenants in the adjacent rooms had reached the same stage of their "treatment" because I could hear the rhythmic slapping of hands against skin punctuated by the occasional grunt and moan of pleasure. There was nothing overtly sexual about the massage, but that is not to say I wasn't aroused. Chu knew well how to keep a man on the brink of ecstasy. Her technique exceeded pleasure and at times bordered on pain. She rubbed sweet-smelling oils on the dry parts of my body and sprinkled talcum powder on the wet parts.

The grand finale came when she flipped off her high heels and hopped up on the table, stood to her full height, which I estimated to be about five feet eight inches, and proceeded to walk on my back. It was then, and only then, that I had regrets about picking one of the larger girls in the house. But it had been worth every baht. I had never in my young life experienced such pure pleasure and physical bliss. And this had been achieved without her actually making love to me.

An hour had passed when Mama San knocked on the door and entered. Her timing was perfect. I had just finished dressing. I was light-headed, numbed by the beer, and relaxed by the hot bath, my body feeling totally drained from the massage. "You enjoy?" Her question was accompanied by the now familiar smile.

"Oh yes," I answered weakly but with enthusiasm.

"You like to take Chu home?"

"Oh yes!" I said, now very enthusiastically. The negotiated price was twenty-five dollars a day. The two lieutenants and I had already discussed how we would conduct the business side of things. I told Mama San, "I will come back here with my two friends at five-thirty this evening. I will pick up Chu at that time and we'll all go out to a restaurant that the girls recommend." I looked at Chu. She smiled holding my gaze with her dark, almond eyes.

"Very good," Mama San agreed. "Then Chu stay with you in your hotel tonight?"

"Yes." I looked over at Chu. "If that's OK?" I felt corny saying that knowing perfectly well it was Chu's job to stay with me. I wanted to make the experience seem less sordid than going into a meat market and taking home a side of beef.

"Good. Chu will be waiting."

Chu shook my hand and left the room while Mama San and I dealt with the finances. Mama San was disappointed that I would pay for only one night and not for the whole week. I explained, "If Chu works out, Mama San, I will pay for the rest of the week. I want to be sure we will be compatible before I pay for her services for seven days."

Her face suddenly took on a look of scorn. "You no

butterfly are you?'' she asked, her polished English suddenly eluding her.

"Butterfly?" I didn't know what she meant. "No. I'm a pilot but . . ."

"You don't go from flower to flower. Like butterfly. You choose one girl. Stay with her."

I understood her meaning. "Yes, I will choose only one girl, Mama San. But she must like me. I must like her. Chu seems lovely. But maybe she will not like me. Maybe, just maybe, we will not get along."

"Humph!" Mama San studied my face, then said, "Ok. But I hope you not butterfly." Her facial features softened. She became pretty again. "No problem. You'll like Chu. You see. She make you happy. Very, very happy."

We took our taxi back to the hotel. Our recollections caused the silliest grin to form on Sam's face. "I told you you'd like. I told you. I told you," he said happily.

We returned to the massage parlor at 1730 as we had arranged with Mama San. The young girls were even more beautiful in western clothes. They wore miniskirts and were immaculately made up and lightly perfumed. So perfect did they seem, they reminded me of little dolls.

They recommended a restaurant which they told us served the best Thai food in Bangkok. We sat on floor cushions at a low table and ate a delicious dish of marinated beef and rice. The dinner was followed by a traditional Thai floor show. Ladies in traditional costumes of brightly colored silk moved in the slow, fluid motions of the national dances, the long golden appendages on each finger exaggerating their graceful hand movements. It was enchanting.

Following dinner, Sam drove us to a bar recommended by the girls. With our girls clutching our arms we entered the dark, smoky bar. A loud stereo system was playing "Purple Haze" by Jimi Hendrix. In the thick heat it blasted the music from huge black speakers with such heavy bass that each drum beat felt like the eight-inch gun concussions at Sally. At the far end of the room, on a packed dance floor, a throng of gyrating dancers moved up and down as one, in sync with the beat.

We sat down at a vacant table littered with half-empty bottles of Singha and awash with spilt drink. A heavily made up waitress in a short, frilly dress cleared the mess and took our drink order. The song died away.

The next song the DJ played was a song that neither the two lieutenants nor I had ever heard before. It was a Beatles number, and for that reason I paid particular attention to the words. I could not believe what I heard. It made my blood pressure rocket. My heart began to pound. The song being played was "Back in the USSR."

I acted more on instinct than by anything else when I stood from my chair incensed with rage. "What's that they're playing?" Confused thoughts swirled through my brain. Was this some sort of propaganda? Was it really the Beatles singing such an anti-American song? Was it playing in America now? If so, how could Americans back home listen to, or condone, such a song? Why was it allowed to be played here in a country that was supposed to be against the very ideals we Americans were fighting against and losing our lives for in Vietnam? The new pilots coming to the Blackwidows had told me about the shifting tide in public sentiment back home, but for God's sake, this was sacrilege. My friends were "over there" trying to stop the spread of communism to the free world, and here were the Beatles singing "Back in the USSR!"

Now angry and out of control, I started for the booth where the DJ sat. The two lieutenants followed closely. Chu flew to my side. "No, no, no. Please. It's a popular song. There is nothing meant by it. Nothing. Please, stop, please, please!" She was tugging at my arm trying to stop me.

"It's an outrage, Chu," I explained. "It's not right and I'm not going to sit here and listen to it."

I arrived at the DJ booth. The two lieutenants arrived at my side just as I reached over to pull the skinny DJ toward me. I dragged his body across the tonearm of the record player, grinding the song to an ear-splitting screech. All activity on the dance floor ceased. My actions were now dictated by the adrenalin pumping through my veins. My voice was not loud but firm and direct. "I don't want to hear any more of that record, understand? I got friends fighting against the communist-backed VC in Vietnam right now. My friends wouldn't appreciate it. Furthermore, my friends and I don't appreciate it. Play something else, but not that. Do you *understand*?''

In the dim light all I could see were wild, frightened eyes and huge buck teeth. ''Yes sir, yes sir, I understand. I understand. I understand,'' he said quickly, nodding affirmatively.

I let him go. Chu pleaded, ''Come. Please. Sit down!'' I could now feel every muscle in my body shaking with rage. She tugged at my arm. ''Please, please. Let's sit down.''

One of the lieutenants said, ''I think he got the message. Come on. Let's get us a beer.''

Our return to the table was quickly followed by complimentary drinks from the manager. The two lieutenants and their girls again took to drinking and laughing and enjoyed happy small talk over the loud music, the incident seemingly quickly forgotten. I could not forget it, though. My violent overreaction to hearing the song troubled me deeply. It was not like me to lose control, to make a public scene. I'd never, until tonight, acted in such an impudent and foolhardy way. The more I reflected on what I'd done the deeper the feeling of contempt and embarrassment became. In my gut I knew I'd probably react the same way again, but knowing that did not help. Such strong opposite and confused emotions occupying my mind was something foreign to me. The shame I felt was greater than the feeling of any accomplishment for my corny, patriotic outburst.

I took a long drink from my bottle of beer and decided that what was done was done, and that my gnawing feelings of guilt and humiliation would not serve to undo past actions. I would not let my nagging guilt feelings spoil the remainder of the evening for the others.

An hour or so passed and as we were getting ready to leave I excused myself to use the toilet. I was still feeling guilty about my outburst. I snaked my way through the crowd to the DJ's booth. The skinny man had his back to me and was thumbing through a stack of records. ''Excuse me?''

The man turned when he heard my voice. When he saw who I was he sat bolt upright, eyes blinking in obvious alarm.

I extended my hand. "Just wanted to say I'm sorry."

He looked at me, then at my hand for a long moment.

"I lost my head earlier and I want to apologize."

The man cautiously took my hand without speaking and we shook hands. He nodded closing his eyes, then opened them again showing me he'd understood. He smiled, exposing his huge buck teeth. I nodded, half smiled back, and returned to the table feeling marginally better.

We arrived back at the hotel around 0100. Although I'd had a lot to drink I now wanted desperately to make love to Chu. My body ached to make love to her. I was, in the immortal words of Blackwidow 14, Bob Coulshaw from Arkansas, "hotter than a two-peckered owl in a forest fire."

The first time was almost an air burst. I was so excited I nearly came before I entered her. The second time the experience was more civilized. It could almost have been described as tender, even loving. I tried to be considerate and worked hard to please her. Afterwards, she appeared to fall asleep in my arms. I wanted to make love again and she clearly did not. My attempts to persuade her otherwise were futile. Her only response was to grunt and curl up with her back toward me and feign sleep. I tried to arouse her by stroking her body tenderly, working my caresses from her firm, round breasts, downward. When my hand came close to her pubic region she would tighten her legs, pull them up to her chest, and edge away from me. When I would try to form my body to hers, she would scoot to the edge of the bed, curling up into the fetal position. I finally tired of the chase and rolled over in frustration. Tomorrow, I thought, I'll get another girl. To hell with this butterfly shit. I was glad I hadn't paid Mama San for the whole week.

Chu was gone when I awoke. She knew it was not going to work between us. I told the two lieutenants what had happened over breakfast by the pool. They had had better luck with their girls and had arranged to see them again that evening. We decided to look at some of the sights, but before setting out I had Sam take me to the massage parlor.

I chose another girl by the same voyeuristic process, had another massage, and made the deal with Mama San. The young woman, whose name was Lee, was very short, unlike Chu. With my arm around her the top of Lee's head was well below my chest. We made an incongruous looking couple, but I found her high spirited, happy, and loving. She had silky black hair that flowed to the middle of her waist. Lee's most distinctive feature, which I could not have noticed when I chose her because she'd had her mouth closed, was her gold tooth, the one to the left of her front teeth. Again, Mama San was a bit put out that I would not pay for the remaining six days, but, as I would find out, she was not as put out as Lee would be.

After I had given Mama San the money, Lee insisted I take her to the hotel immediately and make love to her. When we entered the hotel room I was made to sit on the bed while she performed a slow striptease in front of me. She peeled off her clothes as if unwrapping a wonderful present. I sat on the edge of the bed with an uncontrollable grin on my face. She removed her red silk blouse and tight black skirt, then turned her back, took off her low-cut, black-lace bra, and slowly turned again to face me. She slowly lifted her arms, cradling her head in her hands to show off her two beautiful upturned breasts to best advantage. She then stepped out of her black lace underwear as a prelude to a sexual attack, which was the closest a man can come to being raped. Her wet, uninhibited animal passion was almost frightening. She was, as it turned out, apparently insatiable and extremely enthusiastic and vocal during our lovemaking. At one point I was quite alarmed when she began breathing in short staccato breaths, each breath getting louder and louder to the point of orgasm, when she arched her back and yelled, "Oh, Ohhh, Ohhhh, Ohhhhhh, I'm I'mmm, I'mmmmmm cooommmmmmiinnngggg!" at the top of her lungs. I half expected the hotel manager to come pounding on the door to investigate what the ruckus was all about.

Lee and I seemed to be suited to one another. She even suggested that I take another girl, but I obviously said the right thing when I told her she would be enough woman for me.

After Lee's acrobatic audition, the two lieutenants, Lee, and I piled into the back seat of our taxi. To my extreme embarrassment Lee kept massaging my groin and giggling at my state of arousal. My efforts to discreetly swat her hand away to keep the two lieutenants from noticing were to no avail. They knew. I knew they knew, and the driver, Sam, kept nodding and smiling at me knowingly in the rearview mirror. It was a relief when we finally dropped Lee off to do some shopping. We arranged to pick her up that evening with the other two girls before going off to see some of the sights.

The remaining days seemed to melt into one another. We dined and drank at a different restaurant every night. For the duration I did not have to touch a knife, spoon, or fork. Lee fed me, even in the restaurants. I do not consider myself a chauvinist. I did, however, consider myself a man who may not live to see the end of his combat tour, so I did not protest when she insisted she attend to my every whim. She even shaved me each morning. We took the girls dancing every night, and each night Lee made love to me until I was too exhausted to move.

The two lieutenants and I saw all the sights Sam could think to show us. He even took us to a jewelry store one afternoon. We protested at first. We told him we did not want to buy any jewelry. He insisted. We knew he was given some sort of kick-back for bringing GIs to that shop. We finally relented.

When we entered the store the familiar Singha beer was offered to us on a tray. The day was so hot and sticky the beer came as a welcome refreshment. I drank two beers in quick succession and was hopelessly drunk. I sat down and the Thai jeweler convinced me I ''needed'' to buy a star sapphire ring as a memento of my R&R in Bangkok. So I did. I was pleased with my purchase, initially. But after I sobered up I discovered it was much too large for my finger. (I would lose it within the first thirty seconds of swimming in the Gulf of Tonkin).

* * *

On the third morning of my R&R after Lee and I had
made love she fastened the clasp of her bra and said, "Why
you butterfly? Why you no keep me for all time?"

Here it comes, I thought. I stood up and put on my
boxer shorts. "Lee, I like you very much. I just had a bad
experience with the first girl, that's all."

"No! You butterfly," she spat. "You no like me. You
pay each day. You no want me whole time."

"I do want you. It's just . . ." I knew that whatever I
said was not going to sound right. I was caught in a losing
situation no matter how I tried to reason with her. The
only way to make her happy was to pay Mama San the
money for the rest of the week. But then she'd have me.
No. I wasn't going to be taken. "We'll just see," I told
her.

Lee rummaged through my suitcase at the side of the
bed. She pulled out my Buck knife and opened the blade.
She looked at me strangely. I laughed. "What are you
doing with that?" I held out my hand and approached her.
"Here, give it to me before you hurt yourself."

She held the knife out at arm's length. "No! You butterfly. You no like me. I good to you. You no good to
me."

"That's not true, Lee. I do like you. I told you I had
a bad experience with the first girl. Surely you can un-
dersta . . ."

Her eyes were suddenly on fire. "No! I do not understand. You say you like me. You say you not butterfly. I
not believe you. You bad man. Bad!" she lunged.

I stepped back just in time. "Lee, this isn't funny. Now
give me the knife."

"No! You bad. You butterfly." She sprang at me. I leapt
over the bed using it as a barrier. She jumped over it and
took a quick swipe at me with the knife. The blade passed
within inches of my right arm. I looked at her in disbelief.
She thrust again. I turned in time to avoid the blade. Then
she chased me.

We did several circuits around the room. At one point
I pulled out a small dresser from the wall to keep her at
bay. She kicked at it and with a smash it fell over. The

lamp on top of it crashed to the floor. I grabbed a pillow from the bed. "Cut it out, Lee, goddamn it. Someone's going to get hurt!"

"You, Mr. Butterfly. You going to get hurt. I will cut *it* off. Then you will be butterfly that cannot fly." She stabbed at me again.

The blade darted at my bare chest. I turned. She missed. In the same motion I hit her arm hard with the pillow. The force of the blow momentarily knocked her arm to her side. I grabbed her wrist, disarmed her, threw the knife to the far corner of the room and threw her to the bed. I quickly tossed the pillow aside and threw myself on top of her. She kicked and struggled. I tried to avoid her knees aimed at my groin. I was afraid if her arms got loose she'd gouge my eyes out. I held her wrists and pinned her arms over her head. She fought for a moment, then suddenly stopped squirming and looked up at me, searching deep into my eyes. We were both breathing hard. Time seemed suspended. Her expression softened, her breathing slowed, and I could feel her muscles relax. Now I was really confused. I dared not release her. One moment she wanted to kill me, now she seemed to be beckoning me with her smoldering eyes. Her lips parted slightly as if she were going to speak. She slowly arched her head up to me, still staring. She closed her eyes. I hesitated, then brought my lips down to meet hers. I released her wrists and embraced her and she embraced me. For the next half hour we made tender and passionate love. Later that day I gave Mama San the money for the rest of the week.

The Boeing 707 taking us back to the war landed at Tan Son Nhut air base on April 26. It was a quiet flight from Bangkok back to Vietnam. The mood that hung in the cabin of the aircraft was morose. I felt the depression as well. Like the rest of the men I surely did not want to go back. I thought of Lee. It had been a tearful goodbye, on her part anyway. She had made me feel that she was genuinely sorry at our parting. I could imagine her now, sitting in one of the tiered rows at the massage parlor, waiting for another GI to choose her. I pushed that thought from my mind.

The two lieutenants and I went our separate ways at Tan Son Nhut airport. I left them waiting for another flight out. My flight to Bien Hoa would not leave for another two days. I was shown the BOQ where I met another warrant officer helicopter pilot who was stationed in II Corps. He had just returned from a one week R&R in Singapore.

We were both awestruck by the modern facilities we found at the air force base. It was like something you'd see back in The World. I overheard in passing a candid conversation between two air force officers when one said to the other, "This is an air-conditioned war, goddamn it. If I can't get that silly gook from maintenance to fix the AC in my hootch, they can get someone else to fly their fucking airplane."

Air conditioner? I remember thinking. Such a thing was unheard of in Charlie Company.

Two air force captains who flew F-100 jets befriended us and asked us along for dinner in the officers' mess. It was a properly constructed building accommodating several hundred officers. I was shocked to see that the interior was as nice as anything I had seen stateside. A full colonel joined the four of us at our table.

During the meal waiters attended to our every need. Our hosts were curious about the war we fought and asked many questions about our mode of operation and experiences to date. They were particularly impressed with the number of hours we had logged so far and could scarcely believe that the average flight time an army helicopter pilot accumulated in one year was somewhere around a thousand hours. They wanted to hear about our various roles, combat assaults, and the ass-and-trash, search-and-rescue, and dust-off missions we'd flown.

At the end of the meal when coffee had been served the colonel stood, held his water glass in the air, and clanged the edge with a spoon. "Gentlemen, gentlemen, please!" The conversations in the room hushed. "Gentlemen, we have the great honor this evening of having with us two army helicopter pilots who, I have learned after talking with them, are fighting a totally different kind of war than the one we're fighting. Their war is more intimate. More hairy. And a hell of a lot more dangerous than anything we see. Their war is real flying, gentlemen. And there may be a time when we ourselves may need their services if we ever have to punch out. We can feel a lot more confident knowing men like these could one day save our lives. Therefore, I want to propose a hearty toast to these two gentlemen sitting here tonight." He raised his glass looking down at us. The rest of the men stood and raised their glasses also. "To our two young army helicopter pilots—who, I might add, have balls as big as grapefruit!"

"Here! here!" everyone replied in one voice, then drank. I was embarrassed, but at the same time honored that these air force pilots, these jet jockeys, should think so highly of us and be so impressed with what we did. It remains to this day one of the highest and most cherished compliments I have ever been paid in my aviation career.

I managed to stay in the Tan Son Nhut BOQ for three days before taking my leave of the warrant officer from II Corps and hopping on a C-130 bound for Bien Hoa. That same day I caught a C-123 to Phu Bai. When I arrived back at Charlie Company I found that I was on the schedule to be the stand-by flare pilot that night.

At midnight Spec-4 Flowers rushed out of ops to the flare tent. "Welcome back, sir. You've got a mission to fly to the A-Shau."

"Fucking great!" I said sarcastically.

He handed me a piece of paper with the coordinates. "Division wants you to drop flares over that area because a company we inserted yesterday has lost all communications with the TOC. Last HQ heard they were in contact with a force of NVA, size unknown."

"Who's my peter pilot?"

"New guy. A first lieutenant named Andre Gower."

I walked over to my aircraft following the beam of my flashlight. This was Gower's first flight as copilot in Vietnam. We strapped in and he began to recite the lengthy flight-school pre-start checklist. I stopped him when he was reciting, "Seat belts and pedals adjust."

"Whoa! You can forget that, lieutenant. We kick the tire and light the fire over here." I reached over and set the DCVM on battery, turned on the fuel switch, reached overheard and flicked on the inverter, checked and set the throttle, hit the clock, and pulled the starter trigger.

It was darker than the inside of a Vietcong tunnel complex on our flight out. There was no moon, a slight overcast, and no visible horizon. As Joe used to say in similar situations, "It isn't just dark. It's fucking dark!"

We approached the coordinates where I thought we should be on the map, and I told the crew chief, "OK, Taylor. You can get ready to push out the flares."

"Roger, sir."

The twenty flares were long aluminum tubes that were stacked laterally on top of each other on the Huey's floor. Each had a stainless steel lanyard that was tied to one of the many attaching rings on the floor. When a flare got kicked out, the weight of the flare caused the lanyard to pull out a pin, setting off a mini explosion of burning magnesium. It had often occurred to me that if one of those flares inadvertently went off in the back of the aircraft I would most certainly die. And it would be an extremely unpleasant way to die. Even if it was possible to get the aircraft down, you would probably be burned so terribly you would wish you had died.

In the darkness Taylor stepped from his position behind his M-60 and over the high stack of flares. I heard a loud "POP" and knew instantly he had caught his foot on one of the lanyards. He had only seconds to get rid of the flare before it would ignite and we would go up in a cataclysmic ball of flame. I turned around in my seat in instant panic and yelled without pressing the intercom, "GET IT OUT OF HERE!"

I thought, This is it. We were going to die. But in an instant Taylor kicked the tube with all his might. It sailed off the stack of flares and out the door into the blackness. After clearing the door it ignited a micro-second later next to the chopper, blinding me as if I had looked directly into the sun. I shut my eyes, but when I looked at the instrument panel I still saw the flare, a ball of fire, etched on my retina. We were level. I could tell that much by the instruments. My heart was ready to beat out of my chest.

"Sorry, sir," the crew chief replied weakly.

"Thank Christ you got rid of it, Taylor. To hell with

you guys. I'm going back to Bangkok. I'd rather take my chances with VD and the possibility my pecker could fall off than come back here and put up with this."

My night vision slowly returned to normal. We circled over the jungle at two thousand feet occasionally drawing enemy fire from below. The green tracers floated up at us in slow, graceful arcs. The lost company never responded. We learned the next day that they had been overrun. There had been no survivors.

29 April 1969

Dear Mom:

Hi. Well, I'm back. Ugh! Can't say I'm overjoyed to be here. I'm not so sure R&R is such a good thing. It makes you remember what it's like to be back in the real world.

My first night back from R&R I had to go fly into the mountains and drop flares to try and locate a company of men that were air lifted in and they had lost radio communication. I flew till 0230. Boy, was I tired. Then I flew over eight hours the next day.

Tell Nancy I received the "Laugh-In Book" she sent. Thank her for me.

Bangkok was unbelievable. I took a lot of pictures and I'll send them to you when I get the chance. When I came back here I had eleven letters waiting for me. What a treat. I managed to stay away from the company for fourteen days. I spent a lot of time at the Tan Son Nhut officer's club down south.

I'm getting back into the swing of things here now. Today I flew nine and a half hours.

Not much else for now. Five and a half months to go. I'm over the hump. At least that's something.

Randy

I waited for the burning, the dripping, a raw sore to appear. Each day in the shower I would inspect myself for any sign of *it* turning black, atrophying, and falling off.

But my luck seemed to be holding. I was certain that I had not joined the 60 percent after all. I had come through my R&R without contracting any sort of infection. It was another thing to be thankful for, and indeed I was, as I entered the second half of my tour.

CHAPTER 9

May 1969

Assault on Hamburger Hill

It was about this time in my tour that I began smoking cigars again. I suddenly had the desire to smoke small Hava Tampa Jewels which, with their wooden mouthpiece, gave me something to gnaw on while flying. I didn't have a great need to actually smoke them, but the habit was a diversion during the long hours of flying over there. I hated cigarettes. I never could inhale without coughing. I had begun to smoke cigars several months before I joined the service, but stopped immediately after an embarrassing incident that took place in the Los Angeles reception station. It happened in a room where about a hundred men were seated waiting to in process.

A sergeant yelled out my name. "Mains!"

I stood up and strolled to the front of the room smoking a long, angular cigar called a Wolf's Brother's rum-soaked Crook. I took a big puff, blew out a cloud of smoke and sat down next to the sergeant's desk. After studying me for a moment he announced to everyone in the room, "Hey everyone, goddamn if this guy doesn't look just like a fucking movie star!"

Because L.A. is so close to Hollywood I figured the sergeant really knew what he was talking about. "Yeah?" I said. "Who?"

"Well, when you're smokin' that cigar, you look just like Lassie taking a shit." The room broke out in laughter.

"Now, hot shot, what's your date of birth?"

That was my first introduction to army humor. It had put me off cigars from that day to this.

I was with several of the other pilots sitting in a circle

on folding chairs in Joe Sulak's hootch. It was sometime after evening chow and Ernest was trying to persuade Tom Shonehour to tell us his incredible war story, a mission he'd had that day near the DMZ. I struck a match and lit the end of one of the small cigars, blew out the smoke, took a sip of the cold beer I acquired from Shonehour's small refrigerator, and waited with the rest of the group to hear him spin his yarn.

Ernest prodded excitedly. "OK, Tom. Go ahead and tell us what happened."

"OK, Ernest. I promised you I would so here goes. Well, we were flying for the marines out of Quang Tri," he began. "It was supposed to be a routine insertion ten klicks east of Khe Sahn. That is until Ziker got the shit shot out of him and took a bullet through the wrist on takeoff and crashed. They were lucky the aircraft didn't burn." Shonehour took a quick drink of his beer then continued. "From then on the whole operation turned into a Mongolian cluster fuck. I broke off my approach. No one knew where the enemy fire was coming from. The guys were scrambling out of the downed aircraft. Then we spotted it. It was coming from a ridge line to the north. We called in the gunships and they blew the shit out of the place. The firing stopped and I landed by the wreckage to pick up Ziker and the crew. Ziker's wrist was fucked up pretty bad and he'd been knocked half unconscious in the crash. We could see Ziker's crew chief on his knees near the wreckage waving for help. That's when both my crew chief and gunner ran from my ship over to Ziker's. I just about had a shit fit! I started yelling at them to get back. Neither of them heard me. Then the most fucking incredible thing happened. Scared the shit right out of me and my peter pilot. From the tree line to our south, four NVA soldiers dressed in black pajamas came charging our aircraft."

"Damn!" exclaimed Ernest excitedly. "What'd you do then?"

"What the fuck could I do, Ernest? If I took off I would have left my gunner and crew chief on the ground with the crew of the crashed Huey. If I stayed with no one behind the M-60s to defend us, I could see we were going to be overrun.''

"Shit!" Joe said.

"I nearly goddamn did!" Shonehour said downing another gulp of beer. "I pulled out the old pearl handled M-1 . . . ," he slapped the obscene semiautomatic sawed-off weapon he kept there in his holster, ". . . and I aimed it out my window at the charging NVA."

"I don't fucking believe this," Leach said in disgust. "This sounds like something out of fucking Hollywood."

"Tell em, Dryhurst. Am I shittin' my friends here or is this the gospel truth."

The FNG peter pilot, recently infused into the Black-widows from the 158th, scanned the expectant faces around him. He raised his right hand, "He's telling the truth. I swear to God."

"OK, Tom," Joe said. "What happened next. You've got your M-1 out the window of your helicopter like John Wayne and you're single-handedly going to take on four NVA regulars rushing you in black pajamas. Now what?"

"I'm not shittin' you guys. This fucking happened. OK, anyway, I take a bead on them, site right down the barrel, and before I squeeze the trigger I notice they're unarmed. They are now running at us with their hands reaching for the sky."

"You mean they're going to Chieu Hoi?" Leach said from his bunk, meaning they were giving up.

"Goddamn right, Leach. That's exactly what they did. Right on the spot. They were running at us screamin' and hollerin' in Vietnamese with their hands raised. Then, as if things weren't fucked up enough already, we started getting shot at from the same ridge line the gunships were supposed to have neutralized. So now we're being shot at from our left, and the four NVA are charging us on our right."

"Sounds like a nightmare," Ernest said shaking his head.

"Oh, but it gets better."

"Better?" Ernest screwed up his face.

"We're on the ground running at full RPM waiting for the crew of Ziker's ship, plus my crew. We're being shot at from two hundred meters away with no one to fire our guns. I can tell now that the NVA are definitely Chieu Hoiing. They jump on my aircraft, and two of them get behind the M-60s and begin firing back at the enemy on the ridge line who are firing at us.''

"Now I've heard everything," Leach said from his bunk.

"It's the truth, Jeff. Swear to God. Anyway, by now my crew has Ziker's crew out of the wreckage and the six of them scurry aboard my aircraft with the NVA still firing.'' Shonehour stopped his story to laugh at the recollection. "They didn't know whether to shit-or-go-blind. They thought the NVA had captured *our* aircraft. I had to yell at them to get on before they turned around and ran the other way.''

"What a mess," Ernest said. "You had to be awfully heavy with Ziker's crew, your crew, and the NVA soldiers on board.''

"It was a flat LZ. No real obstacles. That was the least of my problems. I figured I was going to get the machine out of there if I had to carry it out on my fucking back and flap my wings like a goddamn eagle.'' He finished his beer and took another from a small refrigerator next to his bunk.

"That's some war story," Ernest said. "You lucky bastard.''

May 1969 seemed to be a particularly lively month for war stories. May was the time of year the weather was good, and Charlie Company was flying its combined tails off. One evening during the first week of May all Vietnamese help was cleared from our mess hall and we sat through a three-hour briefing for a future combat assault code named "Apache Snow." We were told we were going into the A-Shau again. This time I discovered I would be flying the lead aircraft in Yellow Flight to land and deliver troops to a hill named Dong Ap Ba several klicks east of the border. Dong Ap Ba would later be known as Hamburger Hill.

Several weeks ago our CO, Major Posey, left Charlie Company for good to return to The World. He had completed his one-year tour and had DEROS'd. He was replaced by a major named Torq. It was during the week of the Hamburger Hill assault that our brand new company commander flew up a female Dutch correspondent he'd met in Saigon to write a story on the Blackwidows. Her name was Henny Schrode. She was blonde, with a short hairstyle typical of the late sixties, like Doris Day's, and she filled out a pair of tailored jungle fatigues like a Playboy playmate. She spoke seven languages, and her favorite drink was straight Vodka. In the three days she stayed with the Blackwidows she adopted Ned Kelly, Joe Sulak, and me. She had quickly come to the conclusion that Major Torq was a jerk and that we were a lot more fun. We would stay up until the early morning hours talking and just plain enjoying her lively female company. It upset Major Torq that she avoided him, a major, for three lowlifes like us. During one of these late-night drinking sessions I invited Henny to return for my birthday party to be held on July 2. She said she would try to make it.

On May 13, the day of the CA back into the A-Shau, the operation to insert troops into Dong Ap Ba went without a hitch. We met with little resistance from the enemy and took few hits. Several aircraft did get shot up, but those were in Alpha and Bravo companies. The Blackwidows had been lucky. It was just a very long day of flying that was otherwise unremarkable. But, as I would later find out, it would turn into one of the biggest political circuses in the history of the war.

On May 20 I flew a routine mission that turned into a living nightmare. That's how combat flying is. It shifts from the mundane to the horrendous most often when you least expect it. This particular memory has become part of me. I have relived the mission hundreds of times in my mind. It is as clear to me now as if it had happened yesterday.

It was like a sauna in the cockpit. The sweat was dripping down my forehead in rivulets forming salty pools in the hollows created by the hard plastic bridge of my army-issue sunglasses. My helmet felt like a green oven threatening to cook my skull and fry my brain. My green Nomex flight suit clung to my skin like a wet plastic bag. My back, the itchy fire-retardant material soaked through with perspiration, stuck to the green mesh of my armored seat. A small, half-smoked cigar hung from my mouth. I chewed aggressively at its wooden tip. I was flying at fifteen hundred feet, an altitude safe from small arms fire, toward our objective, an LZ one klick south of the DMZ.

Four marine reconnaissance team members sat impatiently on the hot, gray metal floor of the bumpy chopper going over the last minute checks of their weapons and equipment. Their young, serious faces were grotesquely painted with green and brown camouflage grease paint. You could tell the four men were hyped up and tightly strung like football players before a championship match. In a few minutes they would be dropped into the LZ and disappear into the jungle to stalk the elusive enemy. The remaining four members of the eight-man team were flying in the second Huey trailing a mile behind, commanded by Warrant Officer Bill Rickter.

With an airspeed of 110 knots the LZ came into view quickly. It loomed out of the thick mantle of twisted jungle a half mile ahead. It was one of those LZs blasted out of the triple-canopy jungle by a five-hundred-pound bomb dropped by a sky crane helicopter two weeks earlier.

I turned in my seat. "You guys ready?" I said over the intercom.

My crew chief pulled back the bolt of his pedestal-mounted M-60 machine gun and released it, driving a 7.62-mm round into the chamber with the heavy clank of metal slamming against metal. He raised a sweat-stained Nomex flying glove and gave the thumbs up sign. "Right behind you, sir."

"How about you, Garrett?"

The gunner also chambered a round. "Ready, sir."

I glanced at my copilot. He was an FNG lieutenant, straight out of flight school. This was his third mission in country. "You ready, O'Connor?"

"Ready." He looked and sounded nervous.

"Relax, O'Connor. This should be a piece of cake," I said trying to put the man at ease.

Through habit, as I had done hundreds of times in the

seven months I had been flying in Vietnam, I swung the holstered .38 revolver to my groin as added protection and tucked it comfortably between my legs. In the same motion I adjusted the "chicken plate," a twenty-pound, acrylic, three-quarter-inch armored chest protector, under the two webbed shoulder straps of my seat harness. O'Connor watched me and quickly did the same.

I pressed the red trigger on the cyclic control stick and radioed to the second helicopter, "We're beginning our approach, Bill."

"Roger, Randy. We're a mile behind you."

Two heavily armed marine Echo-Model gunships circled five hundred feet above us ready to offer suppressive fire around the LZ's perimeter. They were armed with 2.75-inch rockets and miniguns capable of delivering three thousand rounds per minute. Two F-4 Phantom jets were on station circling at twenty-five thousand feet, loaded with napalm just in case. "We'll cover you, Blackwidow 25," one of the gunship pilots radioed. "Whenever you're ready you can begin your approach."

"Here we go," I said on the intercom to the crew and rolled the chopper into a hard right bank.

The green horizon appeared to turn ninety degrees against the blue sky strewn with white, puffy cumulus clouds. I added right pedal, kicking the aircraft out of trim, and lowered the collective pitch lever, causing the machine to descend at more than three thousand feet per minute. With both large cargo doors open on the side of the aircraft the wind howled through the chopper as it plummeted out of the sky. I guided the craft in a downward spiral.

A gunship dove past our falling Huey. Puffs of smoke trailed from its rocket pods as the 2.75-mm rockets ignited and snaked their way to the perimeter of the landing zone. They found their mark and exploded with great orange flashes, flinging moist red and brown dirt and green foliage high into the dank Southeast Asian air.

"When we're on short final for the LZ, open fire," I instructed the crew.

"Roger, sir," Taylor and Garrett answered in unison.

The howl of the hurricane-force wind on their boom microphones nearly blanketed their replies.

"Watch the gauges, O'Connor, and stay close on the controls."

O'Connor didn't answer. His eyes were transfixed outside the chopper watching the jungle rush rapidly toward us.

"O'Connor?" I said again, glancing at him momentarily.

"Roger. I'll follow you through. Goddamn, they sure didn't teach us this type of approach in flight school."

"They should have." I banked the machine from a steep, tight right turn to a steep left turn. "It could save your life one day. Charlie looks up at us falling out of the sky like this and thinks we're out of control so he thinks why waste bullets on a helicopter that's going to crash anyway? Or if he does decide to shoot at us he'll have a hell of a time hitting us at this rate of descent. And all these unusual attitude changes make a nearly impossible target to hit."

The second gunship began its run on the LZ. I straightened the ship out and slowed the rate of descent for a normal approach fifty feet above the treetops. The small landing zone was encircled with trees ranging from seventy-five to one hundred feet high. The taller ones were up slope along the planned departure end of the ridge line. I picked my spot to land, not to the center of the zone, but slightly to the right of center where the exposed roots, twisted trees, and chunks of moist earth were less dense.

The perimeter, forty meters to the left of our aircraft, exploded at regular intervals from the impacting rockets from the gunships. The shock waves from the blasts rocked our descending helicopter as it made its way to the planned touchdown point.

I flew our ship over the tree line and began to descend into the gash carved out of the jungle that was the LZ. I gave the command to open fire. Taylor and Garrett sprayed the surrounding tree line with metallic defoliant to keep the enemy's head down if in fact the Vietcong were there.

The ratt-tat-tat-tat-tat-tat-tat-tat from the two M-60s filled the cockpit with their synchronous clatter. I planted the skids of the chopper in the soft soil. The four-man recon team leapt off like clockwork.

"We're clear!" Taylor yelled. "They're gone!"

"Coming up," I said.

With the weight of the four men, their weapons, ammunition, and supplies off-loaded the Huey climbed slowly but steadily until it cleared the hundred-foot jungle thirty-five meters to our front. Once clear of the trees, the gunner and crew chief stopped firing their weapons.

I pushed the cyclic stick forward accelerating the aircraft to sixty knots and began a maximum performance climb to fifteen hundred feet. The second helicopter began its approach behind us. O'Connor began breathing again.

"What'd I tell you O'Connor. Piece of cake, huh?"

The lieutenant managed a smile, a smile of relief.

"Receiving fire! Receiving fire!" came Bill's frantic cry over the radio, filling the crew's headsets. The radio transmission jolted my senses. I instinctively threw the aircraft into a quick 180-degree turn to view the LZ we'd just left.

"They're breaking off the approach," the crew chief yelled.

I radioed, "You all right, Bill?"

"Everything looks all right, Randy. We took a few hits. The gauges look all right. It's hotter than a goddamn hornet's nest down there. Charlie has your four men pinned down in the center of the LZ."

I lowered the collective pitch lever to begin a descent. "Taylor, Garrett."

"Yes, sir."

"We're going in after them. Open fire when I give the order. We'll approach low level from the north, the way we came in. When we cross the tree line I'll give the command to start firing."

"Yes, sir."

"O'Connor, follow me closely on the controls and . . . ," I paused to look directly into the lieutenant's eyes to emphasize what I was about to say, ". . . if anything happens down there be prepared to take the controls and get us out. Do you understand?"

O'Connor's eyes got large. The color disappeared from his thin, sweaty face. "Yes, I understand."

I radioed the second chopper. "Bill?"

"Go ahead, Randy."

"We're on our way in to get those guys. Coordinate the gunships to cover the perimeter. I'll be approaching at treetop level from the north. Have the F-4s drop their sortie on the zone's eastern and western perimeters."

"Roger, Randy. Good luck."

I dove the chopper at 110 knots, leveling the ship at treetop level and flying in the direction of the LZ. The jungle below was now a green blur. "OK guys we're almost there. Hold your fire until I give the command."

"Roger, sir."

I pulled aft on the cyclic control stick, flaring the chopper. Its nose reared back to a thirty-degree attitude to kill the forward airspeed before we reached the tree line on the zone's northern perimeter. Suddenly we crossed over the naked opening in the trees. "Open fire *now*!"

We descended into the zone.

The helicopter's machine guns rattled. Hot shell casings flew from the breaches, bouncing off of everything in the chopper—the floor, the back of my helmet, our armored seats—while Taylor and Garrett sprayed the landing zone with bullets in an effort to keep the enemy's head down.

I maneuvered the craft, descending below the high surrounding jungle tree line. In the zone lay three Vietcong soldiers dressed in black pajamas, now drenched in their own warm blood that oozed freely from fresh wounds.

Dirt kicked up by the bullets fired from the tree line flew in the air around the four pinned men. I could see them below, lying on their stomachs facing the cardinal points of the compass. They fired into the jungle with everything they had. O'Connor hovered over the controls as I guided the chopper into the cavernous LZ.

The scene turned into a flaming holocaust. The first napalm bomb dropped by an F-4 exploded sixty yards away along the western perimeter, shaking the craft with a sudden jolt. The heat wave and blast from the explosion swept across our hovering helicopter like the searing blast from a jet's exhaust. The noise from the gunfire was deafening.

The hot, acrid smell of napalm mixed with the expended gunpowder, smoke, and thick Vietnam heat was nearly suffocating. I landed where we had dropped the men. They were now pinned down thirty yards away.

A screaming Vietnamese soldier bolted from the tree line. His clothes, skin, and hair were ablaze from the fiery napalm. The gunner quickly cut him down. His body collapsed to the ground in a fiery heap, twitching and writhing in spasms until there was only an amorphous mass of lifeless, burning flesh offering yet another pungent aroma to the already putrid stench.

The first two recon team members sprang up off their bellies, jumped to their feet, and ran backwards towards us, reloading and continuing to fire their weapons at the faceless enemy. I could hear bullets occasionally hitting the ship. I watched the engine instruments intently, my hands vice-tight on the controls.

First one, then a second man scampered aboard the chopper. Sweat rolled down my forehead and my sunglasses, immediately leaving wiggly streaks of dried salt on the glass. The third and fourth man jumped up and ran backward toward us. The third man stumbled on an exposed tree root and nearly fell.

For God's sake hurry up, I screamed to myself. The scene unfolded around us in slow motion, surreal, confused, distorted. Rockets fired from the gunships overhead hammered the perimeter with bone-jarring tremors that shook the craft with each blast. "WHUMP! WHUMP!" The rockets exploded in pairs followed by falling debris of soil, foliage, flesh and bone.

The last two men threw themselves on board. "Get the fuck out of here!" the team leader screamed from the back. His shrill voice carried over the sound of gunfire.

I pulled up on the collective pitch lever. The helicopter rose from the ground, climbing slowly through the smoke, stench, and heat. The two F-4 Phantom jets streaked by low level on either side of the landing zone at three hundred knots within seconds of each other. Like two silver bullets, they dropped their remaining sortie of napalm. The two simultaneous explosions that followed caused a deafening explosion of heat and light that shook the helicopter as it slowly made its ascent to clear the tall trees to our front. I could tell the aircraft was heavy. Maybe too heavy. The helicopter strained for altitude. Twenty feet, thirty feet, fifty feet, she rose slowly. We'd refueled in Quang Tri prior to the mission and had topped up to twelve hundred pounds of fuel. The approach into the LZ takes less power than a vertical take off out of the same landing zone. Without the four men the Huey had no power problems, but with the added weight she was severely limited.

The four soldiers continued to fire their automatic weapons from the chopper's open doors into the flaming LZ. Taylor and Garrett continued firing, the barrels of their M-60s now glowing red hot.

Her ascent was slowing. Sixty-five feet, seventy feet she clawed, shook, and struggled for altitude. The turbine engine strained and whined trying to develop enough shaft horsepower to pull the weight of the heavily laden craft vertically over the hundred-foot trees. All the power instruments were well into their red lines. The aircraft stopped climbing twenty-five feet below the tree tops unable to ascend one foot more.

Is this how I'm going to die? I thought in horror. Hovering here like a tin duck in a shooting gallery ready to be picked off by the enemy seventy-five feet below?

O'Connor began to panic. "Goddamn, let's get the fuck out of here."

"Not enough power!" I yelled.

I pulled in more collective and the rotor RPM began to decay spilling lift. The ship began to sink back down into the LZ. Back into the holocaust below.

Whoop! Whoop! Whoop! Whoop! the dreaded low rotor RPM audio warning rang loudly through the pilots' headsets. I fought for control, fought to maintain altitude. One of the machine guns stopped firing.

"My gun's jammed, sir," Taylor said frantically. "I, I . . . I can't clear it."

Suddenly the green plastic window over O'Connor's head exploded, showering plastic splinters everywhere. O'Connor tucked his head down instinctively. He threw his hands over his flight helmet to avoid the shower of debris caused by the Vietcong bullet fired at us from the jungle below.

Two of the enemy ran from the trees carrying Russian-made AK-47 machine guns. Before they could stop to take aim one of the recon team members threw a fragmentation grenade between them. The blast flung them in the air and back into the jungle's smoldering eastern perimeter.

The helo sat hovering seventy-five feet above the zone at full power, the engine straining to deliver every bit of its 1250 horsepower, unable to climb, too heavy to power up any higher in the thick tropical moisture and burning heat.

I suddenly remembered that as a last resort if you added right pedal it takes pitch from the tail rotor giving more engine power for the main rotor, and when power is marginal it just may give the extra edge to get out of a tight situation.

Desperate, and out of ideas, I kicked in right pedal. The aircraft swung violently to the right. I dipped the nose, guiding the machine through the sporadic enemy fire. The skids dragged through the tangled branches of the lower trees to the rear of the zone. Thunk! Thunk! Thunk! several more VC rounds punctured the aircraft. We cleared the trees with no room to spare, accelerating down the jungle-covered mountain slope to safety.

The machine-gun fire ceased. All that could be heard was the loud, low guttural roar of hot air rushing through the gaping hole over O'Connor's head. I accelerated to sixty knots and began a climb.

Bill radioed, "You guys all right? Shit, that was some show!"

I radioed back and told him everyone was OK. The chopper shimmied, vibrated, and shook violently. The caution warning light segment on the instrument panel was lit up like a Christmas tree with red and yellow lights, but the Huey managed to stay in one piece for the twelve-minute flight to LZ Vandergrift where we landed safely on the strip.

* * *

23 May 1969

Dear Mom:

Hi: Received your letter telling me you heard about the 101st Airborne Division and our air assault on the A-shau Valley. Yes, we put the troops on the mountain they call Hamburger Hill you say you're hearing so much about. It was a clean combat assault. We lost no aircraft.

Tonight we had a USO show with Australian entertainers. I took one look at the round-eyed girls and my body began to shake. God, they were beautiful.

I've been told I have put in for the Distinguished Flying Cross for a mission I flew three days ago. I pulled some Marines out of a hot landing zone and got them back safely. The copilot told the Awards and Decorations Officer about it and he is writing me up for the DFC.

Please don't worry, Mom, you know I always look out for number one. I still enjoy the flying. Keep writing.

Love, Randy.

It was always my feeling that if I was going to get killed in Vietnam it would *not* be as a result of being shot down or killed by an enemy bullet, though the incident near the DMZ was one of a few exceptions to nearly make me change my mind. I thought if I didn't survive it would be my own stupid fault. I would let my guard drop and the cause would be pilot error, pure and simple. I nearly proved my philosophy one evening when my crew chief came by my hootch to ask me to move my aircraft from the maintenance facility back to its revetment. It was the one and only time in my aviation career I flew when I was drunk.

I had consumed two double screwdrivers about thirty minutes before Taylor appeared. I felt relaxed rather than drunk. The time was about 2130 and it was dark and drizzling. I walked out to the aircraft wearing an olive drab T-shirt, boxer shorts, and thongs. Taylor was already at the aircraft and I had him sit in the copilot's seat. I strapped in, started the engine, brought the rotors up to flight RPM and took off over the perimeter into the blackness. Climbing through seventy-five feet my head began to spin. I banked the ship to the left. Suffering the effects of the alcohol I lost all spatial orientation, and it was then I began to panic. I thought about the two pilots who had crashed that night outside the perimeter at Sally under similar circumstances after accepting the flare mission. I increased the angle of bank to turn back to the Widow Web in hopes that I would pick up the lights of the company area. A sudden brightness flashed across the windshield reflected in the raindrops running along it. Thousands of tiny star bursts seemed to explode on the windshield further hindering my forward visibility. I forced myself to push the cyclic forward to aim at the approach pad of the Widow Web. A maintenance team was working on a ship in the rain; a bank of spotlights illuminated their working area. They were aimed right at us, and because I was now flying into those lights I was blinded. I thought we were hovering forward toward the Widow Web which was now a hundred yards in front of us. I glanced out of the side window away from the lights, and to my horror, discovered we were hovering backwards. The ship was fifteen feet over a bunker on the berm. I could see the soldiers below running from the rain accelerated down on them from our rotors. From instinct I wanted to say, "You got it," to my copilot because I knew I had lost it. But there was no copilot. Taylor did not know how to fly. I glanced over at him. His face was a mask of fear. Fighting against all the signals my brain was receiving from my body I made myself push the cyclic further forward to make the machine fly to the pad.

I only *just* managed to get the ship down in one piece. I carefully hovered it into the revetment and shut down the engine. That simple little exercise scared me to death. I shuddered to think how close I had come to losing control of the aircraft I knew so intimately from flying it every day. I felt that the ship had become almost a part of me after more than seven hundred combat hours. Flying had become like breathing. But not tonight. I had screwed up royally, nearly succeeding in rolling the helicopter up into a ball. The experience served to humble me. It also taught me, probably at the right time, that if you get too cocky, too blasé about safety, if you reach the stage in your aviation career when you think you've got flying whipped, that's when it's time to beware, because something will reach up and bite you to remind you to keep your guard up. Without this awareness you will doubtless be rewarded by having an accident. At that moment I vowed never to mix alcohol and flying again. It is a promise I have kept to this day.

27 May 1969

Dear Mom:

Well, everyone sure is hearing a lot and talking a lot about Hamburger Hill. To tell the truth a lot hairier things have gone on over here, but for some reason the press has decided to lock onto this story and whip everyone up into an emotional frenzy. The reason they are publicizing Hamburger Hill so much is because people are saying we were the aggressors in taking it. Damn right we were! We had to be. How can you expect to fight, let alone win a war, without being aggressive? The people's protests back home really make a lot of guys over here mad, including me! If the people in the States were over here, they'd see what's going on for themselves, then they'd offer the support we need to fight and win this war.

The flying's been hectic. I've been getting over 120 hours a month. Let me close by saying please don't worry about Hamburger Hill any more. We have it. It's secure. No sweat. Not much else to say, please keep writing.

Love, Randy.

CHAPTER 10

June 1969

Tigers, Elephants, Deer, and ROKs

I couldn't remember the last time I saw my company area in daylight. It felt as if I had spent a lifetime getting up at 0500, taking off before first light, flying for eight, ten, or even twelve hours, and arriving back at Phu Bai after sunset. One day I logged more than sixteen hours of flight time, flying from daybreak until after midnight.

I was now sitting in the second row of our makeshift outdoor movie theater on a metal folding chair that I brought out from the mess hall. It was 2030. I was drinking a lukewarm can of beer, waiting for the movie to begin. The air was hot and thick. I was exhausted. I had not had a shower since last night. I hadn't even had chow. I landed a half hour ago and I was still wearing the sweaty Nomex I put on at 0500 that morning.

Because movies are sent so infrequently to Charlie Company the projectionist changes the sequence of the reels each night to add variety to the same movie. This makes it seem like we are watching a different movie every night. The movies are projected onto a white plywood screen nailed up on two vertical, twelve-foot-high four-by-fours.

The first night the reels are played in their proper order. The second night the second reel is shown first, the third reel is shown second, and the first reel last. The third night reel three is shown first, reel one second, and reel two third, and so on.

During the break between reels Captain Ernest James walks around the outdoor theater and calls out the names of the ACs and passes out mission sheets from ops for the next day's missions. The sheets contain the particulars of the mission such as lift-off time, unit to be supported, position of the unit's support base, call sign, and radio frequency codes to be looked up in the SOI. The SOI, or Signal Operating Instructions, is a secret document kept by the aircraft commander. It is a small book each aircraft commander wears around his neck on a thick string when he is flying. He usually keeps it in the right chest pocket of his Nomex flight suit.

Ernest was rushing around passing out the mission sheets before the first reel began. "Shonehour!" He yelled.

"Here!" Tom answered back.

Ernest walked over to him and handed him the sheet. "Sulak!"

"Here, Ernest!"

"Kelly!"

"Right here, Ernest!"

Ernest gave him his sheet. "Mains!"

"Here, Ernest!" I yelled.

He was a fair distance away. He searched the crowd of over a hundred men. "I don't see you!"

"In the second row!" I shouted.

I could see him looking for me. "Still can't see you."

"Wait one, Ernest." I replied taking out the emergency pen flare gun from the breast pocket of my Nomex. I screwed in the red flare, held it over my head, and with a warning shout of "Stand by!" fired the flare. The bright red flare rocketed straight up over the heads of the GIs sitting in the outside theater. Peals of laughter and applause filled the company area.

"Ah, I see you now, Randy," he chuckled.

Under the red glow of the descending flare, Ernest approached and handed me the mission sheet.

"Thomas!" he continued and walked away.

A new captain to Charlie Company, Captain Buck Phillips, sent to us by the 158th, marched over. "Give me that flare gun soldier. Just what in hell's name do you think you're doing firing that thing in the company area?"

"Getting Ernest's attention," I explained.

My insubordination shocked him. "That's *Captain* James to you, mister. You don't call a superior officer by his first name."

I tried hard not to laugh out loud. I was dog-tired and my first instinct was to tell him to go fuck himself. I fought to keep my composure before I spoke. "I was just trying to get Ernest's . . . uh . . . Captain James's attention."

"What do you think this is around here, a goddamn circus?"

I began to answer, "Well, sir, now that you mention it. . . ."

"Never mind." He threw out his hand. "Gimme that flare gun."

I shrugged and handed it to the captain.

"This won't be the last you'll hear of this, Mains. That I can assure you!" he shouted and set off toward the orderly room.

His statement set off a barrage of cat calls and boos from the rest of the audience, which accompanied Captain Buck Phillips as he walked away. The heckling did not stop until he had disappeared into the night.

3 June 1969

Dear Mom:

Not much happening out of the ordinary over here. Things have been really jumping in the north and northwest of the A-Shau Valley. I've heard we should be pulling out the troops the 101st has there in August because the monsoon makes it impossible to resupply troops there by air.

I have about eight hundred combat flight hours now. I figure I will see over one thousand hours before I leave here. I think I'm starting to get the hang of the flying over here now. I must close now.

Write soon,

Randy

* * *

The arrival of June marked the eighth month I had been in country. I thought by this time I had seen everything there was to see over here in the way of troop pickups. But this assumption was soon proved to be premature.

The voice on the Fox Mike radio sounded extremely urgent. "LZs cold, Blackwidow 25. You can make your approach, but make it quick."

The soldier's urgency was perplexing. If the enemy wasn't around why did I have to make it quick. "Understand the LZ is not hot?" I queried.

"That's affirmative. But get down here and pick us up. And do it fast." The voice was panting now as if the man were running. I couldn't imagine what was going on. I had been suckered into hot LZs before, told they were cold when they were not. I did not want to have it happen again. "We see your green smoke. Confirm you're *not* in contact."

The voice was definitely panting now. "That's . . . affirm. But . . . hurry . . . get us . . . out . . . of here."

"Roger."

I could see the men running through the high elephant grass. There were five of them. I said on the intercom, "Keep a close eye out, Taylor. I don't want to be flying into an ambush."

"Roger, sir."

The gunner added, "LZ looks OK to me. I can't understand why those guys are running."

"Me neither. Be ready to shoot," I cautioned.

"Roger that, sir." I heard him chamber a round.

I flew one of my dizzying descents toward the LZ and guided the machine on approach to head off the first running man. I maneuvered the helicopter next to him and he threw himself on board. The other four men piled in after him. The last man screamed, "OK, let's fucking dee-dee out of here!"

I pulled pitch. We began to rise. I heard Taylor yell to the team leader. "What's the rush?"

"Tiger!"

"Tiger?"

"Yes." The team leader pointed to the LZ. As I circled in the climb I could see a large tiger standing in the tall grass looking up at our ascending chopper. We had robbed him of his lunch. I had never seen a tiger in Vietnam before.

The team leader hollered, "The son of a bitch stalked us for nearly one klick. We fired a few rounds at it to try to scare it away, but he wouldn't leave us alone. He kept on stalking us. Shit, if Charlie isn't fucking bad enough to contend with the fucking animals over here'll eat your ass." He shook his helmeted head. "What a fuckin' crazy goddamn place this is!" I had to agree.

Elephants were a common sight in Vietnam. The NVA was said to use them like trucks to carry equipment on the well-concealed jungle highways. I frequently saw the huge, gray beasts roaming lazily in the open areas near the Laotian border. What angered me were the stories about gunship pilots firing down on them and blowing them apart with rockets and miniguns. I actually saw it happen only once. When I realized what was taking place I came up on the radio and chastised the crew of the offending gunship for their barbarism. They took no notice of my pleas for them to stop. As they saw it, it was their job to disable the enemy in any manner they could. In their eyes they were just doing their job.

I had finished doing some personal administrative chores at Camp Eagle late one afternoon when a CH-47 Chinook helicopter flew in from the A-Shau carrying a large dead deer in a cargo net slung under its huge, flat belly. It dropped the deer on the pad and flew off. A Korean soldier waved thanks to the pilot and walked over to the carcass. I could see the animal's brown coat riddled with bullet holes. The man stuck his knife in the deer's belly and gutted it on the spot.

I had heard how tough the ROK, Republic of Korea, army soldiers were. The stories made them sound totally ruthless. The NVA and VC were deathly afraid of them and the Koreans were universally respected for the top-notch soldiers they were.

The story of the technique used by the ROKs to interrogate a group of prisoners has passed into Vietnam lore.

They would ask a man a question once. If he did not answer he would be shot in the head. Then they would move to the second man and ask him the same question. If he did not answer he would be shot in the head, and they would move to the third prisoner and so on. The ROKs were famous for their practice of throwing prisoners from helicopters if they did not cooperate. The ROKs, as you can imagine, had a higher success rate in obtaining information from prisoners than any other service. If they took a Vietnamese village and found VC present they would cut the heads off the enemy and place them on long poles outside the entrance to the village as a warning. I had never met one of these hardened ROKs, so I was not ready for what I saw the Korean soldier do next.

The man had an empty gallon tin can with him. After he cut open the deer he reached into its chest cavity with his bare hands and scooped out the animal's entrails, placing them in a pile. He then dipped the can in the gaping hole of the animal's chest cavity and filled it with blood. I watched in disgust as he walked a few yards away from the small group of us who had come to watch and he squatted down. Next, he brought the can to his lips, tipped his head back, and cradling the can in both hands, he gulped down the animal's warm blood. I could well understand why the enemy feared those soldiers so.

Although I was not a dedicated dust-off pilot there were many times I flew wounded to the hospital because I just happened to be at the right place at the wrong time, as was the case when I picked up the soldier who got hit on the head with the rotor blade during the A-Shau Valley assault. The opportunity came up again when Joe Sulak and I were supporting the marines up north.

I was making a routine approach to one of the pads at LZ Vandergrift. I was on short final when the landing pad suddenly exploded in front of me in a great orange flash followed by a tall plume of white smoke. The concussion really jolted the ship. I instinctively threw the cyclic to the left and began a steep turn. I could see and hear several more explosions peppering the surrounding air base.

Joe radioed. "It's a mortar attack. Christ, Randy, you'd

be fucking dead if it happened ten seconds later. We're getting the hell out of here and flying back up the valley."

I was in the middle of guiding the machine around in a steep, 180-degree turn. "Roger that, Joe. We'll follow you." I nosed the aircraft over and began to fly low level behind him back the way we'd flown in.

The unit on the ground radioed, "Blackwidow two-five! Blackwidow two-five! This is March-Bandit. We've got wounded. Can you come back and pick them up? Over."

I turned the aircraft around. There was no sign of further explosions. "Joe, I'm going in to pick up the wounded."

"Good luck. I'll be circling three klicks to the north."

I landed to one side of the pad next to a gaping, smoldering hole in the steel planking where the mortar round had impacted. The marines approached quickly carrying three wounded soldiers. Two of the men loaded on board did not appear to be too badly hurt to me. They were conscious and had half-walked with the assistance of their buddies. But the third man was unconscious and in two pieces. They laid him gently on the floor, his right leg, which had been blown off above the knee, with its white bone, the femur, sticking out several inches from the raw flesh. The man who had carried the leg stuck it onto the exposed bone. The booted foot stayed upright for a second then flopped over at an obscene angle. One of the soldiers ran up to my door and yelled over the noise of our screaming engine, "They were in the shit house when it got hit."

I looked up and saw the remains of the plywood structure. Seeing how much damage the mortar had caused made me wonder how anyone had survived the blast. The soldier gave me the thumbs-up sign, and I pulled pitch to take off immediately. As we climbed away in the turn, the pad exploded again behind us with a direct hit from another incoming mortar. We made it to the hospital in fifteen minutes.

There were other instances when I carried young soldiers who had no hope of making it. They were already gone. My most vivid recollection of such a mission is the morning I was called to pick up ten dead soldiers outside the perimeter of Camp Evans.

From three hundred feet on approach I could see the green body bags arranged neatly in a row along one of the dikes of a rice paddy. As soon as I landed, several soldiers wearing green boonie hats and no shirts, their grim faces camouflaged with dark green and beige grease paint, began loading the five bags that made up our load onto the Huey's gray metal floor. I could smell the stench of death immediately.

The sharp outlines of the bodies were visible through the bags. One of the shirtless soldiers walked around the front of the chopper and opened my door. I slid back the armored plate on my seat. The soldier stood on the helicopter's skid to yell his message so I would hear it through my green flight helmet.

"Take them back to the surgical hospital at Phu Bai, sir. They'll know what to do with them."

"What happened?" I yelled over the whine of the turbine engine and quick WOP-WOP-WOP of the wide rotor blades beating the thick, humid air.

Sweat dripped off the soldier's tan, mud-streaked chest. "Fire fight."

"How many'd you lose?"

The soldier held up ten fingers.

"How many VC did you kill?"

"None!"

"None?"

He explained, "These guys you're carrying are part of a platoon that split up to ambush Charlie last night. They opened up on each other some time in the early morning."

"Was the enemy anywhere around?"

The soldier shook his head in reply.

"You mean these guys killed each other thinking the other group was the enemy?"

The soldier nodded.

The Peter Pilot flew the ship to the hospital at Phu Bai. Sometime during the flight I turned in my seat and glanced back at the body bags. Four of them lay neatly on the floor, but one of the bags was propped up against the transmission island as if the person inside were sitting upright. The hundred-knot wind entering through the two open cargo doors whipped at the top of the body bag. A tuft of blond hair suddenly appeared from the top of the bag and snapped in the breeze. In the wind the bag started to work its way down the form entrapped inside until a full head of blond hair was visible. I could not tear my eyes from the sight. The bag worked lower exposing the forehead, blond eyebrows, closed eyes, then a straight nose, until finally the whole head was visible. The boy would have been about my age. There was no blood, no gore, nothing on the smooth face to suggest mortal injury. It seemed crazy to me. He appeared to be only sleeping. The blond hair was now whipped wildly by the wind, adding to the illusion of life. I turned to look straight ahead out the windshield and pushed in the floor mike switch with my combat boot. "Taylor?"

The crew chief answered, "Yes, sir?"

"Would you reach over and cover up that guy's head?"

"Roger, sir."

I turned around again thirty seconds later. The crew chief had closed the top of the bag and was now securing it with a short length of stainless-steel safety wire. Several strands of blond hair still protruded from the top.

"It's secure, sir," said Taylor who resumed his place behind his M-60.

"Thanks."

My Peter Pilot looked over at me and said, "You OK? You look white as a sheet."

"Yeah, sure." I looked out the side window for a moment at the high jungle peaks to the east bordering the A-Shau. Then I looked across at the peter pilot. "What a waste, huh? Really a waste. God, he looks so young."

"We're not exactly ready for social security ourselves now, are we?"

"No, I guess you're right." I thought about it for a moment before replying. "I just hope I live long enough to collect it, that's all."

It seemed that there was one whole week in which I flew nothing but medevac missions, carrying men that had been killed or wounded in some equally crazy, senseless manner. I had to fly one dead soldier from Firebase Birmingham to Camp Eagle who had survived both the A-Shau Valley assault and the slaughter on Hamburger Hill and was due to leave country after completing a full year in Vietnam. He was on a truck taking him to his base camp to out process when he accidentally leaned against the muzzle of his M-16 and it discharged. The bullet tore through his heart and killed him instantly.

Then there was the soldier whose platoon had come under fire by the VC. He pulled out a grenade, pulled the pin, and threw it. It hit a tree, bounced straight back at him, and blew him up.

Probably the worst incident was that of the soldier who had been shot accidentally by his best friend during a fire fight. We had to carry both the body and the unfortunate assassin. You could tell instantly by looking at the man that his mind had snapped. He sat in the back of our chopper rocking back and forth staring with a disbelieving gaze at his buddy encased in the green body bag. He hummed a tune that I did not recognize. From time to time he would break down and cry for perhaps thirty seconds, and then he'd stop crying and hum the tune again. The war was definitely over for him, I thought. Or was it? He looked so disturbed I imagine that to this day he is still affected by that traumatic event.

Not all the injuries I saw were severe, and some even had an element of humor. Lieutenant Andre Gower, the new copilot who had flown with me on the flare mission on my first day back from R&R, was flying with Ned Kelly over the A-Shau on a routine resupply mission when they got shot at with a 50-caliber machine gun. When a 50-caliber tracer round comes at you it looks like a red golf ball. At least that's how it was described by Andre Gower after one came crashing through the Peter Pilot's chin bubble and blasted the toe off his jump boot. The toe of his boot looked like something worn by a clown in the circus. The leather on the toe was blown outward as if the exlosion had occurred inside the boot. He was lucky. He suffered nothing worse than a blood blister on the end of his big toe. But that was not all. He would become eligible for a purple heart if he shed blood, so once back at the company area he pricked the blood blister with a pin and hobbled over to show the awards-and-decorations officer his wound. Sure enough, he was put in for a purple heart. But better yet, the pin-pricked wound festered in the Vietnamese tropical heat. It became so infected he eventually had to be medevaced to Japan for several months. His wife flew over to join him. All the time he remained in Japan recuperating, his remaining days to serve in Vietnam were clicking off. Everyone considered Lieutenant Andre Gower to be a lucky son of a bitch. And that he surely was.

16 June 1969

Hi:

I have been getting a lot of mail from you guys. Sorry, but this is actually the only time I have had to write in the last week. I finally got a day off because I have been flying so much lately. The regulations state they must give you a day off if you have exceeded 120 flight hours in a thirty-day period.

You asked me in your last letter what date I expect to get home. I should be in the U.S. the 15th of October. Seems like a lifetime from now.

I'm glad you liked the small photo album I sent to you. I will send more when I receive them. Gotta go. Take care.

Randy.

It was in June that Joe Sulak nearly got killed. He, Ned Kelly, and I were flying back from Mai Loc after extracting an eight-man team out of Laos on the Mcguire rigs. We were given orders that on our ferry flight down to Phu Bai we were to check in with a small unit who needed extracting south of LZ Sarge, and we were to fly them back to Quang Tri.

It was around 1600 in the afternoon. We flew a loose trail formation to the coordinates given to us. Joe was flying the lead aircraft. I could hear him on the radio making contact with the ground unit. "I have your yellow smoke, unit seven-oh-two. You had any enemy contact recently?"

"Negative Blackwidow Double-Deuce. Not since yesterday. Only thing is the LZ's a bit tight. We had a resupply ship in yesterday. You should have no trouble getting in and out."

"Roger, be there in two mikes."

Ned Kelly and I circled our ships to the west at fifteen hundred feet and watched Joe make his approach to the jungle. Ned made the usual macabre remark over the radio, "Hey, Sulak. If you get killed can I have your stereo?"

"You can have it all, Kelly," Joe answered back good-naturedly.

I looked down through my side window and watched as Joe hovered over the dark hole in the jungle and disappeared down into it. It look tight, real tight. Ned Kelly began his approach a klick away.

The radio suddenly crackled. I could hear the clatter of machine-gun fire in the background. "Blackwidow Double-Deuce, goddamn, you OK?"

"We're hit! We're aborting. We're aborting," I heard Joe say forcefully but coolly.

The soldier on the ground radioed, "It was an RPG. Looked like it hit your tail, Double-Deuce."

Joe replied, "Goddamn, I believe it. Hell of a lot of vibration in my pedals. I'm still trying to guide her out of here."

I could see Joe's ship emerging from the hole in the trees. I nosed my helicopter over and dove to take up a position to fly alongside him. Ned Kelly asked on the UHF radio, "What happened, Joe?"

"I think an RPG went through my tail rotor. Nowhere safe to land around here. Going to try and make it into the strip at Vandergrift. Follow me close."

"Roger."

Joe tried to lighten the weight of the fear we all felt. "Looks like you may get that stereo after all, Kelly."

"Who you kidding, Sulak. You're too goddamn cheap

to let me have it that easy, you sorry Texan.'' Kelly answered back. He couldn't disguise the concern in his voice.

Kelly flew several rotor disks away from Joe's left side. I flew equal distant on his right. Several baseball-size holes could be seen in the aircraft's tail boom. I fully expected to see the tail rotor disintegrate and Joe's aircraft start to spin uncontrollably. But it held together and he made it back to the airstrip at Vandergrift and shut down.

In one of the tail rotor blades there was a hole the size of a golf ball. Joe had seen the RPG come out of the jungle, the white ribbon of smoke snaking its way toward them in the restrictive LZ. He said he'd never felt more vulnerable but could do nothing but scrunch down in his seat and close his eyes to wait for the explosion. When it didn't come he knew his luck held and that he wouldn't have to give up his stereo that day.

Ned and I had to leave Joe at Vandergrift and fly back to the LZ to finish the job. We made three sorties each to extract the men on the ground. On each sortie I had to descend into that same LZ, which looked like a one-hundred-foot, deep-green barrel, and I half expected to see a ribbon of smoke make its way from the dense tree line to finish the job the enemy had bungled on Joe's helicopter. Ned Kelly and I encountered no further resistance, however, and the airlift went without a hitch.

As I discovered on the night I'd stupidly tried to reposition the aircraft having had too much to drink, when you think you have flying mastered something occurs to bring you up sharp, to let you know that if you don't stay on top of it it'll reach out, tap you on the shoulder, and poke you in the eye. I had another such occurrence when I was flying for the marines out of Quang Tri on a routine insertion mission. I dropped my guard and almost bought the farm.

It was an extremely windy day. I was hover-taxiing out to line up for takeoff when an army Bird Dog ground looped then flipped on its back on the runway in the thirty-knot cross wind. No one was hurt. The pilot scurried out of the wreckage and surveyed the upside-down airplane with hands on hips. That accident should have been suf-

ficient warning to be extra careful on take-off and landing
that day. But it wasn't.

My copilot, a short, skinny warrant officer named Costello, was a senior peter pilot who had survived three helicopter crashes to date in Vietnam. He was cool, quiet,
and cynical.

I began my approach to the ridge line where the C&C
aircraft instructed us to insert the five marine troops. Because of the high winds whistling over the mountain I
should have made a steeper-than-normal approach to avoid
the severe down draft on the lee side of the mountain.
Instead, I made my standard low, flat approach. On short
final the gusting down draft hit the machine with a loud
Woooosh! It was as if I had flown into an invisible claw
that gripped the machine and tried to pull it down into the
jungle below. I instinctively pulled in the collective pitch
lever to check our alarming rate of descent. The engine
could not deliver the power to fly us out of the strong down
draft. The rotor RPM began to decay. Usually it is in the
green at 6600 engine RPM. The low RPM audio wailed
in our ears. The nose of the aircraft began to yaw to the
right even with the full left pedal pushed in. The pedal hit
the stop. That is when I lost total yaw control and the nose
of the craft turned right ninety degrees to our approach
path. The RPM gauge read 5500, well below the flight
range. Costello, thinking this was going to be crash number four, coolly reached over and switched off the low
RPM audio, and waited for impact.

One hears of aircraft commanders so composed during
emergencies that, as they are about to crash, they manage
to keep their voice calm and unruffled even as they broadcast their mayday call. I hoped I would be able to cope in
a similar way, but as it turned out this was far from the
case. I keyed the mike switch and broadcast to God and
everybody in support of the mission, and that included two
marine gunships, the second Huey carrying the remainder
of the team, two army ARA Cobra gunships, and two
F-100s at fifteen thousand feet. I yelled as I watched the
ridge line rush at us sideways, ''Jesus Christ, Jesus Christ,
Shit! Shit! Shit!'' before the skids of the Huey hit the floor
of the LZ side on.

I will never know how I managed, after performing a semi-autorotation to the LZ, to miss the surrounding trees, drop off the troops, "milk" the engine RPM back to 6600, and get out without further incident. Although I was elated to have avoided crashing, I felt like a fool.

For my comic outburst on the radio that day I had to buy all the rounds in the Quang Tri officers' club that night. If I was asked once, I was asked fifty times, "Hey . . . aren't you the guy who broadcast 'Jesus Christ, Jesus Christ, Shit! Shit! Shit!' on the radio today?" I just nodded trying to act as humble as I could and bought the man a drink. I took the ribbing without comment. I was just thankful we hadn't crashed. Again, I'd been reminded not to let my guard down. I'd been lucky and had walked away from my mistake. I knew of other men who had not been so lucky. Douche Bag Dick Childs was one of those men.

The CO had seen the golden opportunity to get rid of First Lieutenant Dick Childs during the swap in personnel with the 158th. Childs had proved to be a lousy Huey pilot and the Blackwidows were glad to be rid of him. We learned several weeks later that he didn't want to be with the 158th, and after a week the 158th discovered they did not want him, so he requested and got transferred to Delta Company, the gun platoon.

One clear day in June, when all the other pilots in Charlie Company were flying, a sleek Cobra gunship landed unannounced in the Widow Web. The pilot who climbed out of the machine was Douche Bag Dick Childs. He sauntered into my hootch. It was one of the few days I was not flying. I was grounded with a mandatory day off because I had flown more than 120 hours in the preceding thirty-day period. He greeted me like a long lost brother, and I offered him a soft drink. Ernest James had seen the Cobra land and rushed over from ops to join us.

Ernest asked Douche Bag to tell him about the action he had seen so far, so we heard how he got shot down during the assault on Hamburger Hill. He'd had to make a forced landing to a hillside. The Cobra had rolled down the hill and was a total write off. He and the copilot were pulled out by a ship from Alpha Company. He told several more war stories, and he finally announced that he had to be leaving.

I was glad to hear it. He made me uncomfortable. He was a poor pilot and full of bullshit. A deadly combination. A lot of pilots I met were full of bullshit. The trouble with Douche Bag is that he *believed* his bullshit. Safe pilots knew where the bullshit ended and reality began. That was the difference.

Before he left the hootch he turned and pointed with his thumb, "Either one of you two want to go for a ride in that Cobra I got parked out there?"

The thought frightened me. "No thanks."

Ernest nearly fell over himself in his enthusiasm. "Hell yes, Dick. Goddamn, I'd love to."

"Come on then, Ernest. I'll show you how the gunnies do it." He winked at me. "Beats the hell out of flying slicks."

I resented his remark and his pompous air but said nothing. Good natured competition between gunship pilots and slick pilots had always existed. But it rubbed me the wrong way knowing the kind of pilot Douche Bag Dick Childs was.

He said, "Should have Ernest back in a half hour."

"You do that," I replied like an overprotective parent.

Leaning against the sandbags surrounding my hootch wearing green boxer shorts, green T-shirt, and shower shoes, I watched the sleek machine nose over and take off from the Widow Web. Ernest waved at me from the front seat. Childs sat behind him in the narrow, two-pilot machine. The nose pulled back abruptly and the helicopter rocketed upward in a maximum performance climb to about fifteen hundred feet, banked, and headed toward the coast.

I walked back to my area and lay on my bunk under the hot breeze of my fan and waited. An hour passed. They did not return. An hour and a half passed. Still no sign of them. I walked over to ops and told Spec-4 Peoples I was worried. He picked up the mike of the FM radio and put out a call. Nothing.

After nearly two hours and still no Ernest, Captain

Crunch called headquarters at Camp Eagle. We found out a Cobra gunship had been seen swooping through the sky over the coast near Vinh Loc. Headquarters was trying to figure out who it belonged to.

According to the eyewitness report the Cobra dove, doing about 190 knots, then pulled straight up, losing airspeed, and at the top of the climb did a hammer-head turn. The witness to the accident, an LOH (light observation helicopter) pilot from Division Arty out of Camp Eagle, said that the pilot blew the maneuver because he caused negative Gs on the rotor head. The rotor system became unstable causing its hub to slam against the mast which then snapped off and separated from the aircraft. The LOH pilot said they were at 1500 feet when the rotors went one way and the aircraft nosed over and fell to earth. Douche Bag Dick Childs and Ernest James died instantly when the rotorless Cobra airframe slammed into a rice paddy at more than 200 knots and exploded on impact.

Numbed by the tragic news, I walked back to my hootch and, although it was only midafternoon, I poured a double vodka and threw it down, following it immediately with another. I flopped down on my bunk and played Ernest's favorite song, "Love Is Blue," on my reel-to-reel. My mind and body were torn by the opposite emotions of extreme anger and deep sadness. I wanted to punch my fist through something, to scream out that it wasn't fair. Thoughts of Ernest's contagiously happy personality and his enthusiasm for combat flying filled my mind. His senseless death sickened me. If Dick Childs hadn't died in the accident I thought I would have rung his fucking neck. But that wouldn't bring Ernest back.

I played "Love Is Blue" one more time and, when it came to the part where the violins reached their crescendo, Ernest's favorite part in the piece, I began to cry. I cried for the selfish reason that I would deeply miss the smiling, baby-faced captain, and I cried at the knowledge that his death had been so completely futile.

CHAPTER 11

July 1969

Miniskirts, Flares, and a General Court-Martial

On 2 July 1969 I celebrated my twenty-third birthday. On that day I received one of the most memorable surprises of my life. The occasion is well documented in the letter I sent home six days later.

8 July 1969

Dear Mom:

Sorry I haven't written for a while, but I have really been flying a lot lately. I have been receiving all your letters though. Thanks for the birthday goodies. Let me tell you what happened on my birthday. You won't believe it. I don't believe it and it happened to me!

The captain responsible for scheduling the missions knew that July 2nd was my birthday so he gave me July 2nd and 3rd off. The 2nd for my birthday and the 3rd to <u>recuperate</u> from my birthday. On or around June 28th the commanding officer gave us permission to remodel our hootches if we wished. The words were barely out of his mouth before we had built a bar and sitting room in our hootch. We installed a small refrigerator behind the bar and we were ready to go. On July 1st I took a hop to Da Nang for a booze run and by the 2nd I was ready for a party. But the best is still to come.

I was walking by the front of my hootch when Joe Sulak stuck his head out the door and told me to come in because there was a birthday gift waiting for me. When I walked through the door, Joe stepped back and from behind him this blonde woman dressed in jungle fatigues was coming at me with arms spread and lips puckered. She grabbed me and planted one of the biggest kisses on me I've ever had, then she wished me a happy birthday. Where did she come from, you ask? About two months ago the CO flew her down from Saigon to do a story on the Blackwidows. She is a Dutch reporter traveling around Vietnam giving the people in Holland the scoop on what's happening over here. As it turns out, she thought the CO was sort of a clod so during her stay she used to end up in our hootch talking to Joe Sulak, Ned Kelly, and me. I remember asking her to come to my birthday party and she said she would try to make it. I had forgotten about her promise, but, sure enough, she flew up from Saigon to be here for my birthday party. You could have knocked me over with a feather. Her name is Henny Schrode. She's a beautiful girl with an accent that melts my heart every time I hear it. She knows seven languages too.

To continue. The CO was away doing business at Camp Eagle so ops gave me an aircraft and I flew us to the beach. This particular beach is like an in-country r&r center for the troops of the 101st. She and I stayed there all day. I knew some of the Sea Bees stationed there and one of them let me use his surfboard. So Henny and I went surfing in the Gulf of Tonkin. We had to walk far down the beach because you can imagine what a blonde in a bikini in Vietnam would do to the other guys here. I was the envy of everyone.

After a full day at the beach we got dressed, me in my Nomex flight suit and she in her form-fitting jungle fatigues, and we got in the helicopter and I flew us back to base. Practically every guy in the company greeted us as we landed and escorted us to my hootch where we freshened up and changed for the party. Henny emerged wearing a bright pink miniskirt, and I mean miniskirt. I about passed out every time I looked at her beautiful, strong, tan legs. It was much too much for me. The party broke up around 0230. Every guy stayed to the end even though most had a 0430 crank time that morning. It was a dream. Great party, stereo going full blast, beautiful girl, good friends, sunburned from a day of surfing at the beach and knowing I didn't have to fly the next day. The experience made me homesick. Only three months and I'll be home. I can't wait.

Love, Randy.

In my letters I made no mention of an incident that took place just after my birthday, on the Fourth of July to be exact. It served to make my remaining three months in Vietnam miserable and nearly ruined my career as an officer in the United States Army.

Apparently it had become the custom in Vietnam to celebrate the Fourth of July with flares, gunfire, and cannon fire. The CO called the company together and gave specific orders for no one to celebrate this year in such a visible manner. He informed us that intelligence reports indicated the enemy might be waiting for such an opportunity to strike. So I played poker in my hootch with three other pilots and proceeded to get drunk on whiskey and Coca Cola.

At 2230 Captain Buck Phillips entered our hootch and said, "OK, everyone out. There's a company formation."

I checked my watch, pulled the cigar from my mouth and said, "At 2230?"

"Get out there, Mains!" he barked.

His hostile attitude confused me. Why was he so uptight? I left the hootch with the others and joined the rest of the company personnel assembling outside the orderly room. I was a lot drunker than I'd thought. I'd had perhaps four, maybe five, strong whiskey and Cokes and had trouble walking. I puffed on my cigar and milled around the crowd of men looking for members of my platoon so I could join them in the formation.

·Another captain, who had been sent to Charlie Company from the 158th, Captain Pratt, walked up to me, stood nose to nose and screamed in my face, "Get over there, Mains."

I looked in the direction he was pointing and looked back at him stupidly.

"Move!" he screamed.

In my drunken state I took a deep puff on my cigar and blew the smoke out slowly into the man's face. It was dark, but I could see the burning rage in his eyes. I turned and walked away from him and took my place in the formation next to Joe.

The CO, Major Torq, standing in front of the assembled men with Captain Phillips to his right and Captain Pratt standing to his left, announced, "Someone here disobeyed my direct order tonight and set off a flare. I have called this formation to find out who that someone was?"

No one spoke. I stood weaving from the effects of the alcohol and took another puff on my cigar tying to focus on the outline of the man standing in front of me.

The CO continued, "I have a pretty good idea who it was, but I want to hear it from the man himself."

Again silence. A few men coughed. No one spoke.

Anger charged his voice. "The man will wish he'd never disobeyed my orders. I'll find out who it is. When I do he'll wish he'd never been assigned to my command." He turned to Captain Pratt. "Dismiss the men."

Back at my hootch the four of us resumed the poker game. As the first hand was being dealt a corporal from the orderly room came in and said, "Sir, old man wants to see you."

"What for?"

"He just said he wants to see you. Don't know why."

I looked at the other three men seated at the table, shrugged and left with the corporal. I was so affected by the alcohol I nearly stumbled climbing up the three wooden steps leading into the CO's hootch. I knocked on the door and was given permission to enter. Buck Phillips and Captain Pratt were standing behind the desk of a seated Major Torq. The three men looked far from happy. I approached the desk, snapped to drunken attention and slurred, "Sir, Candidate Mains reporting as ordered, sir." I was by now so drunk I replied as if still in flight school.

Before I could correct myself Major Torq said, "Just sit down, Mains."

I took a chair facing his desk. He leaned forward with hands clasped tightly together on top of the desk. His eyes narrowed. "I know it was you. You're the one who shot off the flare tonight, aren't you?"

His accusation served to sober me up a bit. "No, sir."

"It's no use denying it, Mains. I have a witness who says he saw you shoot off the flare on the perimeter tonight and that goes directly against division orders."

Buck Phillips, his arms crossed across his chest, smirked with satisfaction behind the Major. I tried to focus my hazy vision on Torq. "But . . . I was playing cards with three guys in the hootch tonight. I never left them. I've got witnesses."

Major Torq slammed his hand on the desk. "I don't care if you say you've got witnesses, Mains. I have a witness that says you were the one who did it." He now pointed a finger at my face. "I'm going to court-martial you, Mains. I'm going to make an example out of you. And if I can, I'm going to drum you out of the United States Army."

My brain swirled with alcohol-clouded thoughts. Why was he doing this? Why was he out to get me? Was it because of Henny? Because I took his girl? Surely not.

Torq continued, "And you owe Captain Pratt here an apology."

"Apology?"

Torq leaned forward in his chair, "You seem to have no respect for superior officers do you, Mains. You call them by their first name . . . ,"

I glanced at Captain Phillips. He still had the same smirk on his face.

Torq continued, ". . . and you blew cigar smoke in Captain Pratt's face during the formation tonight in flagrant disregard of his rank. Now I want you to apologize."

I looked up at the man, trying to focus on his face. "I'm sorry . . . I blew smoke . . . in your face . . . sir." I felt like an idiot. What I really wanted to do was tell all three miserable, rear echelon sons of bitches to go somewhere and fuck themselves. I couldn't believe this was happening. It had to be some sort of nightmare. Here I was, risking my life, flying my rear-end off in a combat zone. Hell, I could be killed on a mission tomorrow, and here were these three FNG clowns making me apologize for getting drunk on the Fourth of July, of all days, and for blowing a little smoke? In my drunken state I wanted to leap to my feet, rip the wings from my chest, and make a rude gesture before turning on my heels and storming out. I wanted to tell them to fly eight or ten hours a day themselves while I stayed back in the rear sitting on my butt to deal with their trivial bureaucratic BS for a change. Why didn't they go off and get shot at! But of course I remained silent. It was one of the rare occasions in my life when, thoroughly provoked, I kept my mouth shut.

Major Torq filed charges against me. My army records were flagged, frozen in limbo, until the matter was settled. The worst news was that I was grounded.

I was flown to HQ at Camp Eagle two days later to meet with the Judge Adjutant. He advised me that if I had, in fact, been in the company of my friends that night that I should obtain statements in triplicate from each man. So I did. There had been two others in the hootch that night and they also wrote out sworn statements to the effect that I had not been absent during the time in question. I took the five statements to Camp Eagle.

A colonel there saw the handful of evidence supporting my case and told me, "Now son, we all have friends. You know, and I know, that friends will do a lot for us when the chips are down. I suggest you submit only three of those statements. That'll be enough."

The most painful part of the ordeal was being grounded. I hung around the company area like a bird with clipped wings, feeling as useless as the maintenance officers who never flew outside of autorotative distance from the Widow Web. They were the only pilots I saw during the day and I made every effort to avoid them. As each day passed my self-esteem slipped another notch until I felt even less significant than they. At least they were flying.

The other pilots sympathized with my position, but that didn't make things any easier. I felt like a leper, an outcast. I felt like a freeloader not pulling my weight. I now knew the agony Ernest James must have felt watching all the crews take off on their combat missions to return hot, sweaty, and tired with their war stories from a full day's flying.

I would lie in my bunk at night frustrated and angry, fantasizing about taking the unregistered .45 I'd acquired from the marine lieutenant in Quang Tri and sneaking into Major Torq's hootch, placing the barrel against his temple and whispering into his ear, "Quit fucking with me, Torq, you understand? Just drop the bullshit charges you've fabricated against me, let me go back to flying, and I won't pull this trigger and blow your miserable fucking brains out." I replayed the scene over and over in my mind while I waited. This insane fantasy gave me some perverse sort of satisfaction.

One day while I sat in my hootch writing letters home a captain from Second Platoon came in to talk to me. He was a nice guy named Eric Farlow. I'm not quite certain why he came to talk to me but I suspect Major Torq probably sent him. Farlow told me he sympathized with my unfortunate situation.

"There are some people that are just not cut out to be in the military, Randy," he told me in apparent sincerity. "I'm afraid you are one of those people. You are what we call 'route step' " (that is to say, I marched at my own step, out of time with everyone else). He continued, "I sense, although by all reports you are a highly competent and respected pilot, that you do as you please when on the ground, that you have difficulty accepting authority. The army is the wrong place to have an attitude like that."

"Yes, sir, I agree with you."

"You do?"

"Yes. I admit I have difficulty accepting authority when I have no respect for the person behind the rank. Buck Phillips and Captain Pratt are two good examples. A man has to prove his worth to me. He has to earn it. They're two sorry excuses for captains in my book. And I'm not alone when I say that."

He looked at the plywood floor, shook his head and let out a small laugh. "It's that attitude of yours that's got you into the trouble you're in now. And I can promise you it'll continue to get you into trouble until you either change it or you get out."

I chuckled, "I doubt if my attitude will change, sir. It's the flying I really care about in the army. And flying's taught me that it's your performance that talks and the bullshit that walks. Flying does an excellent job of separating the bullshit from the bullshitter. What I've learned is that the BS may work in a command on the ground but that same kind of thinking will get you killed in the air. Douche Bag Dick Childs was a perfect example of what I'm talking about."

"Yes, you're probably right, but while on the ground we have to learn to 'play the game' in order to survive. You, unfortunately, do not play the game."

And he was right. I could not play the game. In my mind it was hypocritical. Childish. And by sticking to this moral ground my remaining time in the army would be as a swimmer fighting against the tide. And like that swimmer I would eventually become exhausted and give up, or hope I could hold out until the tide turned in my favor.

The days of waiting for a court date dragged on forever; each day seemed longer and hotter than the next. I remember lying on my bunk under my fan listening to AM radio on 20 July 1969 and hearing the news that we had landed a man on the moon. The irony of that feat overwhelmed me at the time. The twenty-five billion dollars spent to accomplish Neil Armstrong's "one giant leap for mankind" was being hailed as the greatest technological mobilization the world had known. Yet here on earth we could not sort out the problems embroiling me and half a million other Americans in war. OK, we'd won the space race. So what? We had broadened our horizons when we couldn't even control the frontiers here on earth. It was laughable. I wondered what were the military ramifications of such an endeavor. I was now cynical enough to believe that the *real* purpose behind landing a man on the moon had some far greater tactical meaning than the self-righteous reason given by the United States. Okay, we had proven that America was the leader in the space race. But as far as I could see we were still falling behind in a primitive war that was losing popularity each day it was being fought.

In my growing depression I was convinced mankind had gone totally mad.

I had been grounded for a full three weeks before Major Torq finally called me into his hootch to give me the verdict.

He thumbed through the file in front of him then closed it and folded his hands. He looked angry. "I'm afraid we don't have enough evidence on you to prosecute on the flare incident, Mains. However I am pressing for non-judicial punishment under the UCMJ (Uniform Code of Military Justice). I am issuing you with an Article-15 for insubordination to a superior officer because you blew cigar smoke into the face of Captain Pratt."

I was actually relieved at the news. "When can I go back to flying, sir?"

"Immediately."

I could not help smiling. I think my obvious enthusiasm must have taken him by surprise. "Is that all then, sir?"

"Yes, that'll be all. You're dismissed."

I stood, snapped to attention, saluted, and turned to walk out. Then I stopped, turned back around, and asked, "Sir, may I ask you a question?"

"You may."

"Exactly what is it I've done that gives me the feeling that you have it in for me, sir?"

His face revealed his astonishment at my forward question. "I don't 'have it in for you,' Mains. I simply detest your kind."

"My kind, sir? What do you mean?"

"Most of you warrants have no military bearing whatsoever. You're a mockery to the United States Army. I sense that you personally do not respect authority and I think, as an individual, you are highly irresponsible."

"Irresponsible, sir?" I laughed. "Irresponsible? I've flown more than eight hundred combat hours over here and I've managed to bring Uncle Sam's property back day after day. No one's been killed on my ship, sir. Not even scratched. I've risked my life and the lives of my crew to accomplish the missions I've had to fly over here. And you say I'm irresponsible?"

"I'm talking about the childish flare incident in the movie theater last month."

"I see. And that makes me irresponsible? You naturally figured that if I shot off the flare in the movie theatre I was surely the one who did it on the Fourth of July. Is that it, sir?"

"I don't need to explain myself to you, Mr. Mains. Consider yourself damn lucky you got off as lightly as you did. I'll give you fair warning now. I'll be watching every move you make from here on in. If you screw up the least little bit, and don't play the game, or you make one minor military infraction," he held out his hand and closed it into a tight fist. "I'll have you. Remember that. Now, dismissed."

I flew my first flight, after being grounded for three weeks, with Buck Phillips as my copilot. I did not mind because although I had zero respect for him as an officer and as a leader of men, I was elated to be flying again.

We flew for nearly eight hours for the marines out of LZ Vandergrift. At one stage in the mission we picked up eight troops in the field. As it happened, when I lifted the aircraft up to a hover I had to push in full left pedal to stop us from spinning to the right. The pedal hit the stops and we began to turn to the right anyway. I snapped off the throttle to stop the turn and did a hovering autorotation to the ground. I asked the crew chief to off-load three troops, and we took off without further incident.

At the end of the day back at the Widow Web, as we were walking to the company area, Buck Phillips told me that he had been checking me out all along. If he had seen me do anything unsafe on the mission he had been instructed by Major Torq to take away my AC orders rendering me a permanent copilot. He went on to inform me that he'd been impressed by my flying ability and that I had passed and that I could continue to exercise my rights as aircraft commander. I was infuriated. What gave him the right to check me out? He was neither an instructor pilot nor an aircraft commander. He had less than fifty hours of combat time in country and he was checking me out? There was no one to whom I could complain as he was under orders from the CO. Phillips even had the audacity to imply I should be thankful he was not rescinding my AC orders. His presumptuousness not only enraged me but also the other pilots in the platoon when they heard what had happened.

Several days later Major Torq appointed Captain Buck Phillips our platoon leader. A week later Phillips made himself an aircraft commander against the protests of the other ACs in the platoon. That act would be his final undoing.

For his first flight as an aircraft commander Phillips assigned himself the brand new H-model Huey that Junior and Captain Paulson had flown up from Cam Ranh Bay. That fact, in itself, made a lot of the other ACs in the company angry. It was customary for a new aircraft to be assigned to one of the senior ACs.

When Phillips picked the brand new aircraft up to a hover he overcontrolled the tail rotor pedals and smashed both of the aircraft's synchronized elevators into the steel walls of the revetment. He landed, shut down, and the aircraft was then out of service for a week for repairs.

The arrival the week before of that same new aircraft was an event that itself caused a shroud of mystery to fall over Charlie Company that would remain unsolved for several days. The mystery began when Junior and Captain Paulson landed in the Widow Web in the brand new machine. It was in perfect condition except for one small thing. There was an unexplained bullet hole in the tail boom. Junior and Captain Paulson seemed as surprised to see it as we were.

Ned Kelly cornered Junior in the club that night and asked, "How did you guys manage to take a hit on a routine ferry flight, anyway?"

Junior and Paulson looked at one another and feigned ignorance. "Don't know," Junior said innocently. "Must have been when we were flying over the jungle."

Kelly eyed Junior suspiciously. "Yeah, but you were flying coastal to I Corps and, knowing you two like I do, you had to be flying so damn high to avoid getting shot at you probably needed oxygen. So, how'd you manage to take a hit?"

Junior seemed nervous. He chugged half his beer before answering, "I told you, Kelly, I don't know. It was just there."

"You mean it just suddenly appeared? When'd you notice it?" Kelly asked unwilling to let up. Most of the officers in the club were now listening to the interrogation.

Junior looked at Captain Paulson who looked away from him quickly and sipped at his own beer. "I don't know," Junior whined. "I didn't notice it till we landed back here."

"You were on a three-day ferry flight and you didn't notice it till you got back here? You two are maintenance officers. Didn't you see it on one of your daily preflights?"

"Nope."

"And you mean to tell me you didn't hear the bullet hit your ship?"

Paulson butted in, "He told you, Kelly, he doesn't know when it happened. We didn't hear anything. We landed here and that's when we saw it. The round didn't hit anything vital. It's repaired. Why can't you just drop the subject?"

Kelly eyed Junior and Paulson for a moment, then he said, "Because it intrigues me. I think you two know something and you're not telling us. I think you're covering up something, and I want to know what it is. Your story's too flaky. Now tell us. We're all friends here. What happened?"

Some of the men now listening joined in, "Yeah, come on. Tell us what happened."

"Drop it, Kelly. Nothing happened. We just took a hit. That's all. Hell, it could have happened when we took off from Bien Hoa after refueling for all we know. Who the hell knows? Just drop it, OK?"

Kelly smiled, took a drag from his cigarette and squished the butt in an ashtray on the bar. "I'll find out. Don't you worry. You guys are hiding something and I'll get to the bottom of it—Flowers!"

The bartender rushed over. "Yes, sir."

"Set up a couple of Blushing Assholes. One apiece for my two friends here."

Flowers beamed, "Yes, sir!"

"We gotta get going," Junior said. "We can't stay. Really. We have test flights to fly tonight. We can't hang around and get bombed."

"We'll let you guys go when we hear the story."

And a good one it turned out to be. Though they protested long and hard we would not let them out of the club until we had heard it. Paulson and Junior had met some nurses in the officer's club in Da Nang and Junior had promised one of them a ride in the helicopter. The next day Paulson and Junior landed the showroom-new H-model Huey on the beach. Junior placed the giggly nurse in the copilot's seat, put a flight helmet on her, and was standing on the skid leaning over adjusting her seat belt when they began taking enemy fire. Captain Paulson, taking full stock of the situation, panicked and yanked in a handful of collective pitch. The light machine rocketed upward as if fired from a cannon. Junior was still standing on the skid and had a death grip around the now screaming nurse. His feet were slipping off the skid and he literally held on for his life. The copilot's open door was flapping wildly in the breeze and slamming him in the ass as they passed through five hundred feet. Just envisioning the incident had us rolling on the plywood floor of the club with uncontrollable laughter. The operation was thereafter known as the "Combat Assault on Heartbreak Beach." Paulson and Junior had to buy the rounds in the club all night long and never made it out to fly their maintenance test flights.

One of the combat yarns I had heard in flight school was the story of the helicopter pilot who landed in an LZ and looked up to see he was staring down the barrel of the enemy's submachine gun. Having, by then, flown in Vietnam for nearly nine months, I could not imagine being able to sneak up on anyone, much less the enemy, considering the loud racket a Huey made. So I discounted that story as implausible, that is, until it happened to me.

I had picked up a super grunt team out of Quang Tri and was to insert them a klick north of Khe Sahn. The marine super grunts looked like a gang of thugs. None of them carried the same type of weapon. They even dressed differently. Some wore sleeveless fatigue shirts, others were bare-chested. A few wore green headbands, while others had camouflaged faces and bandoleers of ammunition crisscrossing their chests.

The landing zone was located in a clear area on a ridge line. There were few trees. Most had been bombed out over the years. It was covered mainly by tall elephant grass. I was hovering the machine over the grass, just about ready to land, looking through the chin bubble between my pedals to set the aircraft down. A thick, sweaty arm suddenly appeared next to my helmet, the finger of the hand pointing out the windshield in front of me. I looked up as the inside of the chopper exploded in gunfire. Two startled Vietnamese had stood up, and one was aiming an AK-47 at my face from fifty yards away. I froze, feeling the pressure of the invisible bull's eye between my eyes. I watched as both men were hit with a solid curtain of gunfire from our ship and were thrown backwards. I yanked in the power, pulling aft on the cyclic stick. The machine rose and leapt into the air backwards from the grassy knoll, the nose pointed to the sky, the tail toward the jungle. I continued to accelerate backwards, then kicked in right pedal turning 180 degrees and flew down the mountain slope to safety.

23 July

Hi Mom:

I received a letter from Michelle today telling me she is attending summer college in Guadalajara, Mexico. She says she is really enjoying staying with a Mexican family there. She is with three other girls. I think it does a person good to see how people in other lands live so you can appreciate how good we really have it in the USA. I know I'll never look at the U.S. the same way again. It's the best place to be in the world.

We had an awards and decorations ceremony and the battalion commander gave out some medals. I got the

Army Commendation Medal and an air medal. Not much else.

Keep writing,

Randy.

For months Captain Curly had been trying to persuade the head nurse at the hospital at Phu Bai to come to Charlie Company for a cocktail party. When he finally succeeded in convincing her to attend, he decided the best place to have the party was in our mess hall.

Ten nurses showed up. It was a very stilted affair at first. It reminded me of my awkward days attending high school dances. We tried to make polite conversation without incorporating our usual four-letter words and Captain Curly tried to persuade the women to drink the lethal punch, a sweet variation of Spec-4 Flowers's Blushing Asshole concoction. But the women were savvy to such devious tactics and sipped weak wine and soda instead, leaving the deadly punch for the officers.

Things deteriorated as the night wore on and the level in the punch bowl receded to reveal soggy and discolored fruit lying at the bottom. To liven up the party Captain Curly thought it would be good fun to drop his pants and moon several of the nurses, offering the horrified ladies a full view of his dangling genitalia. Then someone broke not one, but two, raw eggs over Captain Curly's bald head for being uncouth in the presence of ladies. Another officer was found in a ditch outside the mess hall suffering from alcohol poisoning. Another had a piece of his front tooth knocked out by a half-empty beer can which had been hurled at him for following Captain Curly's example of mooning the nurses. The women stormed off enraged. Luckily for them they departed before the food fight began.

The next day Captain Curly received a short, scribbled note from the head nurse thanking, in her words, "the assholes of Charlie Company for a perfectly horrific evening," and added, "in the future do not ever attempt to invite the nurses back again."

CHAPTER 12

August 1969

Poetic Karma Strikes the Brass

3 August 1969

Hi Mom:

I've been receiving your letters regularly, but to be honest I just can't think of anything interesting to write about.

It's hot here now and it feels good when I fly because I can climb to three thousand or four thousand feet and cool off.

I bet things are beautiful in southern California right now. The beaches, beautiful girls, and you're in the height of summer. I miss it.

I sure enjoy your letters. I do receive every one even though it seems like I don't by the way I don't answer each one. Please keep them coming.

Love, Randy

I still bore a lot of resentment toward Major Torq, Buck Phillips, and Captain Pratt for needlessly making my life so difficult. As if following some grand scheme to balance right and wrong in the universe, Karma took over and each man in turn seemed to receive his just reward. Captain Buck Phillips was the first to receive his.

Captain Phillips flew for only one week as AC in the new H-model Huey after it came out of maintenance. On a combat assault we had near LZ Vegel he decided to fly flight lead. It would be the last time he would fly.

After the three-hour CA to insert the grunts, we were flying back to the Widow Web in a flight of ten. Buck Phillips elected to break formation and buzz a Vietnamese village. He performed a wing over and dove at one of the homes he had singled out from the rest. The house was made of bamboo and scraps of wood and was covered with a corrugated tin roof. When he pulled out of the dive he did not lead the maneuver with forward cyclic, but instead pulled in collective pitch. When he noticed the rate of descent was too great to stop, he flared the aircraft. The new machine fell through the flare and the newly repaired tail boom smashed into the fragile Vietnamese home. The force of the tail boom slamming into the hootch caused the small dwelling to explode into bits of kindling. A large chunk of wood became a deadly missile striking and killing a small Vietnamese boy running away in fear of the diving helicopter.

Instead of landing immediately, Phillips flew the damaged aircraft back to the company area. The maintenance personnel found that three of the four bolts holding the tail boom onto the main fuselage had been sheered off by the force of striking the house. Phillips had been lucky he got the machine back without crashing.

Buck Phillips was immediately stripped of his command, court-martialed, and subsequently sent back to the states. It was later rumored he had been seen at the primary flight-training facility at Fort Wolters in Mineral Wells, Texas. He had been stripped of his wings and assigned to the supply depot where he was issuing flight suits to the new warrant officer candidates. It was also rumored that an allotment was being deducted from his paycheck each month to pay for the damage he had caused to the new aircraft.

Major Torq had his own problems. A general from Division Headquarters landed in the Widow Web the first week in August and performed a surprise inspection of the company. After the inspection the general told Major Torq that he had never seen a company in such an administrative shambles, and if Torq did not want to be stripped of his command he had better shape it up in two weeks, or else.

Another inspection was carried out at the end of the two-week period and Major Torq passed, but only barely. For the rest of the time I was in Charlie Company, Major Torq lived in fear of another surprise inspection. His new worry seemed to take the heat off me.

Although Captain Pratt was a rated aviator he was primarily an infantry officer. For some reason headquarters at Camp Eagle sent him orders assigning him to command the tiny TOC, Tactical Operations Center, on the most remote piece of real estate the 101st owned. It was a tiny, 6500-foot hilltop named Eagle's Nest overlooking the A-Shau valley. He was to command a five-man listening post during the long and wet monsoon season. He was given one week to pack his belongings and ship out.

It seemed to me that all three had received their just reward for having made my life so miserable and that if perhaps they had not tried to make my life so unpleasant some great deity upstairs would not have punished them. I did have some lingering compassion for each man's plight, but nonetheless, I walked around the company area for several days with a smug grin on my face.

Because the monsoon was bearing down on us quickly we began a large operation to evacuate the troops from the A-Shau before the rains began that would make resupplying them nearly impossible. This was a time of endless eight- and ten-hour days in the cockpit. Each day seemed like the previous. I ate, flew, drank a few beers at night, then collapsed into bed to do the same the next day.

26 August 1969

Dear Mom:

I borrowed a Super 8mm movie camera from a friend the other day and bought five rolls of movie film from the PX. We had a mission to support the marines up at Quang Tri so I shot a movie of our mission to send home

*to you. It will show a segment of a day in the life of a
helicopter pilot over here. I sent it off to be processed
so when you receive it you'll know what it is. Please
don't peek! I will edit them into a movie and will show
it to you when I get home.*

*I flew 140 hours in a thirty-day period so I have been
grounded for three days. That's company policy to avoid
excessive pilot fatigue. It feels good to have the time off.
Maybe I'll go to Da Nang tomorrow.*

*The guys that were scheduled to go home in Septem-
ber got a ten-day drop. I don't know why they got the
drop they just did. Maybe the same will happen to me.*

*I haven't received my orders for my next duty station
yet. Should be coming up soon.*

*The weather has been extremely hot with many 110-
degree days. Sounds as if you guys are having a good
summer. Hope Andrea still enjoys her swimming les-
sons. She must be getting good.*

*I received a letter from Michelle and she's back home
from summer college in Guadalajara. She said she had
a good time.*

*Coming home is all I think about now. Our company
policy is to stop flying fifteen days before deros (date
estimate return from overseas). I don't know why I threw
that in. It just came to me.*

*Not much happening. Our company has stopped flying
for one of our divisions and is flying near Quang Tri for
the Marines and the Special Forces. The missions are a
lot more fun.*

*Mom, Happy Birthday. I'll take you out for a belated
birthday dinner when I get home. Fifty days to go. I'm
a two-digit midget!*

Love, Randy

It was in August that I received a letter from my sister,
Nancy. She wrote to tell me that Mom had had a nervous
breakdown. The stress of my being in Vietnam and the
waiting day after day for the mailman to bring her news
of whether I was alive or dead finally got the better of her
until she simply succumbed. Nancy told me the doctors

thought she would be out of the hospital in time to see me when I arrived home.

I had realized the day I medevaced my first dead soldier that the casualties of war are not confined to the battlefield. I wondered how many other mothers, fathers, or family members of the men over here were suffering the invisible wounds inflicted by this unpopular war? Receiving that letter from Nancy shortly after the flare incident was the last straw. I could not wait to get out of it. I'd had enough. I was finished. It was someone else's turn.

I remember scanning my face in the shaving mirror hanging on its nail over the crude plywood table I had built in my area. It was drawn and soaked with perspiration. I no longer had the youthful, naive college-boy sparkle in my blue eyes. They looked back at me with an intensity that frightened me. There was a maturity, a knowing gaze in the reflection. They were short timer's eyes. I was definitely not an FNG any more. All the old guys were now gone. Ned Kelly, Dan Crawford, Bob Coulshaw, Wishy-Washy Bernie Nivens, Les Ramson, Jeff Leach, Douglas Julian Carson—they had all done their year and gone back to The World. I was now the old guy.

I lived daily by my wits and my skills as a combat helicopter pilot. By now I had flown more than nine hundred combat hours. I had made life-and-death decisions on a daily basis as easily as a similar young man my age back in The World would decide what color socks to wear with his suit, or what time to pick up his girl to take her on a date. I looked at myself and felt old before my time. But, paradoxically, inside I felt charged and more alive than I had ever felt before. The lifestyle over here affected me like a strong drug. I thrived on it. I was hooked, addicted.

I would admit it only to myself, no one else, that I was good at what I did. A pilot over here had to have a certain conceited, self-centered attitude or he would never climb in the cockpit and take the machine aloft in such hostile conditions. Nothing I've achieved in my life since has been as rewarding as the knowledge that I had done it—flown combat and come out of it alive. But I could not let myself be swept away by it all. I still had forty-five days left to serve. A lot could happen in forty-five days. A lot could happen on your last day of flying. That could be the day the bullet with your name on it finds its mark between your eyes. No, it would not be over, really over, until I stepped off the plane in San Francisco. Then I could afford to drop my guard and then, and only then, could I pat myself on the back and say, "You've made it."

I woke up, I flew, I went to bed. Day after day it was the same. I felt like I was strapping on a Huey in the morning, like an article of clothing, and unstrapping it after an eight- or ten-hour flying day. All the ACs were dragging. With such monotony quite small things in our lives would keep our spirits up, like the night we told an FNG pilot to sleep in Stony Rutherford's bunk when Rutherford was on R&R.

After evening chow Tom Shonehour led the new guy down the hall to Rutherford's area. It was across a small hallway from mine.

"Afraid it's the only place we have for you to sleep," Tom said apologetically. "I'm really sorry about that."

The new guy was short, about Joe's height. He was thin too and had a high, squeaky voice. "No need to be sorry. This'll do just fine," he said as he threw his duffel bag onto Stony's bunk.

I was just across from Stony's area, sitting back in my folding chair drinking vodka and orange soda, when I said, as we had rehearsed, "Shonehour, you really think it's a good idea for him to sleep there?"

Tom shrugged, "I don't think it's catching. Besides the sheets have been changed."

The FNG's face showed immediate concern. "Whatta ya mean you don't think it's catching? Something wrong with the bunk?"

"Oh no. Of course not. It's fine. Don't listen to Mains over there. He's just ultraconservative on health issues. You'll be just fine sleeping here."

"Health issues? What health issues?"

"You mean you didn't tell him, Tom?" I scolded.

"No need to worry the man needlessly, Randy. Just drop it will ya?"

"Drop what?" the FNG was hooked.

"Oh, nothing," I said flippantly. "Tom's probably right.

You'll be OK. I'm probably overreacting. Just forget it."
I took a sip of my drink and pretended to lean over in my
chair and search for something on top of my plywood desk.

I could sense our victim looking at me and then assessing Tom. "OK, you guys. What's wrong with the guy who
usually lives in this area?"

"Nothing," Tom said innocently.

I turned to face Tom. "Nothing, Tom? Come on, I think
it's only fair to let him know what happened to Rutherford.
After all, if the same happens to him who can he blame? If
you tell him then he can take the necessary precautions."

"Necessary precautions? What necessary precautions!"
We really had this one good, I thought.

Tom closed his eyes and let out a long sigh. "Oh, all
right." He looked into the expectant eyes of the FNG and
said, "Stony Rutherford had to be medevaced for a slight
health problem."

"What kind of health problem?"

Tom looked at me. I nodded as if to say go ahead tell
him. Then he looked back at the FNG. "He had to be
taken out on a stretcher because of . . . well . . . he had
terminal crabs."

"Terminal crabs!" The FNG shouted and quickly grabbed
his duffel bag and dragged it out of Stony's area into mine.

"Goddamn, don't fucking bring them in here!" I shouted.

The startled FNG jumped back into the small hall between the two areas, dragging his duffel bag with him.
"Well, shit, what do I do then?"

Tom spoke coolly. "The place has been fumigated. His
sheets have been burned. The area has been inspected by
the division doctor and given a clean bill of health." Tom
pointed to Stony's crude desk. "See those four green cans
of louse powder?"

"Yes."

"Well, if it'll make you feel more at ease you can sprinkle that powder around the area. If there're any more of
the little suckers around that stuff'll take care of em."
Tom turned to leave. With his back to the FNG he gave
me a wink. I nodded. Tom said, "I'll check to see how
you're doing tomorrow. Sweet dreams," he said, then left.

The FNG stood outside Rutherford's area for several

minutes contemplating what to do. I pretended to be going about my business. Finally I heard him drag his duffel bag into Stony's area. Five minutes passed then I heard the FNG say, "There. That ought to take care of any of the crabs that were left."

I walked over to see what he'd done. It looked as if a snow storm had hit Stony Rutherford's area. Everything, and I mean everything, was covered with white louse powder. All four cans of the stuff.

"Yeah, that ought to do it," I said slapping the FNG's shoulder. A small cloud of white powder rose when I did so. I chuckled to myself and went back to my area to turn in for the night.

Poetic Karma paid Shonehour back in the most bizarre manner for his prank on the FNG. He, Joe, and I were in the club one night drinking beer. Shonehour hollered over the song playing on the stereo, "Be right back. Gotta take a piss!"

Joe and I continued our conversation at the bar. Ten minutes later Tom burst into the club, stomped on the likeness of the Screaming Eagle on the floor, and came over to us. "I'm going to kill my goddamn hootch maid."

"Why?" Joe asked.

"Cuz she caused me to piss in my pants, that's fucking why."

We both looked down at Tom's soiled crotch and laughed. Joe asked, "And how'd she make you piss in your pants?"

To our astonishment Tom unbuckled his pants and let them fall to his ankles. By now most the officers in the club were watching him. He pointed to his fly. "Because the silly bitch sewed my boxer shorts shut, that's why. She must of thought they'd ripped open and sewed them up. I was bustin' for a piss right then and I couldn't find the goddamn hole. By the time I got my cock out of my pants I had nearly filled up both boots." He bent down to pull up his pants. "Wait till I get my hands on her. She's dead. She's dead I tell you!" All the men got a good laugh out of that one.

When Tom returned to his hootch that night he inspected the rest of his green boxer shorts and, as he had guessed, they had all been neatly sewn shut.

CHAPTER 13

September 1969

Ushering Back a Lost Tradition

The FNG who spent his first few nights in Stony Rutherford's area was quickly gaining a reputation. In Joe Sulak's words, "That new guy is turning into a real dildo."

The FNG did have a name. His name was Anthony Ambrose. The second day Ambrose was in company he managed to discharge his .38 revolver in our hootch, firing a bullet through four of the living areas and out the screen door at the other end. On hearing the discharge everyone dove to the dusty plywood floor of the hootch. Luckily no one was hit by the stray round.

Richard Michaelson, a pilot who had been with the Blackwidows for six months and had moved into Ned Kelly's old area, picked himself up off the floor, stormed over, and grabbed the still smoking weapon from the startled Ambrose. "Watch what the fuck you're doing, goddamn it. You trying to kill somebody?"

The FNG smiled stupidly at Michaelson without answering.

"You think it's fucking funny you almost blew one of us away just now?"

"No, it's just that . . ."

"Just that, what? That you don't know how to handle a fucking simple weapon?" Michaelson inspected the revolver ensuring that there were no more rounds in the six chambers before throwing it onto Ambrose's bunk. "You do that again and I'll personally make sure you don't touch another weapon again. Understand?" The FNG nodded dumbly, but it was not to be the last time he would get in trouble for firing his .38 without permission.

Several days later he was flown by the company instructor pilot, along with another new pilot, to the training area outside the perimeter at LZ Sally for their company check ride. While the IP and the other FNG were flying the training maneuvers, Ambrose sat on the dike of a rice paddy waiting for his turn. He spotted some pigs and thought it would be good sport to shoot pigs belonging to a Vietnamese farmer. He shot and killed three of them. The IP spotted him being chased by the irate farmer across the area they were training in. He guided the aircraft down alongside the running FNG, picking him up just as the farmer was about to get his hands on him. That episode was strike two against Ambrose. Strike three would get him transferred to the 158th. The incident in question happened several days later.

Ambrose was given the simple task of loading a two-and-a-half-ton truck with ammunition from the ammunition dump at Camp Eagle. He was to drive it back to Phu Bai. It seemed like a simple enough task, but not for Warrant Officer One Ambrose. He had the enlisted men load the truck so full of ammunition the weight of it broke the truck's rear axle before it could be moved from the ammo dump. Ambrose never flew one mission with the Blackwidows. Major Torq had him shipped out of the company that same afternoon.

7 September 1969

Hi:

Received Nancy's postcard so I thought I'd send a letter to you. Not much happening. I estimate twenty more flying days for me now. I need to fly about sixty more hours to make 1100 combat hours. Twenty days or sixty hours whichever comes first will put an end to my flying. That's company policy. I'll probably get bored not flying the last couple of days here, but if I do fly I won't be assigned a mission where I "hang it out" too much. That's the way it's done.

I finally got my orders and, after a one month's home leave, I'll be going to Fort Wolters, Texas, where I'll become a flight instructor. My friend here named Joe Sulak, who I went to flight school with, received his orders and he is going to Fort Wolters too. We've decided we are going to rent an apartment together in Fort Worth.

Being stationed at Fort Wolters will allow me to be home for Christmas which should be fun.

I'm still waiting to see if the people who Deros in October get a drop. If I do that would get me home earlier than the 15th. Here's hoping, but I'm not counting on it.

Not much else to tell except I am still flying a lot and believe it or not I still enjoy it.

Take care,

Randy

Tom Shonehour and I had a flight over the fence into Laos to pick up a special forces team whose position had been compromised. They had called for extraction because they were being chased by the enemy with tracking dogs.

We were flying at two thousand feet. We had flown past Co Rock and were a few miles into Laos when a large puff of black smoke suddenly appeared between our two helicopters. It was the first time that such a thing had happened to me. It surprised me, and rather than take precious time to analyze what was happening, I had learned that when something did not look right to react first and ask questions later. So I banked the machine hard left. Another burst of black smoke exploded between Tom's ship and mine. I could see Tom banking his ship to the right.

"You see that, Tom?" I radioed.

"Roger that. Was that what I think it was?"

"Flack? Yeah, I think so, Tom."

I leveled out, flying ninety degrees from our original heading. I had only seen flack in war movies, never over here.

The escorting gunship pilot radioed, "We saw where it came from, Blackwidow. We're rolling in hot."

"Roger, Gunslinger."

We watched the two Cobra gunships dive and fire a pair of rockets, 40mm, and minigun bursts on the spot in the jungle from which they saw the 37mm come. There definitely had been something down there, because after the second ship fired and pulled up there were several large secondary explosions.

"That should do it, Blackwidow. I think we've neutralized the position. You can continue heading west."

"Good job, Gunslinger," Tom radioed.

Tom and I joined up in loose formation and returned to a heading to fly to the location of the special forces team.

We were able to hover over the Laotian jungle, drop our ropes, and extract the team without incident. What distinguished this from the other pickups I'd flown with the special forces was that, along with a team member, I now had a prisoner dangling under my aircraft.

On the flight back to Vandergrift, while we were flying at two thousand feet and 60 knots, Taylor leaned over his M-60 gun mount to check on the two men on the separate 150-foot strings. "Sir, they're fighting," the crew chief said excitedly.

"What?"

"The special forces guy's fighting with the prisoner he picked up."

I radioed to Tom. "We got a problem, Tom."

He was flying a half klick off our right wing position and closing. "Yeah, I can see. They're going at it like a couple of tom cats. The gook's got your guy upside-down and he's swinging his fists like a wild man."

"Who's winning?" I could feel the ruckus through the flight controls.

"Can't tell. Wait a minute . . . Now the gook's upside-down. They're locked leg and leg. Wait one . . . now they're both upside-down. Goddamn, it looks like a cat fight in midair. Now the gook's clawing at the special forces guy's face. Wait a minute . . . he's pulling a knife."

"Who's pulling a knife?" I asked, alarmed.

"Special forces guy. Shit, he's hacking at the prisoner's rope. He's trying to cut him loose!"

"What?"

"Shit, the gook's really fighting now. Goddamn, there he goes. Fuck!"

I banked left, away from Tom's aircraft, and looked over the armor plating out the window of my door. I could see the body falling, arms and legs flapping wildly, scratching at the thick, hot air as if trying to fly. The man turned into a speck then disappeared against the green, leafy backdrop of the jungle below. I leveled the craft and took a deep breath. I radioed to Tom. "Shit! What a way to go."

"Guess the gook took exception to being captured."

"Yeah. But even so . . . anything's got to be better than being cut loose at two thousand feet."

"Guess the dink thought differently."

"Yeah," I answered. "Guess so."

I thought about the commitment of the enemy and my own lack of it. I doubted I would have put up a fight like that if the roles were reversed. Or would I? Over here, probably not. But if I were fighting for God, country, Mom, and Disneyland on home soil, yes, I probably would. But not over here. And certainly not now. Let the new guys be the gung-ho freedom fighters. I had nearly done my time. I felt like I had completed a one-year prison sentence. I was reaching the end of my rotation in the seemingly never-ending cycle of faces shipped over here to then be shipped back 365 days later. It was someone else's turn.

I seriously questioned my I-don't-give-a-shit attitude. But why should I be any different from any of my predecessors? They had set the pattern of behavior all along and I, as well as Joe and Tom, had followed it to the letter. We had been good students and we had learned well. I had only one thing on my mind at this stage in my army career: to make it home alive. Let the heroics go to the FNGs who didn't know any better, or to the crazy sons of bitches that thrived on war, like Ned Kelly.

I had heard that Kelly was back in country after signing up for another six months in Vietnam. In a letter he said he could obtain an early out from the army by doing so. But I knew better. He liked flying over here. The crazy, seat-of-the-pants lifestyle had crept into his blood.

* * *

The company instructor pilot still preferred to use the green area outside LZ Sally to perform pilot training and to give check rides. On one of our pilot-training missions outside LZ Sally the instructor pilot was late to recover from an autorotation and the aircraft landed hard and slid into a high clump of earth, tearing off the right skid. The instructor flew the aircraft back to Phu Bai and decided to pull a prank on the air traffic controller in the tower.

"Phu Bai tower, this is Blackwidow One-Three. I've got a landing-gear-unsafe indication warning in the cockpit. I'd like to do a fly-by and wondered if you could check it out."

"Roger, Blackwidow One-Three. I'll be looking for you."

"Roger, tower. Be there in five mikes."

Of course there are no such things as gear indication lights in the Huey. The skids, permanently attached to the airframe, do not move. When the instructor flew by the tower at forty knots and the controller saw that only the left skid was visible he panicked. "Blackwidow One-Three, don't land, I repeat, don't land. I can see only one skid down. You must have a hang up."

"I gotta bring her in," the IP said in his finest Hollywood never-say-die, film-star voice. "The men're waiting for me in the Widow Web. Request permission to land."

"Negative, negative, Blackwidow One-Three. I repeat, I see only one skid. Do not land. I repeat, do not land!"

"Gotta bring her in tower. Sorry. Blackwidow One-Three out."

The controller was screaming now, "Negative! Negative! Do not land! Repeat, do not land! Blackwidow One-Three acknowledge! Acknowledge, over!"

The stunned tower controller watched as the olive-drab aircraft descended behind a row of hootches and disappeared into the Widow Web. I imagine he watched expecting to see a huge explosion and a cloud of black smoke appear on the horizon. What he couldn't see was the maintenance team waiting for the crippled bird. The aircraft landed on one skid and hovered in a level attitude while the team of men rushed forward and piled a mound of sand bags under the area where the damaged skid had been. The IP had to hold the hover for about three minutes before being given the thumbs up sign to shut down. The only black smoke on the horizon that afternoon was from the burning shit and jet fuel from the latrines at Phu Bai.

Ap Trang, a small coastal village five klicks northeast of Sally, had to be evacuated. A sprawling, underground bunker complex had been discovered there and the 101st wanted to level it.

I picked up a full colonel and several interpreters from Camp Eagle and landed outside the ville. When we landed I could see refugees waiting to be airlifted to another village. They had all their worldly belongings with them and were being held in a fenced-in area guarded by a group of idle soldiers. The colonel riding in back asked me if I had ever seen an underground bunker complex. When I told him I hadn't he asked if I would like to take a look. He assured me the area was secure, so I rolled the throttle to flight idle, gave the controls to my peter pilot, and took off my chicken plate and flight helmet before following the colonel into the ville.

It felt strange to be on the ground. My role in fighting this war was to fly over it in my helicopter, entering into the ground portion of combat only sporadically as I dropped off and picked up the troops. Entering the ville, which had recently been the scene of a fierce ground battle, made me feel a little uncomfortable. The .38 I had strapped on my hip seemed woefully inadequate right now.

Grunts were milling about everywhere in what must have been a typical post-battle scene. Most were still wearing camouflaged steel helmets and olive-drab flack jackets. They carried their weapons, M-16s, M-60s, or M-79 grenade launchers, lazily over shoulders, cradled in the crook of an arm or pointed at the ground. Some were walking individually and others talked animatedly in groups. An air of quiet peace pervaded and I began to relax. That is until I heard the crackle of gunfire from an M-60. I nearly dove to the dirt. The colonel and the two Vietnamese interpreters did not seem to be concerned. The colonel laughed at my attack of the jitters. ''Probably just firing to clear out any new tunnels they've discovered," he told me.

I nodded nervously, relieved to hear the explanation.

We passed twenty or so dead Vietnamese lined up outside a hole in the ground. Some were blown to pieces with arms and legs missing. Others had only small puncture wounds, tiny red dots from grenade fragments. Nearly one quarter of the bodies were female. The tops of their black silk pajamas had been pulled up to their arm pits exposing their breasts. The pants had been pulled down below the knees exposing the pubic area. Even after being over here for nearly a year I was shocked at this sight. Somehow, their partially nude bodies marked the final sacrilege of their death. It was a grotesque and cruel affront to their personal dignity and privacy.

I felt a macabre fascination for the death which confronted me, an irresistible compulsion to look closely at the bodies lying there on the dirt. Most of the corpses had gaping mouths and unseeing, half-open eyes. I had never looked into the eyes of a dead man before. Most of those I had carried had been encased in body bags which lent an impersonal detachment to their deaths. I'd only had to deal with green shapes, not the once walking, talking, living, breathing individual encased inside. There had been the blond boy whose young face had emerged from the bag in the wind. But his eyes had been closed. He looked peaceful, as if he were just sleeping. But as I looked at these bodies, I could tell there had been agony, and surprise, in their deaths. I studied the eyes. Like those of a fish left in the sun too long, they were dry and clouded. I noticed that some of the dead had their ears cut off. These would be kept as war trophies, souvenirs. I now recalled the story Lorraine had told me on the beach in Panama City about the pictures of dead and mutilated Vietnamese her husband had sent her. I felt sickened at the sight before me and turned away.

The colonel was given a tour of the bunker complex by the lieutenant whose company had found and destroyed it. We did not enter the various holes scattered around the ville. I would not have been able to bring myself to do so anyway, but we were shown the several entry and exit holes of what, we were told, was an underground Vietcong headquarters. Alongside some of the entrances there were more Vietnamese bodies laid out in a line. Once again, the women had their tops pulled up and bottoms pulled down, and some of the men had their ears cut off. I had seen enough. I asked the colonel if I could begin ferrying the refugees to Tay Hoang, the next village approximately ten klicks up the coast. He gave me the go ahead, and I walked back to the waiting chopper.

I flew for more than three hours moving men, women, children, pigs, chickens, and personnel possessions. On one sortie, whereas we usually carried six fully loaded combat troops, I flew twenty-two men, women, and children plus their belongings. My crew chief, Taylor, remarked that the Huey looked like a Tijuana taxi. He wasn't wrong.

The human waste I'd seen in the village that day troubled me. It somehow brought the reality of the war too close. Up until then, for nearly a year, I had managed to keep it at arm's length. For several days afterward I dreamed of the dead men and women lying in rows and thanked my stars for two things: One, that I had not been a grunt. Two, that my going home date was less than a month away.

19 September 1969

Hi:

Received your September 15th letter. Well it looks like I won't get my drop. I haven't heard anything, but I am so short now that a few days doesn't make any difference one way or the other. I can't wait to get back to the world. I try not to think about it too much, but I can't stop myself. It sure has been a long, long year. It's going to be weird to get back to the world, I tell you. Seeing girls again, being able to go out and buy a good meal any time I want. Go shopping in a real department store, trade my green wardrobe in to wear civilian clothes again, go to a real movie. The freedom will be mind boggling. Right now I can't imagine it. The first week I'm home will probably be dedicated to just trying to adjust and rid my mind of the combat mindset I've had to develop to survive over here. I can't wait to drive my sports car along coast highway with the stereo blasting out "Aquarius" by The Fifth Dimension. That's my favorite song over here.

I stop flying missions in 11 more days. Eleven days! I can't believe it. I guess I won't believe it until it's all over and done with. It's fun being an old guy because if there are any questions from the new guys I'm called on to answer them.

Joe Sulak and I had to write an article for the 101st Airborne newspaper drawing from our experiences. We were asked to write a helpful article that would be of importance to other aviators in the division.

Not much else happening. The monsoon season is moving in now following its normal cycle. The weather is getting pretty bad. I'll close for now but will write again soon.

Randy

Joe, Tom, and I had graduated from flight school 23 September 1968. On 23 September 1969, we received orders promoting us to CW2, chief warrant officer two. The promotion to CW2 was one of a series of events that were milestones in the short timer's calendar. It meant, in effect, that you were next to leave country.

There was a party in the club that night. The bartender, Spec-4 Flowers, had finished his tour and had gone home, but his Blushing Asshole recipe and the tradition of drinking for one's rank still persisted. Tom, Joe, and I drank for our new bars to the cadence of the men surrounding us, all of whom were now FNGs in our eyes, yelling, "GO! GO! GO! GO!" From that night onward, after having seen probably twenty other pilots receive their new rank of CW2, I finally felt like an old timer. The three of us celebrated with beer mixed with three or four Blushing Assholes, our arms around each other's necks, singing our hearts out to the songs emanating from the reel-to-reel. I staggered back to the hootch and fell into my bunk in the early hours of the next morning.

On 30 September 1969 I flew my last mission with the Blackwidows. It was a multiship operation to extract a company of soldiers from a moderately tight landing zone east of the A-Shau. I knew in advance it was my last mission in Vietnam. In many ways it would have been better if the ops officer had just come up to me one day and told me that the mission I'd just flown had been my last. The knowledge that I was now flying my last mission added a nagging tension to what should have been a routine trip. I tried to enjoy it knowing it would probably be the last time in my military career I would fly the Bell Huey, having made up my mind to get out of the service as fast as Uncle Sam would let me.

I was flying with a new peter pilot named Zydel. He was young, smooth-faced, eager, and enthusiastic, just as I had been twelve months before. He had carried out the preflight at first light that morning and was strapped into the copilot's seat ready to hit the starter switch when I arrived at the ship. I did my own preflight and climbed in. Without speaking to him, I asked the gunner and crew chief if they were ready and as soon as they replied I started the engine.

After making the radio call to Flight Lead the six of us took off from the Widow Web. Our aircraft was Chock Two in the formation. I didn't as much as look at the FNG sitting next to me. Besides making the radio calls I guess I didn't talk much either. Finally, having waited long enough for me to brief him or even acknowledge his presence, he pressed the floor transmit button and asked, "What do you want me to do?"

I looked over at Zydel and was about to speak when, suddenly, I remembered my first mission in country with CW2 Crawford. He had told me to just sit there and monitor my bootlaces and that if he got shot I was supposed to fly him to the hospital in Phu Bai. That was more or less what I wanted to say now in the same circumstances. I wondered if I was now staring at him with the same haggard, short timer's eyes? I forced a smile. "I'll take her into the LZ the first time. If it's not too tight, and you feel you can handle it, you can take her in after that.''

Zydel smiled. "Thanks," he said enthusiastically.

I cannot remember how long we flew that day, but I do remember my peter pilot thanking me profusely for letting him take the ship into the moderately tight landing zone. He confessed to me that he'd had problems with his pedal control in flight school. Landing in the LZ that day had helped alleviate some of his fear. I told him I'd had the same anxiety when I was new and that he needn't worry, he would quickly get the hang of it.

In the "old days," when the Blackwidows were based up at Sally, it had been the custom for an AC on his last mission to perform a low, high-speed fly-by of the company area. Since Major Torq took over no one had done it, but I figured it was about time to dust off the old tradition.

We flew back as a formation flight of six aircraft. I radioed to Flight Lead that I wanted to do a fly-by to celebrate my last mission. We switched places so that I was now flying Flight Lead. I guided the echelon right formation at 110 knots and five hundred feet over the Widow Web. On my command I began the steep, right break. The aircraft pealed off behind us at three-second intervals. I kept up the airspeed and dove at the pad, leveling out at 120 knots, and then flew at what, I was later told, looked like about three feet between the rows of revetments. We were approaching a hootch at the end of the Widow Web and I pulled back hard on the cyclic nosing the craft skyward. I vaguely remember seeing a gold television aerial on top of that hootch. I continued to pull back on the cyclic until it felt like the nose of the helicopter was pointing straight up. Zydel grabbed the front of the instrument panel with both hands, pulled his body forward against the G forces, looked over at me and yelled, "Are yoooouuuuuu ssshhhittttinnggg meeee!"

When the airspeed dropped to zero I kicked in right pedal to do a torque turn. Now it appeared as if we were nosed straight down at the Widow Web. I could see the other aircraft on short final landing in single file. In the dive the yellow needle of the airspeed indicator quickly registered eighty knots. I leveled out and set up for a normal approach to the pad.

When we landed Ned Kelly was there to greet me. He walked over to the revetment, threw open the door of the chopper, and slid back the armored plate as the blades coasted to a stop. "Goddamn, Mains, that was some fly-by. Good to see you're bringing back the old tradition. Haven't seen one of those since Sally."

I shook his hand, with mine still encased in a Nomex glove. "Well, goddamn yourself, Kelly. When'd you get here?"

"Got in country two weeks ago. Flew up this morning from II Corps. Thought I'd check in to see how you're doing. I can see you haven't changed. Torq caught the fly-by. He looked pissed off."

"Torq, yeah, I wouldn't doubt that."

I got out and squatted down to glance under the aircraft. Along the belly, forward of where the tail boom attaches to the fuselage, I could see a one-foot-long gold line where I had nicked the television aerial on the hootch. I reached under and rubbed the mark off with my glove. There was no damage. I stood and looked across the Widow Web at the roof of the hootch. I could see the aerial still standing. "Must have just grazed it," I said.

"Yes siree, that was one hell of a fly-by," Kelly said again.

As Kelly and I were walking back from the Widow Web to operations he told me about his signing up for another six months in Vietnam. He said that going back to Fort Wolters to instruct brand new students would be too boring for him after the excitement over here. I could only tell him he was nuts, and he did not dispute my observation.

When I got to Ops I was told to report to Major Torq immediately. I knocked on his screen door, entered his office, walked up to his desk, saluted smartly, and said, "Sir, CW2 Mains, reporting as ordered."

He was sitting at his desk and returned the salute. As usual he looked pissed off. "Sit down, Mains."

"Yes, sir."

"I want you to tell me what in hell that was out there just now?"

I feigned ignorance. "What, sir?"

"You know what I'm talking about. That childish aerial display just now. What do you think you were doing?"

I decided to tell him straight. "Trying to bring back some of the esprit de corps that used to be in this company, sir."

"What do you mean, Mains? You think flying like an aerial cowboy breeds esprit de corps?"

"I think you've missed the point, sir."

His face went scarlet and he pointed a stubby index finger at me, "No, mister, I have not missed the point. You've obviously missed the point. Your military bearing and personal discipline are nonexistent. And I'll tell you something: If you didn't have less than a week left in Charlie Company, and if I hadn't already given you an Article-15, I would bring you up on charges. As it is I'm grounding you for thirty days and placing a letter to that effect in your personnel file."

"But sir, I've flown my last mission. I go on leave for thirty days. I won't be flying during that time anyway. Why bother?"

Major Torq's face molded into a self-satisfied grin. "The written reprimand will let the commander at your next duty station know what he's getting, Mains. That's what purpose it'll serve."

I decided not to argue. There was no point. In part, the reprimand placed in my file read: "Warrant Officer Mains has demonstrated a flagrant and total disregard for government property and for published rules and procedures when he performed the unauthorized fly-by on 30 September 1969." I especially liked the part where it stated: ". . . then the nose of the aircraft exceeded 70-degrees nose-up pitch attitude. Mr. Mains performed a right 180-degree torque turn maneuvering the helicopter in a 70-degree nose-down pitch attitude in the dive."

The rest of the men in the company loved it. My final gesture was toasted and lauded and I was unable to buy a drink in the club that night. It was pleasing to hear that the fly-by tradition would be resurrected and adopted as SOP, standard operating procedure, by future pilots of the Blackwidows, regardless of what the old man said. Joe, Tom, a visiting Ned Kelly, and I drank heartily that night to the legacy I was leaving to the Blackwidows.

CHAPTER 14

October 1, 1969

"One in Three, Candidate.
One in Three!"

Dear Mom:

Just a cheery note to let you know that I flew my last mission yesterday. I also have some good news that I received from the ops officer about a half hour ago. I'll be home three days early! That'll be on October 12th! So expect me to call you from San Francisco International the 11th or 12th. I'll tell you then what time to meet me at Los Angeles International. I am so anxious to get home I nearly can't stand it. See you guys in eleven days!

Love, Randy

Joe Sulak's last flight in country was a memorable one as well. His last mission was a PsyOps mission to be flown over the coastal communities. His mission required him to fly from LZ Tomahawk, a fire support base situated north of Da Nang, all the way up to the DMZ. After finding the large underground bunker complex in the ville northeast of Sally, headquarters thought a PsyOps mission would be in order.

A PsyOps mission, or psychological operations mission, was used in conjunction with the Chieu Hoi program. Chieu hoi means open arms in Vietnamese. An optimistic psychologist somewhere in the Pentagon came up with the idea of the Chieu Hoi program as a psychological weapon that, if used properly, might convince the enemy to give up and, hopefully, switch sides.

The helicopter's role in a PsyOps mission begins when technicians place huge loudspeakers facing at a forty-five-degree angle outward, in the open area where the troops usually sit in the back of the helicopter. An interpreter sits in the back of the helicopter and speaks into a microphone. His message is fed into an amplifier boosting it into megawatts of power. The message is then blasted over the air asking the enemy to give up and promising him good things if he does.

To obtain the best coverage in an aerial PsyOps mission the pilot must fly the Huey over the area at low level and at a low airspeed. Joe was not too happy about the flight configuration, but he figured the area he was going to fly over was secure so he went ahead without complaint.

For two hours he flew over rice paddies and coastal communities, the interpreter's voice blaring, telling the enemy hiding below to lay down his arms and come over to our side. At the same time his assistant was kicking out Chieu Hoi leaflets with the same message printed on them. When the area on the map had been covered and all the leaflets had been thrown out the door, the interpreter told Joe he could return to Phu Bai. That is when Joe had a brilliant idea to cap off his last flight in country. He asked for the microphone and the puzzled Vietnamese interpreter handed it to him. Joe instructed his peter pilot to fly low and slow over the 101st headquarters at Phu Bai. The peter pilot did as he was told.

So, from the slow flying, low flying U.S. Army Huey came the message in Joe's slow Texas drawl, "Attention, attention, attention, yankee imperialist pigs! Throw down your arms, drop all weapons and give up! I repeat. Throw down your arms, drop all weapons and give up! Chieu hoi! Chieu hoi! Chieu hoi!"

He made several passes over the startled soldiers on the ground who were looking skyward, mouths agape, and Joe kept repeating the message.

After he landed back at the Widow Web he walked into ops and called headquarters. He found out that the switchboard had lit up following his PsyOps message. At last count there were thirty-two American soldiers who had called in to lay down their arms and give themselves up!

What most of us considered incredible about the incident was that, for some unexplained reason, Joe did not get into trouble for his treasonable act. We were all genuinely shocked, but glad that the army had finally developed a sense of humor.

4 October 1969

Hi:

I received your letter dated September 30th. I would suggest that the best days to wait for my phone call telling you I have arrived in San Francisco are between the 12th or 13th. I have no idea of what time, though.

The departure routine from here goes like this: I clear company four to five days prior to my return date to the States. I leave for Bien Hoa, our division rear area, where I finish clearing and get manifested on a plane for San Francisco. From there I will book myself on a flight for L.A. When I find out my flight number and time of arrival in Los Angeles I'll call you from San Francisco so that you can be waiting. That's how it works.

This will be my last letter. God, those are beautiful words. I'll see you at the airport.

Love, Randy

The day before Joe, Tom, and I were to leave Charlie Company for Bien Hoa to begin our out-processing, Joe and Tom entered my hootch and asked me if I'd like to join them at the Widow Web to say good-bye to a good friend. I walked along with them to take one last look at the machine that, through its reliability and forgiving nature, had been a patient teacher. She had brought us back home safely from every mission. We discovered that our combined combat flying hours totaled more than three thousand for the year. She had served us well. She had taken us from fledgling FNG pilots, barely able to keep her in control, to the now highly experienced, capable aviators we were. In aviation terms she had nurtured us from the cradle and taken us to manhood. Joe, Tom, and I agreed that we would miss flying the reliable Huey which had become a valued and treasured friend.

Standing next to the Huey in the Widow Web, the three of us reminisced about the year. We told our war stories in shorthand as we knew each other's experiences by heart. Tom began, "Remember when the NVA rushed my aircraft and I was going to shoot the bastards with my pearl-handled pistol?"

Joe and I laughed. Then Joe said, "I keep thinking about that hover hole and the RPG Charlie fired through the tail rotor. Damn that was a close one."

"Kelly and I thought you'd had it, Sulak," I said. "And what about that mortar attack at Vandergrift we flew into with the pad blowing up in front of me on short final?"

Joe shook his head, "A few seconds later you'd have been history, partner."

Then we got onto the subject of the one-in-three odds of getting killed that we had heard so much about in flight school. Tom boasted that we'd beaten the odds. I wasn't yet so sure. I wondered about Stu Lindsey and Bob Lawson to whom I had been closer during flight school than I had been to Joe or Tom. Were they still alive? Had they, too, made it unscathed? I would find out when I got to the out-processing station.

Joe, Tom, and I said our good-byes to the officers and enlisted men in Charlie Company and caught a C-130 to Bien Hoa from Phu Bai. We found it difficult to believe we were going home at last, that we had actually made it through our year.

When we arrived at Bien Hoa to out-process a clerk reviewed my records then said, "You can't leave country until you pay your fine."

"Fine, what fine?"

"Says here you were issued an Article-15 in July. Is that correct?"

"I was told I was going to get one, but I never saw it."

"Well it's right here." He showed me, then held out his hand. "That'll be two hundred dollars."

"Two hundred dollars!"

"Says so right here. You can either pay or stay."

"That's one hell of a choice." I pulled out the money from my wallet. I had just been to the paymaster. This visit to division administration was my last stop. "Here." I paid him using two crisp one hundred dollar bills. "Now can I leave?"

"Yes, sir. Oh yes, wait. There's one more thing."

"What's that?"

He handed me a large envelope then reached under his counter and handed me a small blue case. I opened it. Inside with its red, white, and blue ribbon was a Distinguished Flying Cross.

I looked up at him and laughed. "Why does it seem ironic to me that I pay you two hundred dollars for blowing cigar smoke in a captain's face, then you award me a DFC?"

"You blew smoke in a captain's face, sir?"

"Uh Huh."

"Right on! Oh yes, and congratulations on your DFC, sir. You see, I couldn't give it to you until your records had been cleared. Paying the fine unflagged them."

"Thanks." I chuckled and added, "What a crazy fucking place."

"You got that shit right, sir. This fucking place is fucking loony tunes."

The mood at the out-processing center felt like a homecoming event. The men I had shipped in with a year before and then had become separated from were now shipping out. I recognized a lot of my friends from flight school. The greetings were almost always the same. When you saw a familiar face you rushed over, shook hands, then immediately exchanged news about who had been killed or wounded. After having talked to my friends and from their information I figured we probably lost 25 percent of our class.

I finally saw Bob Lawson. He was standing at the bar in the officer's club. I yelled his name and we rushed toward one another and embraced. I held him at arm's length by his shoulders and said, "Goddamn, Bob, I never thought I'd be so glad to see your ugly face again."

He was beaming. "It's good to see you too, Randy." He started to apologize, "Goddamn, I wanted to write to you but . . ."

I waved him off. "Forget it, Bob. Me too. Hell, I understand . . ."

I was afraid to ask the next question. I took a deep breath and summoned up the courage. "What about Stu?"

He shook his head. "Last I heard he got shot down. From what I could gather they shot out his tail rotor and he went in spinning. There was a fire. He's alive, but I heard he got hurt pretty bad."

The news hit me hard. "Shit."

"He's in the VA hospital in Long Beach. We can see him when we're on leave."

We traded war stories. Bob had been shot down twice and had crashed once. He had been lucky. After hearing about my year he told me I had been lucky also.

The mood inside the Boeing 707 that was to fly us home was electric. As it began its takeoff roll down the runway I got the feeling that every man was mentally willing it off the ground. When it finally gained flying speed the nose lifted and it rotated into the air. As the wheels left Vietnam soil all the men let out a cheer that could have been heard back at Phu Bai. I was going home. I looked over at Bob seated next to me at the window seat. He was watching the hootches, the green jungle, the black smoke from the burning shit, the Vietnamese villages, and the rice paddies disappear beneath us as that big, beautiful freedom bird climbed for altitude. He looked over at me. His eyes were tearing. He clenched his jaw and gave me a hearty thumbs up sign. He turned and looked out the window again. I settled back in my seat. Damn, I was going home! Home to my family. It was like a dream. I could not believe it was happening.

Filled with nervous energy I sat up and looked around the plane. If someone had given me five dollars for every smile I could count I would have been a rich man. Yes, I told myself, I do believe it now. It is truly happening. I am really going home.

* * *

I didn't know what to expect when I stepped off the plane in San Francisco. By the stories I'd heard I half expected to get shot at by an antiwar demonstrator. I wondered about the change in sentiment towards the war. How bad was it really? And were people back home actually hurling verbal abuse at the people who fought in Vietnam? I would find out soon enough.

When I emerged from the plane's door in San Francisco I paused for a moment and took in a deep breath of the crisp night air. I could feel the freedom in the air. It was something tangible. It seemed to recharge me after the twenty-two-hour flight. I was home. Home in California!

Dressed in my wrinkled army greens, pungent with the smell of a year in a mildewed foot locker, I rushed into the terminal. I fought through the crowds of civilians and booked a flight to Los Angeles. I called my folks. Mom answered. She and my best friend and surfing buddy, Greg Omberg, had been waiting by the phone for my call.

She said, "Randy, oh Randy, are you here?"

"Yeah, Mom. I made it. I'm home!" I gave her my flight details. "See you in two hours."

"Two hours." Her voice was full of relief. "See you then, honey. God, we love you." Hearing her voice made me want to cry.

I walked up to the nearest bar, ordered a vodka collins, and when the bartender put the drink in front of me I downed it in one gulp. I had been rehearsing the scene in my mind for a month. The drink was sweet and cold. I slammed the empty glass on the bar startling the customers and said, "Thanks. I've been waiting all year for that," and rushed off to catch my plane.

Mom looked frail and gaunt when I spotted her waving in the crowd. I could see she'd been sick. She really cried when she saw me come down the ramp at Los Angeles. We embraced for a long time. I turned to my friend Greg, shook hands, then hugged him too. The feeling of exhilaration was like an electric charge running through my body. Mom told me that Michelle could not meet me too as she'd had other plans that couldn't be changed. I was disappointed, but I understood.

I did not sleep for three-and-a-half days. I tried to go to bed, but every time my head hit the pillow I just lay there and stared up at the ceiling. Too excited to sleep, I got up and drove my sports car up coast highway, the stereo blasting out "Aquarius" by the 5th Dimension, as I had dreamed of doing so many times when I was over there.

I went surfing again with my friend, Greg. After several hours in the water we stood on the beach next to our long boards propped up in the sand. We looked out over the Pacific and we discussed the war. He genuinely wanted to know what it had been like. He listened. He was on leave from the Sea Bees and was shipping out for Vietnam in two weeks.

Michelle drove over to see me. She hugged me. I kissed her. I closed my eyes and I held her close and breathed in her fresh scent. I had forgotten how beautiful she smelled. She looked lovely and the feel of her body against mine made me ache. But I knew, although we were physically close, I was mentally distant. I was difficult to approach. I needed time to unwind, to get ahold of my feelings. She told me that during the year the memory of me had been to her like the song by Glen Campbell, "Gentle on My Mind." I liked her analogy and thanked her for her letters over the last year and for being there for me. I saw her only one other time during my month's leave. Her life no longer coincided with mine. It did not include me. She had other friends. I did not press the issue. I understood.

Mom took my clothes from the duffel bag and had them cleaned in order to, in her words, "rid them of the smell of the war." They had that dank, mildewed smell of the jungle.

I played with my little sister, Andrea. I visited with my eighteen-year-old sister, Nancy. I gave a hug and hearty handshake to my stepfather. They all watched me. The whole family watched me. I think they were looking for signs that I had changed. And I had. My values had changed. My view of life had changed. Everyone said I seemed much more mature. A neighbor remarked that I had left Huntington Beach a boy and had returned home a man.

I was struck by how clean, orderly, and sterile every-thing was back home. When I thought about the mud, dirt, dust, and filth in Vietnam it seemed like a dream. Not a nightmare. Just an unclear dream. I had a hard time imag-ining the guys in Phu Bai in the officers' club right now, perhaps flying their hairy missions. It all seemed light years away. It seemed unreal.

I set up the new stereo I had had shipped home from the PX mail order company in Japan and concentrated on the new music. I went into a music store in Fashion Island and had the clerk pick out twenty of the most popular current albums and I bought them all. I had never heard of Creedence Clearwater Revival. And Bob Dylan had changed his style considerably. He then had a hit out called "Lay Lady Lay."

Everything was as I remembered it except that now the guys had long hair and wore headbands. Drugs seemed to be more prevalent. The war was featured on the news every night as well as the recent demonstrations against it. I tried to ignore it, to push it from my mind, but of course I could not.

One evening Mom invited twenty family friends for drinks and dinner, a celebration in honor of my homecom-ing. After dinner everyone moved into the living room to view the 8-mm movie I'd taken of the mission to extract six marines out of the bombed-out landing zone near Khe Sahn. The cheerful party chatter turned to silence when I dimmed the lights and switched on the projector. To give the film more "feeling" I'd added a sound track which I played on the stereo—a compendium of songs popular at the time.

When the fifteen-minute film ended and the lights had been switched back on, I scanned the faces staring back at me. Their reaction to the film surprised me. A serious-ness had descended over the audience. The look of aston-ishment was on each person's face. A second or two passed without anyone speaking a word, then the room erupted in applause as everyone stood from their seats.

I was told that my short film had suddenly had the effect of making the war disturbingly close, and very real—that their exposure to the war had been deadened by the constant bombardment of war news footage on the nightly six o'clock news. Viewing my crude, homemade movie had accomplished what the news media had failed to do—it brought the war home.

I had been home for two weeks when Bob Lawson called me wanting to know when we should go see Stu at the VA hospital. We scheduled it for two days later.

Bob drove us in his fire-engine-red TR-6. Traveling in the fast lane northbound on the congested 405 freeway we talked about the likelihood of walking into the ward, confronting Stu face-to-face, and seeing that he had been really messed up. What then? We knew we'd have to face him, and we both felt guilty for not going to see him sooner.

The wards were overflowing with casualties of the war. As we were led to Stu's ward we were followed by the eyes of men who had not shared our luck. They had been wounded and were here recuperating. Some had bandaged heads, others had missing limbs, patched eyes, taped extremities. Some of the men had bitterness in their eyes. Others hatred. Or was I only imagining it? Was I reading in a guilt I felt for making it out of the experience without being wounded? Was I really feeling guilty for making it back to The World in one piece? For not being one of the 58,000 or so men who would die in the war. I looked into the faces of these young men and tried to imagine myself in their place. The thought angered me. Yes, I would have been hostile and bitter had it been me lying on one of those beds.

At last the nurse turned left into a room and held the door open for us. "He's in the last bed on the left. Near the window."

We thanked her and walked in. I could feel the blood drop from my head to my feet. I wanted to turn and run. I suddenly felt I was not at all prepared to see my friend. How had he changed? The eyes of the men in the beds lining the walls followed us. I was ready to scream. We approached the row of windows. Stu was close. I saw a drawn white partition to my left. Stu was there. Behind it. My feet mechanically kept me moving, Bob trailing close behind. My heart was beating harder than it ever had on any CA. I circled the partition and we came face to face. Stu's body was in traction. His face looked back at me blankly for a long moment. He looked startled. Then I watched it transform into the familiar smile. At last he spoke, "Goddamn, you guys, it took you fucking long enough to come see me," he scolded.

Through the numbness I could feel myself smiling too. I was smiling because he was still the same Stu. Hell, he didn't look too bad. Not bad at all. OK, he was in traction, but he looked no different. I arrived at his bed, leaned over, and gave him a gentle hug so I would not accidentally cause him pain. He embraced me in return and slapped my back heartily with both hands. I released my friend, then Bob did the same. "Come on you guys. Cut it out. You'll ruin my image."

Bob had heard correctly. Stu's aircraft had taken an RPG through the tail rotor and he had gone in spinning. There had been a fire and the crew chief had dragged him out of the wreckage. Stu showed us the tender looking scar along his arm from the third-degree burns. His main injury had been a broken back. This would cause him to walk with a permanent limp and he would always need a cane. He told us he had a 100 percent disability from the army. We joked about him free-loading off the government, that he had probably done it on purpose. It was macho talk. That was all. It lightened the atmosphere to talk in such terms. Inside I did not feel light hearted. My good friend had nearly been killed, but he *was* alive. We had beaten the odds and considering those odds, making it back alive was definitely something to be thankful for.

Glossary

AC: Aircraft commander. The AC sits in the left seat.

ADF: Automatic direction finder. A radio aid in an aircraft incorporating an instrument with a needle that points to the direction of the non-directional beacon ground station.

AK-47:   Soviet-produced semiautomatic or automatic 7.62mm assault rifle used by the VC and NVA soldiers.

AO: Area of operation. The geographical area covered by a particular hit.

ARA: Aerial Rocket Artillery. A Cobra gunship armed with 2.75-inch rockets.

Article-15:   Nonjudicial punishment that can be imposed by a commanding officer.

ARTY: Artillery.

ARVN: Army of the Republic of Vietnam.

Ass-and-trash mission: The carrying of men and equipment.

Autorotation: An emergency procedure particular to helicopters that must be performed when the engine quits. Autorotation is when the aircraft is flown like an autogyro. The rotors freewheel powered by the air moving through them with the blades in flat pitch.

AWOL: Absent without official leave.

B-40:   A rocket-propelled grenade launcher manufactured in the communist bloc countries and used by the NVA.

Berm: The perimeter of a fortification.

BOQ: Bachelor's Officer's Quarters. Accommodation on a base reserved for visiting officers.

CA: Combat assault.

C&C: Command and control. Usually a helicopter with a mission commander aboard orchestrating an operation.

C-4: An extremely powerful plastic explosive.

C-ration: Combat rations.

Chieu Hoi: Meaning "Open Arms." A program developed to encourage the enemy to lay down their arms and defect to the other side for indoctrination.

Chicken plate: A twenty-five-pound acrylic chest protector worn by the pilots. Capable of stopping a 7.62-mm bullet.

Clackers: A hand-held detonating device for claymore mines.

Claymore: Anti-personnel mine used in ambushes and perimeter security.

CO: Commanding officer.

Cobra: A gunship helicopter designated the AH-1G. Also called a snake for its long, thin appearance.

Collective: Short for collective pitch lever. A flight control situated to the left of each pilot. When lifted it increases the pitch of the main rotor blades collectively causing the aircraft to rise. When lowered the pitch in the main rotor blades decreases causing the aircraft to descend. The throttle, a twist-grip type as on a motorcycle, is located at the end of the collective.

Conex: Large, square steel containers for shipment and storage of supplies and equipment.

CS gas: Vomit-inducing gas termed "chicken shit" gas by the soldiers.

CW2: Chief warrant officer two. This grade is normally earned twelve months after graduating from flight school.

Cyclic: The control stick located in front of each pilot. With an appearance much like the stick found in conventional jet aircraft at the time, the cyclic controls the tilt of the main rotor. If the pilot moves the cyclic forward the main rotor tilts forward causing the helicopter to follow. If moved left, right, or rearward a similar resulting reaction will follow.

DEROS: Date Estimate Return from Overseas.

Didi: Vietnamese, meaning to run.

Dinks: Derogatory name for the enemy.

DMZ: Demilitarized Zone.

Deuce-and-a-half: An army two-and-a-half-ton truck.

Dust-off: Used to describe a medevac helicopter.

F-4: A fighter-bomber widely used during the war called the Phantom.

FAC: Forward air controller usually flying in a small, prop-driven airplane.

FDO: Flight deck officer. Responsible for the safe operation of aircraft aboard a ship.

Firebase: Artillery sites that would support ground forces in their AO.

FNG: Fucking new guy.

Frag: Fragmentation hand grenade.

Fragged: Term used to describe being blown up by a fragmentation grenade. Usually done on purpose by a soldier on the same side.

Fu gas: Fifty-five-gallon barrels of jellied gasoline usually buried along the perimeter of a fortification and detonated in the event of a ground attack.

GCA: Ground-contolled approach. A radar approach in which a pilot is talked down for a landing to an airfield by a radar controller. The pilot performs the approach given glide-slope and distance information.

Gook: Term used to describe the enemy. NVA, VC, or any Vietnamese in general.

Helo: Helicopter.

Hootch: Usually a 16'x32' dwelling built a foot or two off the ground, made of 4'x8' sheets of plywood, surrounded all around with screening material. The roof is made with sheets of corrugated iron.

HQ: Headquarters.

Huey: The name of the Bell UH-1 helicopter.

IG: Inspector general.

IP: Instructor pilot.

Klick: One kilometer, slightly more than one-sixth of a statute mile.

LOH: Light observation helicopter. Usually a OH-6 Cayuse similar to the Hughes 500 flying in the commercial world today.

LZ: Landing zone.

M-16: Standard semiautomatic and automatic rifle issued to the infantry, 5.56mm.

M-60: Light machine gun used by the infantry. There were usually two mounted on the Huey, one on each side.

M-79: 40mm grenade launcher.

Mcguire Rig: A one-hundred-fifty-foot rope attached to tie-down rings on the floor of the UH-1 helicopter and thrown down through jungle canopy. Used to extract soldiers in terrain where a landing could not be made. Three were normally used at a time. Each rope had its own canvas seat, similar to that found on a swing. There was an adjustable loop above where the man's head would be to insert a wrist to hold him in the event the man fell out of the swing seat. Primarily used in Laos.

Minigun: A Gatling gun driven by an electric motor and capable of firing 2,000 to 4,000 rounds per minute.

MOS: Military occupational speciality. Job title.

Napalm: Acronym for naphthenic acid and palmetate. Jellied gasoline like Fu-gas. When dropped from fighter bombers it produces a wall of flame.

Nomex: Fire retardant material developed by Dupont and used in flight suits and flight gloves.

NVA: North Vietnamese Army.

O-club: Officer's club. The officer's club at LZ Sally and at Phu Bai were modified plywood hootches.

Peter pilot: Name for any copilot. The peter pilot flew in the right-hand seat.

PIO: Public information officer.

Piss tube: An artillery canister buried in the ground as a urination point for soldiers. A narrow fence of corrugated iron was placed in front of the piss tube offering minimal privacy.

POL: Petroleum, oil, lubricants. The term used for any aircraft refueling point.

PSP: Perforated steel plate. Interlocking steel plates used for making runways, taxiways, and aircraft movement areas. Also used for making aircraft revetments.

PSYOPS: Psychological Operations. Leaflets were dropped urging the enemy to give up, or loud speakers were placed in the helicopter with blaring messages urging the enemy to Chieu Hoi.

PX: Post exchange. A retail store for servicemen.

Revetment: Two parallel walls made of PSP filled with sandbags or merely a wall of sandbags where a helicopter parked. The idea of a revetment was to prevent shrapnel damage in the event of a rocket or mortar attack.

RLO: Real live officer. Term used by warrant officers to describe a commissioned officer, second lieutenant, and above.

ROK: Republic of Korea. Used to describe a Korean soldier.

Round: Bullet.

RPG: Rocket-propelled grenade. Also known as a B-40 rocket. Initially designed as an antitank weapon but later used to shoot down aircraft.

Sapper: Enemy demolition and assault teams.

Satchel charge: Usually a canvas pack with a handle suitable for throwing. Packed with explosives and carried by sappers during an attack.

Sea Bee: Naval Construction Brigade.

Snake: Another term for the AH-1G Cobra gunship because they were long and extremely thin like a snake.

SOI: Signal Operation Instructions. A book carried by the pilots containing the secret radio codes and call signs of the units in their area of operation.

Spec-4: Specialist 4th class. E-4

Spec-5: Specialist 5th class. E-5

Tacan: Radio navigation aid that gives azimith and distance information.

Tet: Vietnamese lunar New Year.

The World: The states. America. Home.

TOC: Tactical Operations Center.

Transponder: An electronic aid normally carried in an aircraft that, when interrogated by a radar pulse, will automatically send back an assigned, four-digit number code identifying the aircraft on an air traffic controller's radar screen.

VC: Vietcong
ville: A village

XO: Executive officer. Second officer in command.

About the Author

Randolph Mains flew 1042 combat hours during his one-year tour in Vietnam, where he was awarded the Distinguished Flying Cross, twenty-seven Air Medals, and the Bronze Star Medal. He remained in aviation and currently has over 7500 flying hours.

His twenty-year aviation career has taken him to the Australian Outback, where he lived on a 1632-square-mile cattle ranch, herding cattle by helicopter and delivering meat by small, fixed-wing aircraft to aboriginal settlements scattered throughout the Northern Territory. It was in Australia that he and a colleague purchased, sight unseen, a Cherokee-6 fixed-wing aircraft that had crashed in the remote Simpson Desert. They rebuilt it there in the desert and flew it back to civilization. He has flown seismic survey and heli-rig work over the jungles of Papua New Guinea. It was in New Guinea that he tried his hand at hunting crocodiles. In 1976 he was employed as a senior instructor pilot for Bell Helicopter International in Iran for two-and-a-half years prior to the revolution and managed to flee the country on the last commercial charter flight out. Two weeks later, in February 1979, he began his EMS, emergency medical services, career flying on the Houston Life Flight program. He found himself a pioneer in this new and exciting field trying to prove to a skeptical medical community, and to a doubting American public, that the helicopter air ambulance concept could work and save lives in peacetime as it did in Vietnam. Through the hard work and the dedication of other equally committed ex-Vietnam helicopter pilots like himself the concept was accepted and adopted by other hospitals nationwide.

In 1980 his company sent him to San Diego to help set up what has become one of the most successful hospital-based helicopter programs in the United States today. He acquired his California emergency medical technician certification after seeing a need for an extra pair of hands at the accident scenes to which he flew the medical teams. In 1982 Mains won the first annual Golden Hour Award and was flown to Washington, D.C. to receive the accolade that recognized him as the top medevac pilot in America.

While still working as chief pilot for the San Diego Life Flight program he graduated in May 1984 from San Diego State University, where he earned a degree in journalism and a minor in English and creative writing.

After he, himself, nearly lost his life on three separate occasions, he wrote his first book entitled *The Golden Hour*. The novel addresses the grim realities faced by EMS pilots flying in programs across America who operate their machines in a sector of civil aviation where, while saving lives, the odds of having a fatal accident are as high as any the men faced in Vietnam.

In December 1984 Mains moved to the Middle East to accept a position with the Royal Oman Police Air Wing.

WORLD WAR II HISTORIES
by Edwin P. Hoyt

WAR IN THE PACIFIC

TRIUMPH OF JAPAN   75792-3/$4.50 US/$5.50 Can
STIRRINGS   75793-1/$3.95 US/$4.95 Can
SOUTH PACIFIC   76158-0/$4.50 US/$5.50 Can
THE JUNGLES OF NEW GUINEA
                          75750-8/$4.95 US/$5.95 Can
ALEUTIANS   76316-8/$4.99 US/$5.99 Can

WAR IN EUROPE

BLITZKRIEG   76155-6/$4.99 US/$5.99 Can
THE FALL OF FRANCE   76156-4/$4.99 US/$5.99 Can
THE BATTLE OF BRITAIN
                          76482-2/$4.50 US/$5.50 Can

JAMES ELLROY

BROWN'S REQUIEM   78741-5/$3.95 US $4.95 Can
Join ex-cop and sometimes P.I. Fritz Brown beneath the
golden glitter of Tinsel Town...where arson, pay-offs, and
porn are all part of the game.

CLANDESTINE   81141-3/$3.95 US/$4.95 Can
Nominated for an Edgar Award for Best Original Paperback
Mystery Novel. A compelling thriller about an ambitious
L.A. patrolman caught up in the sex and sleaze of smog city
where murder is the dark side of love.

KILLER ON THE ROAD   89934-5/$4.99 US/$5.99 Can
Enter the horrifying world of a killer whose bloody trail of
carnage baffles police from coast to coast and whose only
pleasure is to kill...and kill again.

Featuring Lloyd Hopkins

BLOOD ON THE MOON   69851-X/$4.50 US/$5.50 Can
Lloyd Hopkins is an L.A. cop. Hard, driven, brilliant, he's
the man they call in when a murder case looks bad.

BECAUSE THE NIGHT   70063-8/$3.95 US/$4.95 Can
Detective Sergeant Lloyd Hopkins had a hunch that there
was a connection between three bloody bodies and one
missing cop...a hunch that would take him to the dark heart
of madness...and beyond.